The Discovery of
SUSSEX

*Marine Court, St Leonards on Sea, 1935–7, strongly influenced by
Le Corbusier's analogy of the decks of an ocean liner.*

The Discovery of

SUSSEX

Peter Brandon

Phillimore

2010

Published by
PHILLIMORE & CO. LTD
Andover, Hampshire, England
www.phillimore.co.uk

© Peter Brandon, 2010

ISBN 978-1-86077-616-8

Printed and bound in Great Britain
Manufacturing managed by
Jellyfish Print Solutions Ltd

The Discovery of Sussex was typeset in Caslon.

*In memory of Yorkshire-born Arthur Beckett (1872-1943),
indefatigable promoter of the discovery of Sussex
and guardian spirit of the Downs he did so much to save.*

Contents

ILLUSTRATIONS

Frontispiece: Marine Court, St Leonards on Sea.

COLOUR PLATES

between pages 56 and 57

ACKNOWLEDGEMENTS

I am indebted to Susan Bickford, Mrs J. Braxton, Philippa Hewitt, Martin and Anne King, Geoffrey Mead, Arthur Shopland, Michael Wickham and Martin Willard for suggestions and assistance. I particularly thank Ann Winser for the index to this volume, meticulous proof-reading, and much general help.

The author is grateful to the following individuals and institutions for permission to reproduce their photographs or other illustrative material. Colin Andrew, 44; Brighton Museum and Art Gallery, 72; Adrian Berg, R.A., 17; Burlington Paintings, illustrations by A.A. Glendening; courtesy of the Chris Beetles Gallery on behalf of the Badmin Estate, II, XV, XXXV; The British Library, 8, 9, 10; The Bridgeman Art Library on behalf of the Firle Estate Settlement, XXIV; Mike Clodd, XXX; Michael Fleetwood, 5, 109, 110; the Goodwood Estate, XXVI, XXVII; Peter Greenhalf, XI; Hastings Museum, 61, 62; the late George Holleyman, 76, 77; Imperial War Museum, XXIV, XL, XLI; Michael and Melissa Lunn, VII; Alen MacWeeney, XXXIX; David Messum, XXVIII; Dr Harry Montgomery, 1, 4, 14, 25, 94, 116, 125, 128, 149, 155; The National Trust, 125; Dr Hew Prendergast, 2; *Punch* magazine, 11, 12, 99, 100, 113, 114, 123, 130, 133, 134; the Railway Museum, York, 38, 39; the Tate Gallery, XXXVII, XXXVIII; Victoria and Albert Museum, 4; the late Alan Wade, 55; John Wade, 87; West Dean College Trust, 95; West Sussex Record Office, 27, 43; Ann Winser, 6, 15, 18, 40-2, 45-7, 49, 81, 83, 84, 86, 88, 90-3, 98, 104-5, 108, 124, 131, 140, 142-3, 145-6, 148 and 111, XIV, XVI, XVIII, XXI, XXIII. Other photographs have been taken by the author.

The author also expresses acknowledgement for permission to reproduce other copyright material to John Copper and the Copper family for extracts from Bob Copper's works; A.P. Watts on behalf of Sandra Perkins and other members of the Perkins family for the publication A.P. Herbert's 'Peach on the Pillion' (1923); Cambridge University Press for the reproduction of an extract from John Arlott's 'Landmarks'; Pendragon Press, New York, for permission to quote extracts from *The John Marsh Journals*, edited by Brian Robbins.

Chapter 1

INTIMATIONS OF EDEN

The green hills stretch before me,
No world of gloom and pain
Looms near, unkind and stormy.
Pen cannot tell
The depth of their alluring,
Their soft enfolding spell,
The comfort of their coming.

G.D. Martineau, 'The Hills Without You', *Old Sussex and Other Poems* (1924), p.16

Sussex was the county beyond the London smoke that more than any other between *c.*1880 and 1939 was thought to soothe over-strained nerves and ease the troubles of a tormented mind, or provide an escape for those grappling with change in their lives. It was easily accessible from London and, as E.V. Lucas, that great man of Sussex, boastfully and inaccurately remarked, other counties may have had their downs but they were not so beautiful nor so high as the South Downs and they did not run down to the sea. Praised by its great and lesser poets in countless verses, the county was honoured in book after book until exalting Sussex was done as a matter of course. It captured the hearts and filled the imagination of the nation, and no part of southern England was so overrun with wide-eyed tourists. The unforgettable glory of its beauty could not be fully grasped: 'It was like a dream of some spirit-land it would appear, scarce fit to be touched lest it should fall to pieces, too beautiful to be long watched lest it should fade away.'[1]

The chalk Downs and the sea air were thought to have health-giving properties, producing resorts, sanatoria, golf courses, and crocodiles of preparatory school children, including George Orwell, Cyril Connolly and John Betjeman, all along the Sussex coast. Moreover, it was a county where old habits and old attitudes were preserved more assiduously than in other places. As late as the early 1930s wide vistas were largely untouched, where old-fashioned country sights and sounds could still be heard. The rooted character of parts of Sussex in a rapidly changing England came to represent the cherished entrenchment of the most truly English traditions and customs. Accessibility by railway, bike, motor-cycle or light car meant that Sussex was increasingly perceived by jaded city workers as 'Not London', somewhere providing a temporary means of escape where one could lie in the sun, walk, go sailing, camping or caravanning, build shanties on the edge of the beach or in 'waste' patches inland, canoe down the Arun, Adur and Ouse, take a 'spin', or go snapshotting – finishing with a cottage tea. Here one could end one's days content in an enchanted world, like Belloc:

> If I ever become a rich man,
>> Or if ever I grow to be old,
> I will build a house of deep thatch.
>> To shelter me from the cold,
> And there shall the Sussex songs be sung,
>> And the story of Sussex told …
> I will build my house in the high wood,
>> Within a walk of the sea,
> And the men that were boys when I was a boy
>> Shall sit and drink with me.[2]

Douglas Freshfield of Ashdown Forest was doubtless correct when he suggested that this idea of Sussex as a place for relaxation and distraction was intensified when First World War veterans came home from the horrors of the trenches 'to enjoy the charm of the wide-streeted country towns, the peaceful villages, the flowery meadows and hedgerows, the beech hangers and the broad, billowy Downs'.[3]

This passion for Sussex is one of the greatest of English romances with place. Here was a liveable paradise where one could forget a world disrupted by modern technology. The county became a symbol of the idyllic English landscape. A source of its magic was the silence and stillness, whether embedded in deep woods or pervading downland turf. To those accustomed to the clatter of wheels, the banging of implements, and the clamorous human voices in their urban precincts, this strange new wonder gripped heart and mind. In towns, standing still or doing nothing was called idleness; in the country it was the only way to enjoy the beauty, and doing so became a theme of Sussex literature. The poet Alfred Noyes expressed this pleasure through a tramp's love of the Downs:

> Never laid in hayfields when the dawn came over-sea, sir?
> … Never crept into a stack because the wind was blowing?
> Laid and heard the whisper of the silence, growing, growing.
>> Watched a thousand wheeling stars? …
> Joshua! But I've done it, sir …[4]

From the medical treatment of the wealthy at Brighton grew the Englishman's love of the seaside, a cult symbolised by tens of thousands of bow windows in Brighton and other coastal resorts thrusting forward to catch every glimpse of the prospect and every ray of liquid sunshine. The greatest literary exponent of the seaside has been Richard Jefferies, for whom it provided three potent medicines – the sea itself, the tonic properties of the air, and the sun. In his essay *The Breeze on Beachy Head* he describes the cliffs as a 'land of health' which he had taken as a self-prescribed medicine that healed totally, though in his case only temporarily. Countless others arrived in search of beneficial air and change of surroundings.

The sea had been the cradle of Sussex activities since open boats of the Bronze Age made for Shinewater near Eastbourne. Sussex ships and seamen had entered the crowded shipping lanes of the English Channel and ventured all over the globe. Where land and sea met at old creeks and harbours, the ancient piers and shipyards imbued with the rank smell of tarred timber, was one of the most inspiring of all places in Sussex literature. E.V. Lucas noted that the life of a harbour, however decayed, as were most of the Sussex ports, had a hypnotic effect on tourists more real and strange than the open sea.[5] Above the sound of hammers, the laughing and whistling of the loafers and the constant movement of shipping, both grimy steamers and sailing barques, was that magical place where the quiet green curves of the Downs met the gleaming white cliffs of England and the Pevensey Levels ran out to the Channel.

Much of the natural beauty of the county arose from its extraordinary natural diversity and the uncommon profusion of every plant and tree. One has only to read the first memorable chapter of Gilbert White's *Natural History of Selborne* to learn that condensed into his single parish was almost every type of scenery to be found in lowland England. The same could be said of parishes in the southern part of Sussex. It would have been difficult to find anywhere in the world an area of comparable size which exhibited the same diversity of plant, animal and human life. Nature, in fact, was abounding, 'heaped up like the produce on a market stall', matching to perfection the Pre-Raphaelite landscape painters' tendency to equate beauty with exuberance, opulence and intricacy of detail. Each of the different rocks and soils had its own distinctive flora and wildlife. In the course of a 45-minute drive one

1   *The cliffs of Beachy Head, an iconic Sussex landscape.*

would have seen more varied scenery than in a day's journey in Germany or in two or three in the USA or Russia. A spectacular mosaic of ploughland, pasture, downland, heathland, shingle beach, sea cliff, salt-marsh, winding river valley and little fields culminated in fold upon wooded fold of Ashdown Forest – all of England in a few square miles. 'Eden grown tiny' was Eleanor Farjeons's rapturous description of this landscape of miniatures.[6]

The variety introduced differences in farming between districts, and the local rock and clay became the building stone for the villages. The remarkable distinctiveness between places was a powerful source of historical and imaginative inspiration. The 'spirit of place' was felt nowhere more keenly than along the sharp boundaries where uncultivated woods, heaths, downs and marsh of the 'wild' gave way to garden-like fields or meadows rich in human associations.

To most people Sussex meant the multitude of quiet places where they could soak in the beauty of their surroundings – the cottage garden, a drowsy river bank for fishing, a village cricket ground, a traditional farmstead, a bridle path for riding, a footpath through a forest glade or over a stretch of heath, or the streets of a little town such as Rye which

2 — View across Ashdown Forest from Old Lodge.

recalled past lives so vividly. It was this 'nostalgic, embracing nookiness' that had inspired the artist Samuel Palmer at Shoreham in Kent in the 1820s. But the grandeur of the Sussex distances has also played a great part. Sandwiched between the urban worlds of London and Brighton, the major hill-ranges lie in an oval shape offering panoramic splendour unmatched in lowland England. An almost unique English landscape feature is the 'round world', views from some vantage points covering the whole range of 360 degrees. Few have failed, since the expressively shaped view was 'discovered' in the 17th century, to have had their spirit uplifted by the beauty and wonder of some thirty miles of England which comes into sight from the bordering hills. H.G. Wells remarked, 'Sussex was not so great, nor so hilly and yet, like the sea, it achieved a greatness of effect, sending a mind into the skies.'[7]

The views across this immense tract of country, remote and dream-like, from Lympne in Kent to Petersfield in Hampshire, were discovered by the diarist John Evelyn, the critic John Dennis and by other professed admirers of the Picturesque. One of the first Sussex poets inspired by them was Eliza Hitchener, an intimate of Shelley, in 1821. To John Constable the view across the Weald was 'perhaps the most grand and affecting natural landscape of the world'.[8] To Philip Webb, the seminal architect of the William Morris circle, the boundless horizon from his retirement home on a ridge near Three Bridges was a perfect landscape, 'as lovely in its way as anything in the wide world, including France'.[9] Landscape artists from the 1850s, notably John Linnell, saw this visual experience as at once a natural marvel and a human epic.

David Watkin remarked of this panorama that the earliest writers 'saw an excited version of a Capability Brown park on the grandest scale with range after range of hills composing themselves as elegantly and harmoniously as a Claude landscape'.[10] In the late 19th century, the novelist George Eliot was so much enchanted by this 'round world' of the Weald that she chose to holiday there and eventually retired to it at Witley, near Haslemere.[11] The Trundle, Devil's Dyke, and Caburn and Firle Beacon also provide extensive panoramas of Weald, Down and sea, and are encountered again and again in literature.

Victorians looking down from one of the vantage points overlooking the Weald to the distant South Downs perceived it as one of the great landscapes of England. More than anything else it established Sussex as a place of consolation, healing and contemplation, either by its physical presence or through reading about it. As an image of paradise it tempted writers and others who wanted to launch, defend and spread thoughts and ideas in a novel forum, by exploring the intimate joys of the Sussex countryside – the rivers, heaths, woods, farms, fields and villages.

To the spectator the view had nothing in common with the famous medieval vision of Piers Plowman, whose extensive vale stretching below a hillside in the Malverns was a 'fair field full of folk', but it was particularly fitted for the spirit of the new age. Wild nature had been seen as an enemy, an obstacle to be overcome, but instead of over-zealously eradicating the forest on the poor lands of the Weald, trees had been kept for commercial forestry. The human occupation of the area is still so sparse that, instead of being spangled with closely spaced village churches in open country, in the view from afar man and his works appear invisible. This apparent absence of man takes on an almost supernatural awe when distances are shrouded in mist or haze, at early dawn and at sunset, or when changing colours are caused by sunlight piercing the vapour-laden air of moving clouds.

3 *The escarpment of the Downs near the Devil's Dyke, watercolour, Roger Pike, 1912. The series of combes and the winding lane at their foot have always made this one of the favourite sections of downland.*

The 'Wood of England', or the 'Wood beyond the World', gripped the public imagination with intimations of that older England before man's reshaping.

As Hilaire Belloc remarked in 1909 from his home in the Sussex Weald, blocked in by hills and the sea the Weald was a perfect refuge, 'exactly the place for a seclusion from men'.[12] Earlier, Louis Jennings, in one of the first books trumpeting the Downs as a Promised Land, found his Eden in the ancient park of Wiston below Chanctonbury Ring, where he was convinced that Mother Nature's healing hand would sooth away the wounds resulting from the anxieties and troubles of life.[13] In H.G. Wells' *Research Magnificent* (1915) William Benham's purposeless life following troubled times in London is clarified on overlooking the Weald and walking through Sussex.

By the time Wells was writing, Sussex was perceived as the sanctuary of England. This is the message of Sussex poets such as Vera Arlett, G.D. Martineau and the Rev. Orde Ward. The man who voiced most emphatically the need for respite in a rural place was author and poet Ford Madox Ford, who recovered his strength of mind and ability to write again by deliberately residing in a hermitage in the depths of the Sussex countryside at Red Ford near Storrington and at Cooper's, Bedham near Pulborough. He went there not for 'beauty spots' but 'just country' – commonplace fields, hedges and country lanes – for he did not want stimulation, only rest:

> And it is only to-day that I see again a little nook of the earth, the tiniest of hidden valleys, with a little red stream that buries itself in the red earth beneath the tall green of the grass and the pink and purple of the camias, the occasional gold of buttercups and the cream of meadow sweet. The plants in the garden move in stiff rows like a battalion on parade – the platoons of lettuce; the head-quarters staff, all sweet herbs; and the colour company, which is of scarlet runners. The little old cottage is under a cliff of rock, like a ginger-bread house from a Grimm's fairy-tale; the silver birches and the tall pines confront it; the sunlight lies warmer than you could imagine in the hollow and a nightingale is running in and out of the beanstalks.[14]

Enriching and embellishing the landscape was the rich past – immaculate villages, the lesser manors with their charming names, great houses, castles and ruined abbeys, vestiges of prehistoric and Roman times, fine gardens together with art collections and museums – the galaxy of which E.V. Lucas sang.[15] The Sussex past inspired Kipling, when he moved to Bateman's in Burwash in 1902, to write of Sussex as 'the genuine England of folklore and song', and it was the traditions and folklore of Sussex which appealed so strongly to Charles Dalmon. Arthur Stanley Cooke thought of the Downs as 'the Everlasting Hills' that had not changed since they met the gaze of a Roman soldier at his hill station, and Habberton Lulham loved the Downs primarily for what he regarded as their changelessness in a world of change. It was on the Downs before its ploughing up from 1940 that the past was most predominant. So many prehistoric, Saxon and medieval sites lay relatively untouched that the past was physically before one and could actually be walked into. This sense of the past was often an illusion, but until comparatively recently Sussex was one of the slowest changing parts of England, and even up to the 1950s, when light industries were beginning to invade the countryside, rural ways of life resembled more those of a century earlier than our present day. To outsiders, the countryside, market towns and the manners and customs of the people were delightfully old-fashioned in comparison with the 'progressive' parts of England that had been remodelled by steam or intensive 'high farming'.

Sussex was thought of by Victorians and Edwardians as the most Saxon of the English counties. The gifted naturalist W.H. Hudson claimed that 'Saxon' characteristics, physical and moral, prevailed in Sussex. He found a strong 'Saxon' appearance in the natives, with their round, moon-like faces, blue eyes and light brown hair. The 'Saxon' air was strengthened by the antiquated agricultural techniques in use, especially the cumbrous wooden plough and the heavy Sussex wagons pulled by plodding oxen, as well as the modest little churches. It was reinforced by the Sussex dialect, essentially broad Saxon, and by continuing superstition among country folk.[16] D.H. Lawrence, finishing off *The Rainbow* at Greatham, near Pulborough, noted in 1915 how strange it was that Old England lingered in patches, 'amidst these shaggy gorse commons and marshy, snake-infested places near the foot of the South Downs, the spirit of place lingering on primeval, as when the Saxons came so long ago'.[17] (See also pp.47-8.)

Even up to 1939, rural life was dominated by the past. Bob Copper, descended from a Rottingdean farming family, has compared a day's work by ploughmen in his time with an extract from a dialogue of Aelfric, a Saxon abbot of the 10th century, and found that for 1,000 years man and beast had teamed up in precisely the same manner to wrest a living from the same acres of downland.[18] Similarly, Maude Robinson of Saddlescombe Farm near the Devil's Dyke observed in the 1860s that her father kept 12 oxen for ploughing, the same number as the Knights Templar who had owned the farm in 1225; his sheep were enclosed within wattles and hurdles, as had been those of the warrior-priests.[19] One could meet literary characters such as Kipling's Old Hobden and Meredith's Andrew Hedger in the flesh in scenes that hardly ever changed. The sheep came slowly down from a hillside to lie in the fold at sunset, as they had probably done for more than three thousand years, the villages and hamlets had hardly grown since the Middle Ages, and smock-frocked farmers still worked the fields. Sussex at the end of the 19th century was still regarded as the home of 'the simple, tenacious Saxon'. George Moore, author of *Esther Waters*, set in Shoreham, and of other Sussex books, was proud of his perceived South Saxon ancestry and remarked that 'the country of my instinctive inspiration would be Sussex, the most Saxon of all'. W.H. Hudson, a stranger to Sussex, thought it odd in *Nature in Downland* that W.B. Yeats, 'the leader of the Celtic school', should live at Steyning, 'the most Saxon district in England'.[20]

Huge Sussex barns, covered with lichen, the enormous Sussex wagons, painted blue or scarlet, the mellow cottages and bright red bricks, all gave an aura to the landscape that was picturesque, reassuring, 'a kindly piece of England to be cradled in'; H.E. Bates likened its effect to the friendly tranquilising of a familiar room.

Chanctonbury Ring has acquired a special magic of its own. Generations of local people and visitors have seen the clump of trees high on the Downs as a symbol of Sussex, conveying a sense of permanence, ancientness and beauty. It was planted on the Iron-Age hill-fort and Roman temple by Charles Goring in his boyhood in 1760 and led to numerous imitative coronals on other downland summits. When R. Thurston Hopkins and others attempted to express what the Ring meant to them they said they never saw it in the 'blue distance' without feeling a thrill in their blood.[21] Its site has long had associations with paganism, and superstition connected with the Devil and other agencies centres on the Ring. On May Day's eve hardy walkers await Morris men who dance at the Ring from midnight to 2 a.m. Night walks by people drawn irresistibly to the mysterious hill to see the sunrise from its slopes are a familiar part of Sussex literature. Walter Wilkinson tells of an organised party from West Chiltington heading with rucksacks and blankets for the Ring in the mid-1930s. Blades of grass on the high part of the black malignant hills were illuminated by the glow-worms' 'fairy radiance of their small lamps'.[22]

The composer John Ireland was struck by the strange sight of dancing children at Chanctonbury Ring. The Ring drew him like a magnet and he felt in contact with a supernatural presence which compelled him to convey his feelings for its mystery ain his music. He found a house to live in with an uninterrupted view of the Ring and with no other house in sight. At Rock Mill near Washington, some 350ft above sea level, he spent the last 10 years of his life. (He is buried in Shipley churchyard near Horsham in view of his beloved Downs.)[23]

Mervyn Stockwood, Bishop of Southwark (1959-81), carried the lonely burden of his ministry for over twenty years with the help of repeated visits to Chanctonbury Ring for reflection. On his visit to the Ring in 1959 he had doubts whether he should take up the appointment of Bishop, and took it as an augury that he would be seldom out of controversy when black storm clouds suddenly blotted out a flaming red sky. On several other occasions he returned to the Ring to turn matters over in his mind. He was on Chanctonbury Ring when considering resignation from his see, and the curtain of his ministry finally came down when he was alone there on New Year's Day in 1981, lifting his depression.[24]

4   *Chanctonbury Ring on the eve of the Great Storm, 1987.*

5 *Michael Fleetwood's drawing of Laughton Tower, built by Sir William Pelham in 1534 and one of the earliest brick buildings in Sussex. The tower is now restored by the Landmark Trust.*

Thus Sussex was regarded as separate. In early Saxon times it had a strong sense of identity, a kingdom set within the framework of the long seaboard, the Downs and the wooded Weald which hemmed it in on the north. As late as the 18th century the primitive roads of the Weald tended to isolate Sussex, so that for centuries it was as self-supporting as rural civilisation would allow and acquired something of the isolation and remoteness of an island. Even after this isolation was broken down by turnpikes and railways Sussex retained something of its deep-rooted identity, as Roman canton, Saxon shire and diocese, that devotees of the county liked to think were older than the kingdom of England itself. Sussex was sufficiently different from, say, Surrey, which was more suburban, and Kent, more metropolitan, to deserve attention in its own right. This sense of particularity has long inspired an intense patriotic sentiment among South Saxons, both of birth and adoption, and it strongly infused Sussex literature from the 1890s. G.D. Martineau's sentiment can be taken as speaking for many of the retired Sussex population:

> Lord, give me but a Sussex hill,
> A book, a blue grey sea,
> And I can pass through life until
> The downland covers me.

'On the Downs', *Old Sussex and other Poems* (1924)

'BELOVED OVER ALL': THE GLORYING OF SUSSEX

Sussex was specially fitted for relaxation or retirement to town dwellers and its champions ensured the world knew that the Promised Land was not like ordinary country. Following Belloc and Kipling, the county's writers never doubted that Sussex earth had something of heaven in it. They set out to convince readers that Sussex was 'the tops', where the air one breathed was the finest in England and the turf trod the best in the world. Hilaire Belloc gloried 'the Sussex which is Eden still';[25] Rudyard Kipling sang of the spot 'beloved over all' and of his joy that the lot had fallen to him to love 'Sussex by the Sea' in *Sussex* (1902). Arthur Mee in his popular 'King's England' series regarded Sussex as 'the county of counties for sheer English beauty'. This depiction of Sussex as a 'matchless land' was taken up enthusiastically by lesser writers.

Bourdillon's *In Praise of Sussex* is brimful of local patriotism which he wanted to impart to schoolchildren:

> What land is like this pleasant land that leaneth
>   to the sea …
> What love is like our love for her? What pride is
>   as our pride?

E.V. Lucas expressed the same idea:

> You bade me (a superfluous thing)
> You bade me of our Sussex sing: …
> No other county has such treasure
> As ours, in overflowing measure.

Charles Dalmon wrote of Sussex:

> Is there any other land so good?
> I doubt it, O, I doubt it!

Journalists became willing propagandists for the county. Sussex was advertised in the early 1900s to people worn out in business or by the social world as stranger and more beautiful than many distant countries and yet 'within a hour's drive of the metropolis of the world'.[26]

6   *The Seven Sisters from near Hope Gap are now in jeopardy on account of severe coastal erosion. The Cuckmere estuary is in the foreground.*

Such literary jingoism reached a peak with R.D. Charques who, in 1936, on a sunny summer's day on the Seven Sisters, felt a sudden love of his country, intoxicated as he was with its beauty and a sense that he was far away from 'war and rumours of war, untroubled by dictatorships and concentration camps, delivered from the theories of Utopia and portents of ruin'. This led to a burst of Anglomania 'which declared England as the salt of the earth, the most beautiful and understanding'.[27]

This pride led to a loud, flamboyant patriotism amounting to Sussex-mania. Writers adopted the literary equivalent of Elgar's 'Land of Hope and Glory', with all its banners waving to double basses, cellos, violins, wind, brass, bugles and full grand organ. There was too much sound and not enough sense. As Edward Shanks noted, Kipling's *Sussex* (1902) 'uses a little too much brass in its orchestra',[28] while Belloc was declaiming 'the great hills of the South Country' as the crown of England, superior to the Midlands, in his poem 'The South Country'.

Such excessive homage inevitably incurred scorn from those who did not live in the land of the blest. A journalist on the eve of the Second World War praised Sussex but remarked that he often encountered 'faint scorn' for a Sussex rather built up and overdone, with acres of 'cosy palaces … period houses under construction, actresses' beamy weekend cottages … the hackneyed tags of Kipling and Belloc', and the banal pictures in the Royal Academy. He countered this criticism by describing the 'real' Sussex of Chanctonbury Ring, the wild daffodils near West Dean, the terns diving off Selsey, and of Petworth House, Arundel Castle and Wiston. For these he was not prepared to leave, 'even though a few more houses should be built in Sussex and even a few more verses written about it'.[29]

Criticism of Sussex also came from Northcountrymen who were unexcited by the gentle landscapes and 'awful' treeless Downs, and they rather thought that a modest set of hills hymned to such tunes was not to be wished for but rather to be lived down. E. Montague in the 1920s went further and, with Sussex evidently uppermost in his mind, thought that 'in some pleasant parts of the south you may reasonably tremble for England'. He pictured Sussex inhabited by feeble, lotus-eating idlers who, by living in the country and doing what they loved, were sponging off the hard-earned wealth created north of the Trent, and jeopardising England's economic and moral standing by giving the impression of living their lives as if on holiday.[30] Harold Nicolson of Sissinghurst was uneasy about living comfortably as a writer in uncomfortable times but was reassured in 1932, when the capitalist system had broken down, that he was justly withdrawing from the wreckage to contemplate reasons for the world's ills.[31]

A county extravagantly praised as the most cherished place on earth inevitably provoked other scornful reactions. Evelyn Waugh and Cyril Connolly detested the vogue for the rustic which preserved ancient monuments, revived arts and crafts, and produced Ye Olde Inns and other pseudo-Tudor buildings along the main roads. To the quaint and the picturesque they added all talk of 'Belloc's beer' and Eric Gill's Ditchling.[32] The most successful literary riposte was Stella Gibbons' comic parody of rural life in the South Downs, *Cold Comfort Farm* (1932), which reminded readers, with tongue in cheek, that 'Sussex, when all is said and done, is not quite like other counties'. Hers was not a Sussex that anyone had met in literature before. Urban readers fed on Sussex landscape were familiar with a countryside described as a sunny and happy Elysium by writers who hid

7   Alfred Glendening, 'Arundel Castle', 1882, depicts the great expanse across the Weald to the North Downs.

the reality of rural life – the muck and drudgery, the dilapidated farm buildings and insanitary cottages, the struggle with heavy clays, thin chalks or hungry sands, and the darker side of life generally. All this Stella Gibbons supplied in full measure in one of the funniest books ever written on Sussex.

But, despite the hype, many Englishmen besides Belloc and Kipling thought of Sussex as 'beloved over all'. Half-doubting eyes and ears, they believed the song-makers and the poets had neither erred nor exaggerated. Many of those who came into Sussex with suspicion or prejudice were evidently conquered by its charms.

Chapter 2

BEYOND THE SMOKE: LONDON'S CRY FOR THE COUNTRY

Oh for space, sweet air, clean rain,
How these streets lie reeking!
Love, let's be our own again,
Hear your own soul speaking;
Let us get these walls beyond,
To wave, and star, and heather,
Feel once more the primal bond
That holds the world together.

Habberton Lulham, 'Escape', in *Songs from the Downs and Dunes* (1908)

The intrinsic beauty and interest of the Sussex landscape goes a long way towards explaining the magnetism of the county for urban outsiders between *c.*1880 and 1939, but it is inter-relationships with the expanding London and the towns and cities around it that largely explain the modernisation of Sussex. London's seemingly unstoppable growth from the end of Tudor times accelerated up to the middle of the 18th century, when it 'took off' in unparalleled fashion. In Henry James's description, the 'dreadful, delightful city' of the 1880s was already of such magnitude that its 'immeasurable circumference' was lost in smoke. Victorian Liberals had the conviction that as London grew bigger it got no better. It spread like a tidal wave over the surrounding countryside, engulfing small towns and villages into one single great conurbation, becoming more acridly smoky and in various other ways a less agreeable place in which to live. Furthermore, it divided the city dwellers from their natural habitat, the prime cause of the alienation of modern technological man. Juxtaposed with one of the world's most artificial environments, the Sussex sea and countryside supplied an antidote to industrialisation and urbanisation, particularly important at a time when most townspeople were country-bred, or descended from parents or grandparents who had lived in the country before the 'rural exodus' beginning in the 1840s.

Intellectual tradition of the 18th century had conceived the city as the formative centre of civilisation. The relatively compact and coherent 18th-century London had inspired Dr Johnson's famous aphorism: 'He who is tired of London is tired of life.' But Victorians and their successors had to come to terms with the spectacular outward expansion of the capital to over 120 square miles in 1901 and to some 200 square miles in 1939, the first world capital to grow so big so rapidly. *Pace* Dr Johnson there was not then in the densely urbanised environment all that life could provide, with peoples' homes distant from work and leisure and open spaces permanently lost.

The preference for a life outside cities that was to transform Sussex so profoundly had been ingrained in English culture for centuries. The Englishman was never instinctively a town-dweller. Fourteenth-century foreigners reported that the wealthy English, unlike magnates in medieval Paris or the Italian city states, did not reside permanently in their capital city. Three centuries later it was still widely accepted in Georgian bourgeois circles that the essence of civilised life was to reside alternately at the worldly centre of London and in the seclusion of a rural retreat, which meant within a radius of some ten miles from London's centre. When London was small and the countryside was at it gates, the typical citizen made do with an hour's airing in nearby fields and riverside walks, as Chaucer did from Aldgate, or as other generations did in Moorfields. The same relatively easy access to London's countryside was still available later, though one had to venture further out to escape the buildings, as is evident from Pepys' *Diary*. He writes of regular family strolls to the Thames riverside at Barnes or Rotherhithe, or to Acton, then a health resort, and of the coach trips he amusingly calls his 'Grand Tours', which were actually visits to nearby fields in Hackney and Islington.

As the bricks and mortar spread, journeys to London's surrounding green fields became longer and less convenient. The journalist Leigh Hunt confirmed that although poorer

8   *Acre Lane, Brixton, c.1820. George Scharf captures the now roaring street when it was a lane shaded by trees and inhabited by nurserymen, cowkeepers and smalholders. London families strolled into the fields to enjoy fresh air on Sundays.*

Cockneys in the 1820s thought of Primrose Hill as their *ultima Thule*, the rising middle class had become conscious of the rural surroundings beyond and had made a 'remarkable discovery, of a large tract of territory as much undiscovered as New South Wales and yet within a short distance of the metropolis which surrounds it on all sides – London's countryside'.[1] It is at this point that the story of Sussex begins a new chapter. The growing number of turnpikes out of London stimulated leisure travel and the first guidebooks on London's countryside were published, the most successful of these being John Hassell's *Picturesque Rides and Walks within Thirty Miles of the British Metropolis* (1817). Shortly afterwards the likes of *Pickwick Papers* and *Jorrocks*, picaresque country literature, satisfied the new hunger for the open air among the wealthier urban population.

One of the first to avail himself of better travel facilities for a temporary escape into Sussex was the philosopher and writer Thomas Carlyle in 1840. After a mental breakdown in the 'great black Malebolge', he wanted to see the green face of his old Mother Earth, 'clear of the bricks and reck' and undefiled by soot. It proved an effective remedy. He eventually reached on horseback the Hares at Herstmonceux rectory and found the Sussex Weald a 'country of miracle'. 'A sense of magic,' he wrote, 'of enchantment, hangs over the whole history. The world of nature is everywhere charged with glamour, silence and appeals which awaken emotion beyond the power of words.' He came back convinced that the sight of a silent green field with a great silent sky over it should not be denied any mortal man. His sentiments are a landmark in the perception of the Weald, which hitherto had not been deemed tourist-worthy (see p.28).[2]

But it was the railway that opened up Sussex to the Londoner and made practicable Carlyle's dream of escape. Mark Rutherford captured something of the novelty when his family took an early excursion train from London Bridge to Hastings in mid-July. They did not mind a most uncomfortable journey in heat and dust in order to see the sea. The pleasure of 'imprisoned Londoners' strolling westward to Bexhill on clean sand was exquisite, for it was free of 'the filfth and litter of a London suburb and its broken hedges, its brickbats, its torn advertisements, its worn and trampled grass in fields half given over to the speculative builder'.[3]

In proportion to its growing size, London became so much blacker that the phrase 'The Smoke' became cockney slang for the name of the capital. As representative of the 1870s as Dr Johnson was of a time a hundred years earlier was (Sir) Leslie Stephen, whose daily experience of London he likened to an endurance test, especially in the penitential gloom of winter. But it was not only on grounds of health and depressed spirits that complaints were being made of smoke.[4] Monet and Whistler had shown that night and fog transformed unsightly things into objects of mysterious beauty, or hid them clean away, and turned noble buildings into fairy palaces, but Lord Leighton, the President of the Royal Academy, grieved at the 'crushing curse' his brother painters suffered at the quenching of light. The 'blotting out of colour' sent artists from Melbury Road to Pevensey Bay in winter to seek purer light. Leighton yearned for the 'fragrance of a thousand blooms, not the soot of a thousand chimneys wafted through open windows'.[5]

By the 1870s Victorians who could remember walking through meadows beyond Swiss Cottage, or seeing cows milked at Kentish Town, West Hampstead, Kilburn, Willesden, or Primrose Hill, before villas violated them, were left with a deep sense of estrangement

9   *Severe congestion at Ludgate Circus depicted by Gustave Doré in the 1870s. Doré contrasted this with the comparative calmness of Paris.*

from natural life. (Sir) Robert Hunter justified in 1880 the rescue of London's commons from the speculative builder by the longing to escape of Londoners whose eyes ached for the sight of green spaces.[6]

Broadly speaking, it was London's encroachment on the surrounding areas that led to the 'discovery' of Sussex in the Railway Age. There are, of course, those who have always found more romance in the 'mighty mass of brick and smoke and shipping' of steam civilisation than in rural scenery. Charles Lamb, an inveterate Londoner, declared at the outset of the Romantic Movement that because he had been born in a crowd he had an almost insupportable aversion to solitude and rural scenes and preferred to see a mob of happy faces at the door of the Drury Lane theatre than 'all the flocks of silly sheep that ever whitened the plains of Arcadia or Epsom Downs'. Lamb also stoutly defended the London fog, 'the true London Particular, as manufactured by Thames Coal, Gas, Smoke, Steam, and Co.', noting that the taste of it when dashed with a fine season of sea-coal smoke was far from inspid.[7] Henry James, in 1876, fresh from Paris via the United States, drew up a tremendous list of reasons, 'and much more', why life in London was insupportable,

10 *A townscape of deprivation, Bermondsey, Gustave Doré, 1870s.*

17

but as an artist whose business was the observation of human life London was to him the complete compendium of the world.[8] Conrad's view was similar, his imagination quickened by the immense possibilities London offered for stimulation and fulfilment in story-telling – 'Room enough there to place any story, depth enough there for any passion, variety enough for any setting, darkness enough to bury five millions of lives.' Virginia Woolf also found poetry in London and, loving it, took possession of it, as in her London novel *Mrs Dalloway*. She wrote in the 1920s of the beauty and excitement of King's Cross and of the neighbouring streets as 'aglow with poetry', although to most people it was squalid and prosaic. 'London itself perpetually attracts, stimulates, gives me a play and a story and a poem without any trouble save that of moving my legs through the streets.' Yet, she always had an outlet in Sussex which was indispensable to her for her writing and periodic recuperation, and her husband Leonard, a fanatical gardener, confessed before her death in 1941 that 'I like country life, even with bombs, much better than London without.'[9]

George Eliot, regarded at the end of her life as the leading English novelist, was never well in London and sought country air in Surrey and Sussex, expressing her despair at being imprisoned in a London drawing-room where outside was yellow smoke, the houses opposite were the only view, and everything was monotonous and shadowless. Everyone hurried past regardless of others and the world seemed one huge prison-house to her.[10] The novelist George Gissing, who lived in poverty in London, provided the most comprehensive account of a Londoner's experience of town and country and its effect on him as a writer. In *The Private Papers of Henry Ryecroft* (1903), where he disguised his own personality in fiction, he noted how for years the seasons would pass unobserved in London and yet those who had never looked upon a meadow, nor travelled as far as the tree-bordered suburbs, felt no hardship 'imprisoned in boundless streets' because they had no idea what they were missing; on a hot August day their thoughts might wander to the sea. His health began to suffer from excess toil, bad air, poor food and many miseries, and he experienced a maddening desire for countryside and sea. When he eventually escaped into the country it was a moment of exquisite joy. Town-born and bred, and scarce knowing anything but street vistas, he found himself before a natural landscape, the light and air of which had something of the supernatural: 'I had stepped into a new life … in a single day I had matured astonishingly … I suddenly entered into the conscious enjoyment of powerful sensibilities which had been developing unknown to me … It gave me a new lease of life, and taught me – in so far as I was teachable – how to make use of it.'[11] Gissing and George Eliot can be seen as precursors of the writers invasion of the countryside; they were followed by, for example, John Halsham's successive removes into 'real' country from the outskirts of London, Habberton Lulham's shift from Sydenham to Ditchling, and the Eric Gill group from Hammersmith to the same place. They rediscovered the ordinary accoutrements of country walking, such as thick boots and walking sticks, most 'ordinary' Londoners knowing nothing of these things, the country being a closed book to them.

The continual noise and movement of London and other big cities were leaving people mentally and physically exhausted and in need of exercise or relaxation, or a change of scene. The notion spread that fresh air was a tonic, and that the quiet of the country induced sleep. Londoners began to dream of Sussex horizons and acquired an ardent longing for 'green country', pining for the pure air and deep country silences, whether Downs – which meant

Sussex to most – the quiet woods and lanes of the Weald, the sleepy rivers for fishing, or the old cottages for painting and weekending.

LONDON'S CRY FOR THE COUNTRY, C.1880-1939

By the 1880s 'going beyond the smoke' meant longer journeys still because the smoky cloud, caused mainly by domestic coal-burning, had mushroomed further outwards, sending its miasma deep into the Weald when the wind blew from the north. It was regarded as an evil oppressing the city and yearly increased in intensity. In December 1890 *The Times* lamented:

> Can we dispel that overhanging canopy of gloom which makes London in winter a city of dreadful and almost everlasting night? Can we divest ourselves of that fetid shroud which makes us all wanderers in an Inferno even more drear than Dante ever imagined? It is difficult to give even a hopeful answer … What would London give, what indeed would it not give, if some man of science would tell it how to get rid of that intolerable winter gloom which destroys now so unnecessarily, lowers its vitality, impedes its labour and destroys its happiness?[12]

The cause of Londoners' craving for the countryside was, however, deeper than the immediate urge to escape from the fog: as Henry Williamson recounted in the early chapters of his *Chronicle of Ancient Sunlight*, it was the moral atmosphere which choked people. His

Tramp. "WELL, THERE'S SOMETHIN' TO BE SAID FOR NOT 'AVIN A SUBURBAN RESIDENCE."

11   *Escaping to the country or seaside provided respite from London trams.*

opinion appears to have been widely held at the time and the comfortably-off Victorian and Edwardian intelligentsia, increasingly uncertain of their Christian convictions, were turning to the countryside for spiritual inspiration and transcendental excitement, particularly to long-distance walking and mountain climbing, and this filtered down to mass rambling and hiking in the inter-war years. Against a background of general concern at the conditions of urban life, Ruskin's pen had been a powerful weapon in bringing the idea of the Victorian city into disrepute, and William Morris, and other prominent writers on national identity such as Sir Leslie Stephen, sowed the notion that the 'real' England was provided by the natural beauty of the countryside. This had been the message of George Meredith, and Sir George Trevelyan, the leading historian of his generation and a prominent member of the National Trust and admirer of Meredith, made the same point when he wrote: 'We are, like it or not, children of the earth, and removed from there our spirit withers or runs in various forms of insanity.'[13] The famed broadcaster and walker S.P.B. Mais returned to the theme as late as 1948 by stating, 'We just have to get back to the country whence we were originally sprung or will wilt away in spirit and body. Unless we can refresh ourselves at least by intermittent contact with nature we grow awry.'[14]

Disillusionment with London in the 1920s intensified among survivors of the First World War trenches, who felt they had been making the world fit only for financial disaster and moral decay. In this jaundiced mood they thought London was no place for them and, rather than end up in a growing London suburb, felt getting away from it all in the country would cure them.

To travel into Sussex was to be transported from the newest phase in English life to one of the oldest, where the Londoner could re-establish contact with a rural landscape not disrupted by modern technology, the countryside of his bygone years. The cockney's vision of Sussex was like a child's wonder experienced when on holiday. This thrill has not been better expressed than by Edward Thomas, who in writing of his childhood in Sussex on holidays from Balham before the First World War remarked on the sense of heightened charm imparted to the green country by its contrast with the metropolis.[15]

Migrant writers responded with the intensity of a first love when they found themselves for the first time before a natural landscape. Edward Johnston, the calligrapher and writer, looking back in old age, recalled his state of mind when he looked around Ditchling, which had captivated his fancy on arrival from Hammersmith. He remembered the time when 'Ditchling' was like music to his ears. He had idealised it and given it some of the love he never gave a woman.[16] Eleanor Farjeon was equally extravagant about the South Downs when she first encountered them, and also placed them above human beings in her regard: 'I don't mean I love them more, and yet in a sense I think perhaps I do … They've healed me more, and given me more strength, certainty and peace, than any other living being.'[17] The poet Vera Arlett felt the same about the 'quiet Wealden country', which she called her most 'beautiful friend' as it had offered to her the same companionship and comforts.[18] Bruce Cummings (pseudonym Barbellion), who died after suffering a long illness in 1917, watched from London the countryside of southern England being prised away from him before he could 'swallow landscapes and swill down sunsets, or grapple the whole earth with ropes of steel', which he had craved to do since walking on the elastic turf of the South Downs.[19] Belloc, who had started the passionate acclaim for Sussex, felt compelled to write

12 *Congestion at Piccadilly Circus, 1940s, from the 1943 Report on the Planning of London.*

rhapsodic verse at his county's 'call', and within a short time of arriving at Rottingdean Kipling had sold his soul to the special balm of the South Downs:

> I've given my soul to the Southdown grass,
> And sheep-bells tinkled where you pass.
> Oh Firle an' Ditchling an' sails at sea,
> I reckon you keep my soul for me!

Such experiences matured them as writers. Their new lease of life gave them sensibilities and powers which were unknown before the release from cities.

But it was not only writers and artists who felt this way. After 1918 the countryside ethic was spread well beyond the middle classes and espoused by such rural elegists as Prime Minister Stanley Baldwin and writer and statesman John Buchan. Businessmen, politicians and industrialists were finding that the fret and continual noise of London got on their nerves. These wealthy migrants elevated the look of leisure to a finely judged art by creating parks and gardens, symbolic of pleasure and retreat, out of profits from the City, from coalfields or overseas. Accompanying them were the misfits, rebels, anarchists and escapists who chose to leave a place committed to capitalism and the world of the machine, things they felt harming human values and religious experience. From their nostalgia and dismay were born the Simple Life and Back-to-the-Land movements, and the followers of Ruskin and William Morris abandoned the city to take up cottage life and rural handicrafts. Doctors prescribed landscape as a potent medicine and Victorians and Edwardians understood that beneficial air and fresh surroundings was a tonic.

An issue gathering strength was the problem of outdoor recreation and leisure for the urban poor. It was addressed by the Commons and Open Spaces Society and by the National

13 *'York Street leading to Charles Street',*
Manchester, Pierre Adolphe Valette, 1913.

Trust following suggestions by Octavia Hill in her 'More Air for London' campaign. In *The Condition of England* (1909) Charles F.G. Masterman compared the monotonous daily lives of the people in ghettos such as Lambeth, Clerkenwell, Deptford and parts of Wandsworth, their long journeys to work, hurried meals, engine-like activity and morose attitude to pleasure, with the beauty and opportunities for leisure of young people in the countryside, with its 'long stretches of quiet downs standing white and clean from the blue surrounding sea'.

Thus when, on the declaration of war in 1914, Robert Blatchford thought of the England which would ultimately triumph, as recalled in his book *England and Germany,* he thought of the opal blue sea and the green curves of the Sussex Downs and the gleaming white cliffs of England, on which the hearts of exiles languished.[20] The same attitude continued into the next generation. During the Munich crisis in 1938 the *Daily Mirror* printed photographs of rural England to remind everyone what was at stake in the fight against 'the bully of Europe', and on the outbreak of war Frank Newbould painted the South Downs for war posters having the same purpose. Meanwhile, tram conductors at Brighton station would call out 'Here come the Londoners' as trainloads of trippers headed excitedly towards them to rock down the Queen's Road to the pier.

Chapter 3

CHANGING WAYS OF SEEING AND EXPERIENCING LANDSCAPE

Two of the circumstances explaining early visitors' delight in Sussex were the qualities of the landscape as perceived in the 19th and early 20th centuries and the impact of urbanisation generally. One further aspect needs consideration. Much of Sussex away from the coastal districts stayed broadly the same in outward appearance up to recent times, but the ways in which people looked at landscape and experienced it altered profoundly. Until the mid-19th century visitor responses were determined by fashionable notions of landscape beauty which have since been discarded. To understand how and why Sussex was so drastically changed in the 20th century we need to consider what the changes in public attitudes to landscape were, and to embark on one of the thorniest tasks of a cultural historian by explaining them.

14 *'The Vale of Pevensey', J.M.W. Turner, 1820s, one of the outstanding Sussex 'prospects'.*

HUNTING FOR 'PROSPECTS'

When scenery-seeking first became a passion, with the coming of the Romantic Movement, survivors of the Grand Tour made deliberate excursions in search of extensive and variegated panoramas or 'prospects'. The enjoyment of landscape had become established following Sir John Denham's 'Cooper's Hill', a 'prospect' or 'hill' poem (1642). Artists such as Claude Lorrain and Salvator Rosa, who painted idealised Italian scenery, were at the height of fashion and the newly invented Dutch term 'landskip' was synonymous with prospect. English views were not usually evaluated for their own sake but in terms of landscapes seen on the Grand Tour, notably in Italy, or those Italian scenes composed by revered artists. Tourists lived solely in the eye and rapturously drank in sweeps of prospect, spinning it out in their letters 'as the silkworm makes silk from the mulberry leaves' in the phrase coined by Romantic poet John Keats, who revelled in it himself.[1]

Travellers tried to find in the English spread of land and sea, fields, villages and towns, a prospect that 'would do' for Tuscany and Umbria as painted by classic artists or later described by, for example, Robert Browning. As late as 1908, in his *Room with a View*, E.M. Forster wrote that people were tending to forget Italy and notice more English things:

> How beautiful the Weald looks! The hills stand out above its radiance, as Fiesole stands above the Tuscan plain, and the South Downs, if one chose, were the mountains of Carrara.

Sussex was eminently suited to a game like this, for much of the county lies in the oval bowl of space of the Weald within a frame of the North and South Downs, whose vantage points over the wooded expanse affords, almost uniquely, views over three-quarters of the whole horizon circle, to furnish an unforgettable panorama which remains many people's favourite in all the world.

A defining moment in the cultural history of Sussex occurred in 1717 when John Dennis considered the prospect of the Sussex Weald and the line of the South Downs from Leith Hill in Surrey more extensive and surpassing in beauty anything he had ever seen in Italy. His was the first observation of its kind and signalled a new era in the appreciation of Sussex. John Macky also wrote admiringly of the prospect of the Weald by comparing it with the Lombardy Plain.[2]

Views across the Weald from his Aldworth home high on Blackdown also recalled Italian scenes to Tennyson. The poet William Allingham wrote in his Diary that Tennyson said of the landscape near his own home: 'It is like one at Florence. The south of England is like Italy. When I came back this summer and looked from the terrace at Blackdown, I thought it was exactly like Italy.'[3]

Even as late as the 1920s visitors to Aldworth returned with the same perception. In the sunshine the terrace had a 'curiously Italian look' and the scarlet flowers blazing on the balustrade were striking set against 50 miles of the chequered green of the Weald and the grey-blue of Chanctonbury Ring and the South Downs. Another Sussex view which recalled Italian scenery to 18th-century and early Victorian visitors was the vantage point of St Roche's Hill (now better known as the Trundle) on the Downs high above Chichester. A foreground of highly cultivated plain meets the sea in the headlands and

I   *Gill's Lap, Ashdown Forest, photographed in 1924.*

II   *Amberley Mount, S.R. Badmin, watercolour exhibited 1976.*

Clockwise from top left:

III *Wild daffodils in spring on the West Dean estate in the West Sussex South Downs.*

IV *The Arun, George Vicat Cole, 1880s.*

V *Pett Farm near Hastings, Vincent Lines.*

VI *An illustration of the South Downs from S.P.B. Mais's* Hills of the South, *1930s.*

VII *Landscape at Cooper's Farm in the High Weald, 2009 (photograph by M. Lunn).*

VIII *Kipling's 'Run of the Downs' (illustration by Donald Maxwell, 1926).*

IX *Belloc's Arun valley, an illustration by Donald Maxwell from the 1927 edition of Belloc's* Hills and the Sea.

X *Moated Herstmonceux Castle, the earliest brick-built mansion south of the Thames.*

XII *'Windover in Winter', Frank Wootton, 1945.*

XI *Kipling's downland dewpond, illustrated by Donald Maxwell, 1926.*

XIII *Hastings Stade up against the funicular railway climbing the sandstone cliffs.*

XIV *Pulpit, Berwick Church, initially panted by Vanessa Bell and restored after vandalism by her son Quentin.*

XV *Stopham Bridge, S.R. Badmin, 1980.*

XVI   *The shell of Buckingham House, Shoreham-by-Sea, the setting of George Moore's novel* Esther Waters.

XVII   *Cover illustration of S.P.B. Mais's* Hills of the South, *1930s.*

XVIII   *The Dacre tombs in Herstmonceux Church.*

XIX *An aerial view of Shoreham-by-Sea and its downland setting, 1980s.*

XX *Beach hut, Rye harbour.*
Photograph by Peter Grenhalf.

XXI *Splendour at Leonardslee.*

XXII *Gravetye, a garden created by William Robinson.*

XXIII   *Penns in the Rocks, Withyham,*
home of poet Dorothy Wellesley.

XXIV   *The 3rd Earl Cowper, Johann Zoffany,*
1770s, at Firle Place.

XXV   *Kipling's Bateman's, the east front.*

XXVI *George Stubbs, 'At Goodwood', 1759.*

XXVII *George Stubbs, 'The Charlton Hunt', 1759.*

XXVIII   *'Through the archway', Coke's House, West Burton,*
Wilfrid de Glehn, 1919.

XXIX   *Advertisement for the*
Southern Belle, *1890s.*

XXX   *Balcombe Viaduct, 1841, reconstruction by painter Mike Clodd.*

XXXI *Vincent Lines, artist Mrs Proust at Coastguards Cottages, Pett.*

XXXII *George Vicat Cole, 'Harvest Time', 1880.*

XXXIII *Roger Fry, 'Farm Pond at Charleston', 1918.*

XXXIV   *Eric Ravilious, Cuckmere Haven.*

XXXV   *'Amberley Castle from the big barn',*
S.R. Badmin, exhibited 1981.

XXXVI   *Paul Nash's Shell poster,*
'The Rye Marshes', 1932.

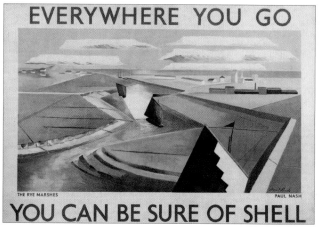

XXXVII *Lytton Strachey, by Duncan Grant, c.1909.*

XXXVIII *Leonard Woolf, by Henry Lamb, 1912.*

XXXIX *Charleston interior, Vanessa Bell, 1916–17.*

XL *'Beachy Head', Eric Ravilious, watercolour* c.*1939.*

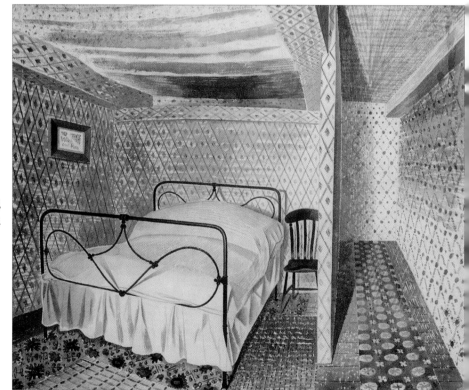

XLI *'Farmhouse Bedroom', Eric Ravilious, 1939.*

creeks of Chichester Harbour and leads the eye to the outline of the Isle of Wight. The focal point of this exquisite view is the spire of Chichester Cathedral. People would ride to the hill to gorge on the view which Horace Walpole remarked was 'in no slight degree the kind of horizon which Claude was accustomed to bound the finest of his pictures'.[4] His suggestion that the scene would have inspired a fashionable 17th-century painter of Italian scenery was enough to give it an iconic significance. It was a scene to inspire Collins' *Ode to Evening*, one of the great poems in the English language. It also influenced the siting of Carne's Seat in Goodwood park, from which the guests of the Dukes of Richmond were charmed by the view. A similar panorama of coast and Downs, but also extending northwards into the Weald, is had from Gumber Corner, on Stane Street high on the Downs, the origin of Hilaire Belloc's love of Sussex. Nearby is the favourite view from Bow Hill of the great naturalist Sir Arthur Tansley, which has the backdrop of the dramatic Kingley Vale and a view extending eastwards along the coast to Highdown Hill, above Worthing, and northwards to the Surrey Hills.

Another extended view that reminded people of Italy was the one from Herstmonceux Church across the Pevensey Levels to the wall of the Downs and a glimpse of sea captured by Turner in his 'Vale of Pevensey'. It was a favourite view of the artist Copley Fielding, a guest at the rectory. The rector Julius Hare was reminded of the fall to the marshes from Ostia, and Augustus Hare's adopted mother, an expatriate from Italy, thought in evening light or a sunlit day that it was the closest in feeling to the Mediterranean she could think of.[5] Her son thought of the view from his home at Holmhurst at the back of St Leonards as a Titian landscape similar to the view of the Roman Campagna from the Alban Hills.[6] However English this and the other scenes were, one could easily imagine oneself looking down from the terrace of a villa raised above the Lombardy plain.[7]

DISTASTE FOR THE BRIGHTON DOWNS TO THE LATE 19TH CENTURY

It took two or three generations in the late 18th and 19th centuries before the South Downs reached people's hearts and imaginations. From a passion for prospects, enthusiasm widened to other kinds of landscape from the end of the 18th century. When the chalk of the South Downs first came under scrutiny it was the more wooded western Downs that were favoured, the treeless eastern Downs behind Brighton and between Shoreham and Eastbourne not being appreciated by fashionable Regency visitors. In the 1820s William Cobbett, ever-ready to expose the frivolities of his age, reported that visitors to Brighton 'flee from open downland as naturally as from pestilence'. Their eyes seemed to have ached at the sight of its featureless convexity, bereft of the trees and water which feature so strongly on Italian canvases. Dr Johnson, for example, could not conceive a landscape without trees, and thought that if a man was overcome at the dismalness of the Sussex Downs he would not find a tree whereon to hang himself.[8] The poet Keats had the same taste: 'Plenty of trees, thank God; plenty of water, thank heaven.'[9] The author of *Excursions in the County of Sussex* (1822) warned visitors to Brighton that for 'the want of trees, and the nature of the soil', the landscape was 'monotonous, and in a degree even arid', disadvantages, it was claimed, that required all the influence of fashion and of royal patronage to counterbalance them. Only the Earl of Chichester's landscaped Stanmer Park had anything locally pleasing to the eye, reached after passing over 'the peculiarly bare and sterile-looking tract' that intervened.

15 *Ashdown Forest is now perceived as naturally beautiful but earlier generations hated it for defying cultivation.*

The source of this disparagement was the introduction of the new visual aesthetic, the Picturesque, by the Rev. William Gilpin. By 'Picturesque' Gilpin meant a scene or object that was actually beautiful and adapted for use in pictures, and the pictures he had in mind were those of the Roman Campagna by Claude Lorrain, Salvator Rosa, Ruysdael and Hobbema. In his 1792 essay Gilpin illustrated two landscapes, one smooth and rounded, with flowing curves and unadorned with trees, a perfect specimen of chalk scenery, and the other broken and varied, with much woodland, like the rugged scenery of the Lake District or Scotland. The latter was pronounced aesthetically pleasing, the former 'ugly' and 'disgusting'.[10]

A generation later, A.B. Granville in his *Spas of England* (1841) thought, 'Nothing can be more dismal-looking, barren, or discouraging than the general aspect of the immediately surrounding country on either side or at the back of Brighton.'[11] Mrs Merrifield, author of the first book on Brighton's natural history in 1860, noted for almost the first time the fascination of downland flora but conceded that visually the Downs were uninviting.[12] The famous preacher F.W. Robertson, of Holy Trinity church, Brighton, was the first to try to re-open visitors' eyes to Brighton downland overlooked by conventional notions about beauty.[13]

In his *Observations* of 1804 (based on a tour made 30 years earlier) Gilpin pronounced that around Brighton 'There is scarce an object either in it, or near it, that strikes the eye with any degree of beauty', adding that 'if the hills were not chalky, Lewes would be pleasantly situated'. Chalk landscapes with a 'blank glaring surface' had little beauty, either in form or in colour. The chalk cliffs of Beachy Head and of Dover, now regarded

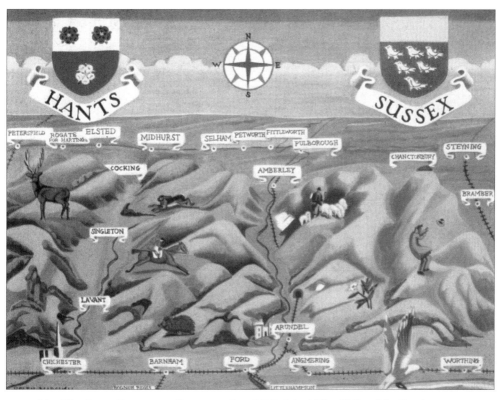

16 *West Sussex Downs, an illustration from S.P.B. Mais's* The Hills of the South, *1930s.*

17 *'Beachy Head', Adrian Berg, R.A., based on intense observation season by season.*

as icons of England, were dismissed as unpleasing objects. To a certain extent Gilpin was influenced by the landscape garden movement led by 'Capability' Brown which urged that open country was a canvas to be embellished with water and trees. (It was this influence which induced Charles Goring to plant the coronal of trees on Chanctonbury Ring in 1760, inspiring similar clumps all over Britain.)

Gilpin's theories would have had no practical importance had not the public embraced them so whole-heartedly, and for so long. He deprived several generations of the enjoyment of downland by means of a misbegotten insinuation which H.J. Massingham called a 'giant worm, trailing its slime over the counties of England'.[14] Gilpin's theories were almost totally abandoned by the generation of the 1870s and 1880s which treasured the Downs in the changed world of English urbanisation and industrialism. Yet Black's *Guide to Sussex*, which reached a 13th edition in 1905, while generally praising the Downs, noted that 'to some their gentle softness has the effect of monotony'. And John Davidson, who wrote a little earlier, thought only Southdown mutton gave him any joy in the bare Downs, which he likened to 'plucked fowls'.[15] It was not until Kipling glorified the eastern Downs that their universal enjoyment became commonplace.

COMPLAINTS OF THE SUSSEX WEALD

To the 18th-century traveller the Weald was the rascalliest of the Sussex districts. It was heaven viewed from a distance, the forest of Saxon Andredesweald, 'always seen in the distance, but which one never reaches', but hell to actually visit, a hill-billy country, sullen, malevolent and untameable. One reason why the Weald was disparaged and demonised was its thick hedgerows, alien to people more familiar with hedgeless open fields tilled in strips by an army of brightly clothed peasants. These formidable barriers were perceived as harbouring vermin and symptomatic of agricultural inefficiency because they got in the way of the plough. An element in 'hedgerow' was used as an epithet for the low, as in hedge-priest, hedge-writer, etc. Hedgerows also symbolised a faint wildness, and it appears to have been an instinctive fear of the 'wild' in natural places that caused this disaffection. The ancient name of 'Weald' was corrupted to 'wild' by 18th-century visitors who passed through it reluctantly on the way to more picturesque places. It is important, however, to bear in mind that the critics of the Weald were gentlemen or academics from comfortable rooms at Oxford or Cambridge. What little evidence we have of the humble Wealdsman's opinion of his existence suggests a certain comfortableness and well-being (see p.40).

From the beginning of the peasants' struggle with its hard-won clays and woods between the 12th and 14th centuries, the Weald was looked upon by critical outsiders as a third- or fourth-rate agricultural region. Deep woods harboured brigands and troublesome natives who were infected by a sense of democratic freedom imparted by the woodland and addicted to nonconformity in religion and outlandish traditions and customs. Heavily wooded districts such as the Weald were regarded as 'wild, blemished places', inhabited by a 'rude and lewd people', which compared unfavourably with fertile open country such as the Sussex coastal plain, a landscape of fruitful fields and hardy tillers that was to the 16th- and 17th-century taste of the English who followed ancient poets such as Horace. It also lacked elegant country seats and inns, and its roads when wet were thick with mire and when dry were unforgiving ruts. Travellers on the move, tossed and turned in the carriage as if in a small boat at sea, were too distracted to notice the prospect opening up before them. Wealden landscape and its ways of life were on the wrong side of the line that divided civilised and uncivilised, refined and unrefined. To the susceptible tourist, it was a place to be avoided rather than visited, and there are numerous malicious complaints and disappointments at not eating well, or travelling comfortably, or finding the scenery they had hoped. Agriculturally, many thought it sullen, untamed and intractable and 18th-century farming expert Arthur Young called it 'effectually a barbarism'.[16]

The Sussex Heathland

Two hundred years ago the profound silence, emptiness and strangeness of heaths filled people with horror and dread. To 18th-century tourists, travel through them was dangerous and 'scenically tiresome' and they were 'horrid and frightful' to look upon. Agriculturalists bewailed them as wastes and yearned for their enclosure into productive fields. Given the prevailing maxims about beauty, people found 'no object on which the eye can repose, even for a moment'.

Yet heather-country came to be regarded as desirable. Ruskin's preference for the 'wild' over the polished neatness of Richmond riverside influenced public perception, and evidence for this are the paintings of young Victorian artists such as Birket Foster and Helen Allingham in the Haslemere district. The new note was struck by Mrs Mary (Humphry) Ward who spent summers at Grayswood near Haslemere. She perceived heathland as wild and solitary, indeed, but rich, luxuriant and friendly to the sense of the

18   *Greenway near Buxted in the High Weald, formerly a highway.*

traveller, even in the loneliest of places. To her the 'untamed, primitive earth, guiltless of boundary or furrow' was not forbidding or austere but a 'hint of the primeval' on heaths and commons.[17] All around southern England the land was 'being tamed and groomed, the wildwood shorn away, the marshes drained, the fields tilled' into the sleek, man-made Home Counties. To the late Victorian middle-class the heath possessed a quality not encountered elsewhere and, as a healthier and more attractive alternative to London and other cities and towns, it created a minor urban exodus. The change in perception can be illustrated by the attitude towards Hindhead and Blackdown. Cobbett in the 1820s had a pact with himself never to set foot on Hindhead, which he regarded as an affront to an agricultural improver.[18] Fifty years later Tennyson was specially charmed by the riotous heather blossom for three months of the year at nearby Blackdown at the rear of his house. By then the expression 'patch of purple' was being over-used in literature.

The Downs that were England

The inspirational annexation into the kingdom of poetry and prose of the rhythmically rolling Sussex Downs, and the 'discovery' of the Sussex Weald by late Victorians are remarkable examples of the startling vagaries and vicissitudes over time of landscape knowledge and appreciation. In the 1940s and 1950s the pre-war South Downs were ploughed up and sowed to the skyline and suffered modern agri-business's over-use of chemicals, but an older generation recalled the endless stretches of springy turf exuding thyme-scented air, thorn trees wracked by the wind, clouds of butterflies, bees and moths, rustling in the undergrowth of crickets and grasshoppers, and the patches of heather, bracken, gorse and scrub. Skylarks and other wild birds were more numerous and the Downs were 'white-over with sheep'. It was with a sense of shock, deprivation and emptiness that they revisited a childhood haunt to find a featureless expanse of weed-free wheat or barley produced by industrial machinery.

The Downs' extraordinary reputation is due in part to the relentless 'booming' of them by the county's writers and artists, but they would have been unheeded by the urban audience without the effects of industrialisation. According to H.J. Massingham, life in cities and towns led to the concept of the South Downs as 'the very core of human life on earth, the pillar of human stability … Home and place and reality in a world of nightmares'.[19] The most rapturous of early appreciations of the Downs is Swinburne's heady late Victorian lyricism. On discovering the view from the summit of the Downs near Lancing Clump in 1887, he described it as, without exception, the most glorious view he had ever set eyes upon.[20] On Christmas Eve 1940, Virginia Woolf, marooned in Sussex by the bombs in London and deeply troubled by war and by doubts about the value of her last book *Between the Acts* (1941), lunched at Court Farm, Alciston amid the remains of its medieval hall and immense barn, the setting of her book. 'An incredible loveliness', she wrote, 'The downs breaking their wave, yet one pale quarry and all the barns and stacks either a broken pink or a verdurous green; and then the walk by the wall; and the church; and the great tithe barn. How England consoles and warms one in these deep hollows, where the past stands almost stagnant.'[21] Her husband, Leonard Woolf of Rodmell, who fell under the spell of the Downs in the unending summer of 1912, wrote of their gentle curves close to which he had lived ever since; he had learnt that 'in all seasons and

19 The hedged landscape of the Weald, akin to the bocage *of northern France and indicative of partial woodland clearance by peasants.*

circumstances, their physical loveliness and serenity can make one's happiness exquisite and assuage one's misery'.[22]

The *Quarterly Review* for 1862 suggests that tourists were discovering what they called quaintness and old-world beauty in the Downs. It thought there was no more tranquillising scene for the overwrought brain than the sight of the Downs on a fine summer's day and noted that the sight of plodding oxen taught a very lesson of patience in the fevered age of steam and electricity. The feeling that the Downs had stood still, and that the past had taken over its undulating landscape, was most exciting to the public imagination and drew scores of downland writers and artists into Sussex in the wake of Belloc and Kipling. Visitors found scenes which were not only mysterious, tender, 'wild' and calming but held traces at every hand of the presence of some of the earliest human beings in England in barrows, lynchets and hill-forts. The grand landmark of Chanctonbury Ring acquired a mystical and symbolic force without equal in southern England and is the most frequently cited place in Sussex literature.

After the thrill of walking or riding on the Downs, and the breeze and the joy of the views, the solitude and tranquillity begin to soak in. Beckett wrote in the early 1900s:

> No noise comes from the plain, but the occasional lowing of kine, the shout of a shepherd commanding his dog; on the Downs there is no sound but the song of the lark, and the musical tinkle of the sheep bell as the flock moves along a slope. I have walked for days on the Downs without seeing a single human being.[23]

To Louis Jennings, in his *Rambles on Southern Hills* (1880), one of the first books written on the Downs, the silence was like an exquisite vessel of porcelain: 'One scarcely dared to breathe lest it break.'[24]

The feeling of ancientness on the Downs engendered the notion of a kind of open-air museum or nature reserve, where one could see, touch and feel the presence of Old England. Helen Thomas, wife of poet Edward Thomas, encountered a thrill which left her feeling she was in the 'heart of England's being'; it engendered a deep and passionate patriotism and a sense of pride in belonging to the Downs and to their history and traditions that was almost religious in flavour, and Virginia Woolf thought of Mount Caburn as 'primeval'.[25] S.P.B. Mais, who knew the Downs well, considered them the quickest way to recover a sense of the long past, and that it was the long continuity of their ancestral links, together with the beauty of their rounded shapes, which made them the 'great consolers of

20 *Edward Thomas's view of the South Downs from Steep, Hampshire.*

the distressed spirit, as they are the inspirers of gaiety among the youthful'.[26]

Older people wistfully recalled a prospect which, in its emptiness and silence, recalled paradise. Miles upon miles of unfenced turf afforded an exhilarating sense of freedom which sent a wave of patriotism through those who trod it. People who knew the Downs then say that those who cannot remember that time do not know what life could hold. Something of their meaning can be recaptured by Hudson's splendid opening to his *Nature in Downland* (1900), a description of the silvery down of the dwarf thistle falling on a hot August day on the unenclosed and untilled earth of the sheep walks of Kingston Hill near Lewes; the sight of 'thousands upon thousands of balls or stars of down', universal then on the South Downs sheep pastures, reminded him of his old days on horseback in the South American Pampas. The site of Hudson's musing is now a sea of grain.

THE COUNTRY OF THE IGUANODON: THE NEW VISION OF THE SUSSEX WEALD

To Victorians the Weald was an English landscape of marked individuality which possessed a powerful visual appeal, arousing strong emotional responses in natural scientists, landscape artists, writers, architects, landscape gardeners and visitors alike. The first to re-evaluate the long-suffering Weald, hitherto 'unsaleable', were country house and villa owners following the new turnpikes down to the coast in the period *c.*1780-1820. The Victorians and Edwardians who followed admired, ironically, the very features they had so long despised, notably the woodland which earlier tourists had shunned. Now people who lived without trees in towns could not have enough of their sight and smell. Their Weald was threaded with railways and better roads, and had multiplying inns and an aura of law and order. An opportunity to re-examine what its landscape had to offer was available.

Many of the newcomers were seduced by painted landscapes showing views from the ranging summits of the Weald which symbolised the Victorian notion of tranquil English scenic beauty and were a method of alleviating the psychological problems which accompanied technological progress. The Victorian landscape artist was thrilled with the Weald's uncommon profusion of trees, shrubs and plants and their luscious varieties of foliage, an exuberance which was the essence of the art of the time; it paradoxically opposed landscape qualities that seemed deeply humanised and utterly 'wild by turns, one melting into another'.[27] This 'unfinished' aspect of the Weald also gained admiration from Rudyard Kipling, who moved to the centre of the Weald at Burwash in 1902 and thought it the most

English country one could ever dream of. Twenty years later Hilaire Belloc felt similarly when stepping out into the Weald at Shipley, near Horsham, where he thought he had entered the heart and essence of the English countryside.[28] The Weald became a rallying point for migrating artists from the 1840s and multiplying artists' colonies subsequently turned it into an open-air studio. No other environment in lowland England had anything like the same significance on shaping the Victorian attitude to the visual arts.

This was inextricably linked with the drama of earth history which geologists and botanists were simultaneously unravelling in a newly constituted open-air Wealden laboratory of field studies. By accidents of geology, south-east England is moulded in a striking earth architecture, the chalk strata of the Chilterns dipping under London, rising again to form the North Downs and reappearing in the South Downs (the over-arch of chalk having been eroded away to expose the older rocks in the intervening Weald). The vast power of nature to create and modify landscape over millions of years, and the mystery and beauty of the natural forces which upheaved the region and denuded it to reveal the underlying part of the Wealden dome, attracted to the region such scientists as Lyell, Mantell, Prestwich, Darwin and Topley, among others, and it became familiar to those absorbed in scientific discovery the world over.

To those brought up to believe the earth was in the state in which it was originally created, apart from the effects of universal deluge, Gideon and Mary Ann Mantell's discovery of the teeth and other remains of a Frankenstein-like herbivorous reptile in Tilgate Forest near Cuckfield, published in 1822, was one of the stunning revelations in a religious age grappling with a new cosmogony which was eventually to incorporate Darwin's theories of evolution. The Mantells found one of the first dinosaurs to be discovered in the world, later discovering a Plesiosaurus and the enormous Megalosaurus. Their reconstruction of the dinosaurs' habitat, with turtles of various kinds on the banks of rivers and lakes, and groups of enormous crocodiles basking in the mudflats of an expansive Wealden delta fed by great rivers, together with countless other forms of animal and vegetable life, millions of years before the creation of the human race, gripped the public imagination.

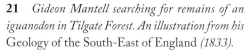

21 *Gideon Mantell searching for remains of an iguanodon in Tilgate Forest. An illustration from his* Geology of the South-East of England *(1833).*

Mantell's lectures on the great changes in land, water, temperature and forms of life were presented with an unmatched facility, and his books laid the foundations of the geology of the Weald more effectively than had been done before.[29]

John Farey had demonstrated in 1806 that along a central axis running east-west across the Forest Ridge in the High Weald, as around the Balcombe Viaduct, the dip of rocks to the south was in the reverse direction to that on the north. Subsequently it was observed that the rocks within the semi-ellipse were disposed regularly, but that north of the axis they were in ascending order and in descending order south of it. This indicated that the Weald had once been thrust high above the present surface. In *The Fossils of the South Downs* (1822) Gideon Mantell considered it likely that chalk had at a remote time covered the space between the present North and South Downs and that 'by some unknown catastrophe the central mass of chalk had been swept away' to reveal the older rocks. In the 1830s Charles Lyell demonstrated the vastness of time needed to create the Weald and showed that for most of its long history the Earth had been unpeopled. Scientific enquiry in the decade 1857-67 established that the erstwhile chalk dome had been reshaped by rivers over millions of years. Further study of the Weald's geology and plant and animal life found that its unusual diversity, down to minute details of stone and leaf, was an exquisitely ordered system. Theregion was one of the best-known denuded domed landscapes in the world and its land forms since have had a special importance in the deciphering of British scenery.[30]

Landscape gardeners attracted to the Weald brought to perfection the woodland 'wild' garden and the nascent 'cottage' style of gardens associated with William Robinson, Gertrude Jeykll, Edwin Lutyens and others. For the generation of Ruskin and William Morris the Weald resembled a surviving medieval landscape. The region, which on account of unresponsive soils had never been driven hard by the farmer, was cut up into an enormous patchwork of little fields bordered by thick hedges and a thickly wooded countryside, mainly by peasant farmers in the Middle Ages. In 1898 John Halsham claimed it was one of the most beautiful landscapes in the world.

This perception was enhanced by Victorian country house architects who followed in the wake of landscape artists from the 1860s. A rediscovered interest in vernacular houses led to the half-timbered and stone-built houses of the Weald becoming fashionable among revivalist architects such as George Devey, Anthony Salvin, Norman Shaw. P.F. Robinson, Philip Webb and, later, Edwin Lutyens, who searched for 'Old English' rustic models in order to weave an imaginary Middle Ages round old 'Gothick' buildings. The so-called 'Wealden House' (the late medieval half-timbered house concentrated in mid-Kent but extending into Sussex) was held as proof that conscious aesthetic effort had been a consideration in domestic building for several centuries. A rash of large and smaller country houses were demanded all over southern England by urban business people and perpetrated in a base form the mock-Tudor buildings of London's suburbs.

The medieval centuries had been idealised as a period of romance by the Pre-Raphaelites, and by John Ruskin and William Morris, and with its close-set fields, crumbling manor houses, lichened castles, ivy-covered churches, ruinous abbeys, moated halls and yeomen's farmhouses the Weald became a world where 'all that is prescribed to your ear and eye is what Medieval England heard and saw'. This led to the revival of handicrafts and concern for the 'organic' setting of domestic buildings, the leader of this movement being Norman Shaw, who built country houses in the 'Old English' style at Withyham in the 1870s. Two of his pupils, Mervyn Macartney and Ernest Newton, incorporated the style of indigenous Wealden architecture in their new mansions, to the extent of having open halls and great hearths and using Sussex oak and exterior decoration such as pargetting, braced beams and mullions. Another of their principles, which has tended to be ignored in modern England, was the use of locally sourced materials. 'We owe it to England and the landscape to build in a reverent way with suitable materials,' wrote Philip Webb, whose main source of inspiration was the vernacular architecture of south-east England.[31]

Webb had a long familiarity with the Weald's buildings and landscapes. As early as 1867 he wrote from Cuckfield that he had spent the last four years hunting up and down the southern counties for houses of all ages for his architectural practice. The old houses of the central Weald suggested to him 'yule logs, jesters, barking dogs, bear-baiting and barbarism', and he cynically noted that the present people were just as barbaric, 'applying energies only to business, colonisation and money. You could not imagine Michaelangelo living at Cuckfield.'

For his generation, travel southwards from London was to be transported to an England of two or more centuries earlier, where as late as 1857 people still lived the self-supporting life on small family farms that William Cobbett had wanted to see revived. From then until the 1920s one could actually 'live' history rather than study it. The Weald came to be regarded as one of the last strongholds of nature at its wildest and most aggressively verdant, an intimation of aboriginal England before its remodelling by man. Lacking roads, this was the landscape of isolated farms known by W.S. Blunt, Michael Fairless, Belloc (from 1913), John Halsham and Eleanor Farjeon. The French geographer Elisée Reclus remarked that the Weald had 'wild woodland scenery unsurpassed in many parts of England'.[32]

The changed point of view transformed a landscape dormant for hundreds of years. Extensive areas of the High Weald within reach of railway stations and main roads were covered with ubiquitous country houses, and traditional family farms went into retreat in the face of landscaped parks and gardens. Parts of the Weald were smart for the first time in history, but 'Londonised' manners and speech rapidly compromised traditional ways of life. 'The great wood of England', or 'the Wood beyond the World', once feared and hated, was now regarded as a salvation.

The change in the perception of the Weald arose primarily from the struggle to cope with technology, newly opened eyes recognising for the first time a region in which people still lived close to nature. With London's countryside no longer at its gates, the Weald was perceived as one of the 'lungs' of London. The minutely tilled fields set in a heavily wooded expanse was identified as an uncommon species of English landscape, the land wrested from the wild in earlier times but a high proportion of woodland uncleared owing to inferior soils and difficult topography. In 1898 John Halsham declared the Weald a precious national heritage and said that man had created what was 'surely in its entirety one of the most notable pieces of man's handiwork which the world has seen'.[33]

All this was to play an important part in the imaginative life of landscape artists, poets and prose writers. In literature the feeling for the Middle Ages was evoked by Walter Pater, who distilled, as fully as is possible in words, its homely and peaceful atmosphere, the trimness

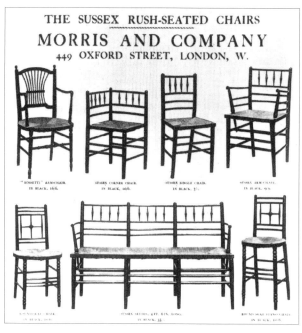

THE SUSSEX RUSH-SEATED CHAIRS

MORRIS AND COMPANY

449 OXFORD STREET, LONDON, W.

22 *The William Morris Company's advertisement for the rush-seated Sussex Chair.*

of its lush meadows and trees, and the fragrance of its hedges; all were reminiscent to him of the enamelled landscapes depicted in vignettes in medieval Books of Hours.[34] From 1898 John Halsham pleaded for the central part of the Sussex Weald and the adjacent Downs to become what we would call a National Park[35] and Kipling's *Puck of Pook's Hill* (1906), *Rewards and Fairies* (1910) and his short stories of the Dudwell valley, which followed later, introduced readers to a hitherto unknown region.

The ways in which people saw Sussex were changing. When Horace Walpole wrote of 'the Saxon air' of the county, he used it disparagingly to indicate a district and people stuck so far in the past that it was as if King George II were the first king of the East Angles.[36] Now the 'old world' atmosphere of country Sussex and its farming folk was most appealing to the Londoner weary of modern civilisation. The change occurred in late Victorian times but the period between the two world wars was the peak of the cult of the Open Air. The era had its own monthly journal, *Open Air*, published briefly by *Country Life* in 1923, specifically to introduce the delights of the countryside to the novice town dweller. This was also the era of countryside anthologies such as E.V. Lucas's *The Open Road* and an immense volume of 'country' writing for an urban readership longing for the purer air forty miles or more from London. In cities there was no rest from hectic hurry. Tired minds and bodies were refreshed by a slower rhythm of life in which one could love slow things. Country speech, soft on the ear, measured and musical, was a most restful thing after the staccato syllables of town talk. The careful, deliberate work of hedgers, thatchers, shepherds and woodmen and the lifestyle of gipsies excited envy, if only momentarily, from men who followed complicated and exacting occupations. Watching a skilled hedger with his half-moon hook plashing the spiked thorn, or coppicers with their hand-tools cutting poles to fall neatly outwards into a star shape, made a strong appeal to the townsman, being examples of human labour more picturesque than that done in factories or dockyards. The joy of finding some place where you could stand alone and remote, quite out of earshot of any road, and in close contact with Nature, was far more difficult to achieve in the crowded space of cities. The urge to escape from the urban jar meant that Saturday to many people spoke of the countryside and led, from the early 1920s, to the desire for a 'little place in the country', or adventures in a reasonably priced 'light car', some walking, cycling, camping, boating or simply loafing.

Chapter 4

WILLIAM COBBETT'S SUSSEX

John Bull-ish and old-fashioned, Cobbett was the champion of the common man and, in G.K. Chesterton's words, 'simply a man who had discovered a crime – that capitalism was a swindle'. He never lived in Sussex but he wrote much about it, and no one has described the landscape and 'ordinary' people of Sussex in such vivid detail and with such depth of feeling. In the 10 years following 1822, his perspective was so individual that he provided information and understanding that we cannot find in any other quarter, and his insight is so intense it is as if he were geographer, sociologist, historian and ruralist in one. Moreover, he wrote before the coming of the railway. His inconsistency, bias in favour of the working man, and crude knowledge of history and economics mean, however, that care must be taken with his testimony. As London grew larger, Cobbett detested it more, not merely for its smoke and rattle, but because to him it was a colossus created by the sweat of working people which destroyed the old rural society he felt in his bones was the real England.

He was never happier in the 1820s than when leaving 'the Wen' and riding off on horseback at a slow pace through the countryside, observing the condition of the land and the working people, never purely as an 'agricultural writer' but to gather material as a political agitator for his *Political Register*. In his eight 'Rides' through Sussex he wrote of the look and feel of the countryside, keeping as far as possible off turnpike roads because of the rapid changes taking place along them. And as he never lost an opportunity of talking to people about their concerns, he was able to write with confidence about local affairs. The accounts of his journey, unique in English, were published as *Rural Rides* in 1830.

An archetypal 'Little Englander', yet no outright reactionary, Cobbett experienced the transformation of an England undergoing the Industrial Revolution, from the age of the stagecoach to that of the steam train. *Rural Rides* is suffused with a sense of the deterioration in everyday life since his boyhood, in the corruption of public life and the pauperisation of the rural labouring classes from which he had sprung. He was always loyal to rural 'Old England' and had an aversion to 'vermin' such as stock-brokers, bankers, Jews and merchants, together with sinecurists, Scots, Quakers, Methodists and evangelicals, and revealed what would now be thought proto-fascist tendencies. London he condemned as a great 'Wen', literally a giant cyst, drawing to itself the goodness of the body – the Body Politic – and sustained by his pet hatred, 'The Thing' – speculation, finance, despotism, high taxation and the non-reform of Parliament. He wrote instinctively and fluently and put approximately ten million words in print. As Dr John Stevenson explained in a recent lecture to the Cobbett Society, 'With so much, Cobbett is a little like the Bible – you will find something of everything in him, which is why writers of so many different persuasions have claimed him for their own.' His particular views were to be echoed repeatedly in Sussex

23   *William Cobbett.*

over the next century and are far from absent today (see Chapter 23).[1]

Cobbett admired Sussex people, the handsome downlanders with their sturdy constitution and pretty women, smaller featured and boned than the girls of High Wycombe he had met earlier, and more fresh-coloured and bright-eyed. He left Lewes in admiration of its setting and its people, finding it 'a model of solidity and neatness', the buildings substantial to the very outskirts, the pavements good, the shops nice and clean, the people good-looking and well-dressed, and the inns good with reasonable charges.

Horsham also cheered him as a nice, solid town, clean like all the other Sussex places, where men and boys wore the smock-frock more than elsewhere. Such survivals charmed him. He met the landlady's small boy dressed in a smock-frock at Billingshurst, which reminded him of his own childhood, and at Wisborough Green he saw a woman bleaching her home-spun and home-woven linen, a sight unseen since he had left America.[2]

It was the woodlanders of the Weald that impressed him most. He found their standard of living, like all working people in Sussex, higher than in other places such as the Hampshire Downs, contrasting the pinched faces of the labourers there who rarely tasted meat with 'the round, red faces you see in the wealds and forests, particularly in Sussex, where the labourers *will* have a *meat-pudding* of some sort of other; and where they *will* have a *fire* to sit by in the winter'. He concluded there was less misery or wretchedness in Sussex compared with what he had seen in other parts of England, though he referred constantly to the low wages of agricultural labourers. As proof of their relative well-being he cited the neatness and beauty of labourers' cottage gardens from Singleton to Sedlescombe, which he considered unmatched anywhere else in the world and an honour to England. He thought them the most interesting objects in the Wealden countryside and gives the impression that the little gardens were full of vegetables and flowers and that roses and honeysuckles perfumed every cottage door.[3]

Cobbett's impressions of the Wealden economy and society are equally illuminating and individual. Agricultural writers such as Arthur Young, an inveterate enemy of the smallholder, bemoaned the 'backwardness' of its farmers, the heavy soils and lack of decent roads. It was on his first Sussex tour in January 1822, when Cobbett rode to Battle, that he became engrossed in the condition of the 'leather-legged race' he called Wealdsmen.

In a few sentences thrown off in the evening after the day's ride he gave an extraordinarily vivid and perceptive account of them. It was a district, he noted, not of high agricultural quality but:

> as to human happiness, I am of opinion, that as much, and even more, falls to the lot of the leather-legged chaps that live in and rove about amongst those clays and woods as to the more regularly disciplined labourers of the rich and prime parts of England. As 'God has made the back to the burthen', so the clay and coppice people make the dress to the stubs and bushes. Under the sole of the shoe is *iron*; from the sole six inches upwards is a high-low; then forms a leather bam to the knee; then comes a pair of leather breeches; then comes stout doublet; over this comes a smock-frock; and the wearer sets brush and stubs and thorns and mire at defiance.

He had always observed that woodland and forest labourers were the best off in the main. The coppices, which were more valuable than in many other places because of the demand for hop-poles, gave them pleasant and profitable work in winter; the woods were warm, too, even in the coldest winters, and supplied free fuel. They had not so great a corn harvest, but had three weeks' harvest in April and May, the season of barking oaks for leather making, called in Sussex 'flaying'. He noted that women worked in the coppices, shaving the bark

24 *Lewes from the castle keep, 1999.*

25 *Elegant flint-buildings at Lewes.*

26   *Cottage life, 1840s, Cranbrook School, Kent.*

off the hop-poles to remove maggots which would eat into the wood, and that little boys and girls assisted their mothers in this.[4]

Cobbett had looked more closely at the Weald, and from a different perspective, and he found something no previous observer had remarked upon – its sustaining power for human beings. The coppices, oakwoods and little fields on the family farms provided work all the year and yielded supplementary handicrafts. Hedges needed hedgers; woods required men to cut them; ditches had to be dug and intractable fields needed many hands to work them. Cobbett put the human happiness of working people first, and found it more abundant in wooded countries and less so in arable England. As for the Weald, he saw it as an Eden, thus turning the conventional notion of the region on its head. His remarks are a symbolic moment in the history of the Weald for they were to mark an historic change in attitude towards it. (Cobbett's thoughts on the general well-being of Wealdsmen, resulting from their way of life, are corroborated by Thomas Carlyle, who at Herstmonceux in 1840 thought life there more supportable than he had seen elsewhere, and John Halsham at the end of the 19th century took a similar view.)

The sight of St Leonard's Forest with its barren, treeless, soil and 'black rugged hideous rocks' repelled Cobbett as much as had the coast of Nova Scotia during his service in the army. He had seldom travelled over eight miles so well devised to fill the mind with painful reflections, the more so because land speculators were enclosing and cutting up parts of it and 'driving labourers from its skirts'. His remarks on Ashdown Forest are notorious: he found it a heath with a few birch scrubs on it, 'verily the most villainously ugly spot I ever saw in England'. Yet he had an eye for landscape beauty, such as that of the common heath in full bloom in spring, grown to a height of four feet at Frant. For coppices he had the greatest admiration. Travelling to Battle on a lovely warm day he thought there was nothing in vegetable creation more delightful to behold or more suggestive of the idea of human comfort and warmth in winter. For two months of the year the coppice frequently changed its hues and was bespangled with primroses and bluebells. As he rode through the woodland his thoughts turn to the wild birds. The opening of the birch leaves was the signal for the pheasant to crow and the blackbird and thrush to sing, and 'when the oak buds begin to look reddish, and not a day before, the whole tribe of finches burst forth in song from every bough, while the lark, imitating all, carries the joyous sounds to the sky'.[5]

It was in the midst of this land of small farmers, at North Lodge, a farmhouse in Worth, near Crawley, that he was inspired to write his *Cottage Economy* (1821), designed to teach the cottager and smallholder how to make the most of his little bit of ground. The farmer's wife, Mrs Brazier, was his heroine. She was nearly eighty years of age and had brought up 40 children and grandchildren and 'had it said of her, that she had done more work herself than any woman in Sussex; and that there was not a working-man or woman in the parish who had not, for or last, either resided or been fed under her roof'. Although she could neither write nor read, she understood the making of bread, the brewing of beer, the keeping of cows, the rearing of pigs, and was able to teach Cobbett practically all that he did not know.

Cobbett thought of the South Downs as the epitome of the Old England he cherished and it was impossible to think of a more comfortable life than that man might lead there. When he deliberately avoided the Chichester turnpike and passed along the lane between Upwaltham and Singleton in the heart of the western Downs, still one of the loveliest of by-ways, he wrote 'of some of the finest farms in the world' between stretches of trees and underwood, and of villages beautiful to behold, owned by the Duke of Richmond or Lord Egremont, both of whom gave their husbandmen fair play and were well spoken of. He noted the well-stocked gardens of the labourers, their good and warm houses, the pigs in almost everyone's sty, and the young turnip-hoer who had a good lump of household bread and not a very small piece of bacon for his lunch. To instruct farmers in Northumberland (who he thought dressed their labourers in rags and fed them on potatoes), he said how childishly they farmed in comparison with the four teams of large oxen he had seen on the Downs near Shoreham, six in a team, all ploughing in one field in preparation for wheat, and the several pairs of horses in the same field, dragging, harrowing and rolling. He had seen on the other side of the road at least five to six quarters of wheat standing upon the acre, and at least nine to ten quarters of oats standing alongside, each of the two fields being fifty to a hundred acres. His enthusiastic remarks on arable farming contrast with later writers who give the impression of the Downs as a pastoral paradise inhabited by sheep and shepherds.[6]

On his journey to Worth in May 1823 Cobbett encountered the new tunnel being built which cut through a hill on the Brighton road at Reigate to save a few hundred yards of travel. This he thought money taken away from the industrious for the benefit of idlers. He was amazed that 'stock-jobbers working in Change Alley' could reside at Brighton and commute to and from London by coach, the journey taking about four hours each way, leaving not very early in the morning and returning not very late at night. Twenty coaches a day plied between London and Brighton by three or four different roads and Cobbett claimed hundreds of men and horses were employed in levelling and shortening the roads to Brighton.[7]

His vigorous defence of the England of his boyhood did not die with him. On the contrary, he became a mentor to Belloc and Blunt, both of whom sought to retain the 'old' Sussex of their youth, and his unorthodox concept of sustainability was prominent in Kipling's Burwash stories and was the essence of the late Victorian 'discovery' of the Weald and of the anti-urban culture of the Sussex poets and writers of the inter-war years.

EMIGRATION

He stressed the labourer's contentment, but Cobbett found at Rogate a hedger earning 1s. 6d. a day and heard that people on poor rate got 7d. a day for the man and a gallon loaf a week for the rest of the family which was 'less than that for gaolbirds', a fact which led him to reflect that Mrs Fry and numerous other persons were intent on improving the conditions of prisoners in gaols but not 'ejaculating one pious sigh' for those sufferers who were doomed to become felons or 'waste away their bodies by hunger' without a change in their fortunes.[8] On the eve of *Rural Rides*' publication a crisis broke out over low wages and the introduction of threshing machines (see pp.51-2).

Cobbett was concerned that labourers were emigrating to Canada and the United States, and indignant towards those who were driving such people from their country. In 1829 he learned that parishes in the eastern part of Sussex near Battle, Rye and Winchelsea were shipping families of labouring people off to the United States to save the costs of public maintenance which they would have drawn on as paupers. One hundred persons had left Ewhurst for America since 1818, and 90 had emigrated from Salehurst within a few years of 1830. At Burwash 50 persons left for New York, followed by another 40 in 1832. These were financed by loans on the personal security of residents which were repaid over three years from the Poor Rate, an arrangement considered satisfactory to the whole community. Cobbett left his home at Barn-Elms Farm in west London to gather information on the subject. A resident of Robertsbridge had collected copies of letters sent home by emigrants to relatives in Sussex with the object of inducing others to emigrate. One of the letters was from a young woman, Mary Jane Watson, who went out to America in 1823 and, writing home to her grandmother and grandfather from Albany, remarked:

> I have now got good clothes, and I can dress as well as any lady in Sedlescombe. I can enjoy a silk frock, or a white frock, and my crape frock and my crape veil and morocco shoes, without a parish grumbling about it. The girls here that are out doing house-work, dress as well as any lady in Sedlescombe; you cannot tell the poor from the rich here. One is dressed as good as the other. I don't think of going to meeting with leather shoes on; we wear morocco, and prunello.

27 *Making roofing lathes, High Weald.*

28   *'Preparing for Dinner,' F.O. Hardy, 1840s.*

Cobbett went to the village of Sedlescombe to find out more of the circumstances, 'filled with melancholy at the thought that such people should be driven from the country'. He found himself in a very beautiful spot, with an ancient church, a straggling wide street bending round in a sort of semi-circle, the houses and little gardens generally very neat; the surrounding land was a mixture of woodland, grassland, arable and hop-gardens. At the inn he found a labourer holding one of his 11 children who took him to the home of Stephen Watson at Footland. Watson was at home with his wife, two daughters and a daughter-in-law. He had come home from work and had eight or ten children and 40 grandchildren, having worked for 27 years for one master. He assured Cobbett that his daughter's letter was genuine and that those beloved children in America would never know want.

Cobbett also had a copy of a letter, to Thomas Cooke of Cripps Corner near Battle, from his daughter and son-in-law who had emigrated to Hudson on the Hudson River 130 miles north of New York. It described the kind treatment they met with on their landing at New York, how readily the husband had found work, and that they were living well. The letter continued:

> We live close by a large river … a very fruitful place for apples, cherries, raspberries, grapes, plums; any one may get them without money. Dear mother, I fear you will be troubled to read that side, it is put so thick, for my paper is not half big enough to say all that I want to say to you; but this I can say, we wants for nothing, bless God for it; for we can buy a leg of mutton every day, and green pease, and French-beans; and we have got in thirty-two gallons of cider for fourteen shillings [8s. 9d. in English money] I wish you was all here to help drink it. Tell my sister, if she was here, she might earn eight or ten shillings

a day [5s. to 6s. 3d. in English money], for they charge so much for work … We had so much meat brought us that we could not eat it while it was good … We are in a land of plenty, and *above all*, we can hear the sound of the Gospel. I only wish I had come here before. Give my love to Elizabeth, and if she wants fine clothes she is to come here; it would be the making of her.

The writer's mother and father were happy that their daughter would never want bread. When Cobbett confirmed that from his own experience in America he thought the contents of the letters true, the parents were delighted beyond all description.

Referring to another letter from an emigrant, Cobbett remarked:

This man (living with a wife and six children) gets to New York, a pauper without a farthing in the world, on the 19th of May, 1828, and in March 1829, he has laid out £22 10s. English money in 'housel', he has a sow ready to farrow, and he is about to purchase a cow or two![9]

Cobbett secured the original copies of many such letters and published them in his *Emigrant's Guide* (1829). One was addressed to 'Mr James Parks, to be left at Mr Benjamin Boot's, Wheelwright, Staple Cross, in the parish of Ewhurst, near Northiam, in the county of Sussex, Old England, Great Britain' and read:

Greenbush, 16 March 1828.

Dear Father,

… It is with the greatest pleasure that I take my pen in hand to tell you that we are all in good health, in a fine country, where I have plenty of work at my trade, and well paid for doing it … I have left Albany; I live across the River Hudson from Albany at a place called Greenbush. Greenbush is a village about like Burwash town.

Josiah has left his place at the tavern and lives in New York; and works at lime-burning, and is doing pretty well.

Albany is a very elegant city, stands on a rising ground on the banks of the Hudson River; it is a surprising place for trade. There commences the greatest canal I suppose that this world produces, which goes above 300 miles into the western country, and was all dug by hand … Tell Thomas Avann to come to America; and tell him to leave his strap (what he wears when he has nothing to eat in England), *for some other half-starved slave.* Tell Miriam there's no sending children to bed without a supper, or husbands to work without dinners in their bags, in this country.

The Rev. Sockett also collated letters addressed by emigrants to their families in the Petworth district and two letters from the Swan River in Western Australia were published.[10]

Chapter 5

THE SOUTH SAXONS, 1830-50

For centuries the majority of Sussex people were agricultural workers. Their work was the basis of the county's prosperity and their well-being was consequently a matter of concern, if only from a money-making point of view. Yet very little is known about them, for the labourers themselves were mostly inarticulate and for a very long time were dismissed as a subject unworthy of the reader so that, for example, they are unmentioned by the earliest Sussex historians such as Thomas Horsfield (1835), despite his time being one of rural unrest. Even today books are written on Sussex places in which 'ordinary' country people do not count, an echo of the days before the last war when there was little to learn about these obscure people at a country-house dinner party or a weekend cottage lunch. One recalls peasant John Clare's wistful line 'I am – yet what I am, none cares or knows.'

An exception to this indifference was William Cobbett, the tireless champion who rose from plough-boy to Member of Parliament and devoted the latter part of his life to the people's well-being. He reckoned that working people, and in particular farm workers, were regarded as an inferior race of beings and treated as such. He described them as unpresuming persons content with their station in life, honest and sincere, and he added: 'I have admired their character and conduct ever since I was able to estimate them; and I would willingly strike dead at my feet the insolent brutes who speak contemptuously of them.'[1] At Lewes he dwells on the characteristics of the 'ordinary' Sussex people, regarding the men as remarkably handsome and the girls pretty, as they were throughout the county, with round faces, little hands and wrists, plump arms and bright eyes.[2]

As mentioned earlier, Cobbett found not a single instance of want of neatness about a poor man's house and regarded this as a proof of his good qualities. Cobbett was sentimental about the working class, and could not refrain from idealising their character. Broadly speaking he was probably correct about labourers' virtues but there were those known as 'shifty' and others corrupted by the beerhouses.

After Cobbett we have to wait more than sixty years before another writer with a similar empathy for farm labourers. George Forrester Scott of Lindfield and Ardingly wrote under the pseudonym of 'John Halsham'. In *Idlehurst: a Journal kept in the Country* (1898), *Lonewood Corner* (1907) and *Old Standards* (1913), he shows himself a miniaturist with a wonderful visual gift and an ear for dialect. Furthermore, he was a rare spirit who had a remarkable empathy for 'ordinary' people and took trouble to record their histories and thoughts. This he did for decades, always with genuine sympathy and concern for his interviewees, unlike Kipling, who had a similar gift for recording working-class people but took no more than a literary interest in them.

29 *A Southwick fisherman, 1890s.*

Halsham would spend hours watching labourers ploughing and harvesting, learning about woodcraft skills and talking over their careers with them. Old Eliel Awcock, who had worked for years in the gardens of the Hall, rose to second gardener at 18 shillings a week before dropping to 10 or so doing odd jobs at the vicarage when he got older. Then illness struck. Halsham assisted him with getting his state pension, for he had difficulty in confirming his age. Finally, a scrawl in the family Bible was declared evidence enough for him to fill in the official form. (Eliel had such a broad accent that although he tried to give directions to a gentleman who had lost his way, the visitor could not understand a word he was saying, and took the wrong direction.)

Mas' Comber, born under Chanctonbury, was underfed as a lad and never learned to read but became a champion mower and 'a rare one' with horses. He was gleaning with his mother before he turned seven years of age and his horizon throughout life was the Hill (the steep of the Downs); he never went to London.[3] Jethro Tully was a skilled labourer used to getting up at four in the morning to walk to work and arriving back

30 *Agricultural workers, La Thangue, 1890s.*

46

home after 7 p.m. Old Nye, ruddy-faced, white-haired and clad in the archaic white frock, posed at the gate for lady artists and 'camera folk' in summer. He viewed daily the process of vehicles down the street – the post-cart, the carrier's tilt, the doctor's car, the parson's cob – and the exodus from the wheelwright's loft in the evening. One of Halsham's most vivid portraits is of Mr Mant of Lindfield, who had a corn chandlery with a post office and was the general factotum of the village, acting as registrar of four adjoining parishes; he changed the tradesmen's cheques, balanced the books for farmers, paid the wages of the estate workers when the squire was absent, was treasurer to local clubs, wrote letters for people, made their wills and was the accustomed go-between and peace-maker in the event of quarrels.[4]

Halsham also observed country people closely at shopping or at fairs and markets and vividly brought to life their countenances, demeanour and clothing. Walking out of Lindfield at dusk on a Saturday he encounters Mrs Bish in ancient black, with a vast basket on her arm, full of her physic, Sunday's flap-of-beef, half a pound of tea and currants; stout young men, light bushy whiskers on florid cheeks, in tail coats and gaiters, the commonest sight; and a man playing an accordion. At the fair are shepherds dealing with the 'ship', lantern-jawed, sandy-bearded Saxons, oldish, worthy-looking men, weather-burnt and rusty-bearded, often wearing the slate-coloured frock and carrying the ancient umbrella with its whalebone ribs. Round the pens lounge the old-job men, 'nomads, hardly less animal-looking than the beasts they follow', bleary-eyed shambling hulks. Then there are the dealers and breeders, some in the John Bull attire of old, the gay neckerchief and low-crowned silk hat. Halsham found most of the men big and stout, stridently aggressive, heavy-handed and hard-faced, many with countenances gross and vacant. A few younger men in the crowd wore smart riding-breeches, fancy waistcoats and bowlers, but the majority wore the traditional tailcoats of greying hue and ample cut, square-topped felt hats, and leather leggings.[5]

Halsham did not disguise his thoughts about the physical constitution of those who remained on the land at the end of the 19th century. The old man with a stoop, labouring with slow painfulness with his hoe, was a type common in the village – with sunken, toothless mouth, rheumy eyes and a sharp, grey-stubbled chin, misfeatured at birth. Although frail and ungainly he had the power of slow, tireless, work with his lean arms and crooked knees. His daughter, slight and flat-chested, had 'the weakest mouth that ever simpered' and a blunt round face, yet was the nearest to pretty of all the girls in the parish. By and large Halsham found the cottage folk of his acquaintance strangely plain and unlovely, with the worn eyes and fallen mouths of grown men and women as well as deformities in the lads and girls in general. This suggested to Halsham 'large causes, perhaps as yet insufficiently explored'.

Halsham's reference to Saxons was followed up by W.H. Hudson, the gifted nature writer who claimed 'Saxon' characteristics, physical and moral, predominated in Sussex people. Shepherds appear to have been particularly 'Saxon' in feature. Hudson met a shepherd boy aged about fifteen with a perfect Saxon face, which he saw more in Sussex than anywhere in England: a large rosy face, brown in colour, with sky-blue eyes and light brown hair worn long, the epitome of child-like innocence.

Hudson also thought Sussex people good-looking, the strongest and hardiest in south England and fairly sober, though they drank more than most people he had met. He thought their good qualities stronger than their vices and found them so good to live with that he forgave their 'amiable weaknesses', including the illegitimate children which in some villages were as 'plentiful as blackberries'.[6] (Earlier overseers of the poor, as at Mayfield which was notorious for prostitution, and at Battle in the 1830s, had not taken such a frivolous attitude to it.)[7] Above all, Hudson admired their 'rock-like stability of character and sturdy independence of spirit and with it a patient contentment with the life of unremitting toil'.

John Cowper Powys, fresh from the Midlands and Dorset, was also struck by the blue-eyed South Saxons and thought there was something about Sussex that was more 'profoundly English in the narrowest sense of the word, than in any other county of the kingdom'.[8] It is a measure of modern migration into the county that such people are almost a lost race, either because they were swept up in the exodus to the city and replaced by strangers from London suburbs or inter-married with other incomers or townspeople. The 'Saxon' heritage had been a source of pride and both natives and visitors liked to think that Sussex people were descended from King Alfred's rustics and had not a drop of mixed blood in their veins.

Another writer with a strong understanding and sympathy for the labourer was George Sturt, who inherited his father's wheelwright's business near Farnham at the end of the 19th century. His chief recollection of the days of his youth was of the generations of Surrey labourers who came in July to harvest the crops in 'the Manor of Sussex' (the Selsey peninsula and its surrounds), the most productive arable district of the county. They mostly came to the same farms, year after year, and worked as long as harvesting lasted. Employment was so certain and pay so good that many of the men took their wives, sons, and even their daughters to win a share of the earnings. Consequently, Farnham and its district was half-emptied of inhabitants through August by what was a folk-migration. One old man talking to Sturt said that two of his children had been born during his expeditions into Sussex. Sturt heard of the long, hot days in the fields and the nights sleeping in barns and outbuildings, and judged from the talk that the harvesters had been in holiday mood, though it was not for health reasons that they undertook the trip.[9]

Ford Madox Ford's descriptions of the working farmers and farm labourers he encountered on the Sussex-Kent border in the 1890s are illuminating and unpatronising. The old lady

31 *The cumbrous wooden Sussex plough, originally pulled by oxen.*

who came weekly to the baker's to heat the ovens with faggots for her cooking and washing held the countryman's distrust of any man dressed in a collar and tie. Another of his discoveries was Old Wilson:

> There was nothing he could not do, patiently and to perfection. He was a wonderful gardener; he could make a stake-and-binder hedge better than any other man; he could get out of the underwood more of the fourteen kinds of woodcraft produce than any other man in the weald of Kent or Sussex, too. Hop-poles, stakes, binders, faggots, wattle-gates, field-gates, clothes-props, clothes-pegs, gate-posts, kindling – there was nothing he could not work up out of your underwood and brush.

He was also an admirable thatcher, a careful waggoner and a wonderfully good shepherd, and he could lay bricks, cut out rafters, plaster, hang paper, paint, make chairs, corner-cupboards, fish, poach, snare, brew, gather simples, care for poultry, stop foxes' earths. He kept tallies on notched sticks with a bill hook and late in life taught himself to read. Ford considered the country folk as happy as they were wise and unlettered. They made good money – 13s. 6d. a week, with a cottage and garden for 18d. and cheap food. They did not want for junketings – sale dinners and excursions got up by the parson – and the village was full of sociability – one chatted over the hedgerows or from orchard to orchard.[10]

By means of the various accounts of the Sussex countrymen we can piece together something of their characteristics. There were significant differences between Downsmen and Wealdsmen. The average Downland farmworker was long-limbed and loose of build and his gait was slow and shambling, heavy and deliberate. A townsman would have thought he suffered from chronic fatigue but his lumbering movement resulted from a long day's work in the fields which demanded economy in activity. (The fisherman's walk was leisurely, as if he were stepping over pebbles, half a step being subtracted from each whole one in his passage.) The faces of old men were generally weather-beaten and ruddy, even brown, the chins shaved only on Sundays. People thought the fair hair, blue eyes and rotund face was a sign of Saxon origin. The men were tired, the effect of long years of drudgery and back-breaking work. By 1900 the round frock, or gabardine, was seldom worn by labourers, and the shepherd in a smock was a rarity, but nearly everybody had once attended church in a tall hat and smock. The farmer's men took to wearing thick corduroy suits on weekdays, and on Sundays and gala days light-coloured suits with collars and bright ties instead of a woollen neck-scarf. The home-brewing of small beer had ceased and tea drinking had become universal.

The Wealdsman also lumbered slowly and was exceptionally long-limbed, presumably with the same economy of movement as Downlanders, although it was popularly considered that it resulted from the pulling of legs out from mires.[11] He was as sturdy and hard-working as his compatriots on the Downs, but reckoned to be in most ways different: shrewder, more resilient and resourceful, naturally stubborn, independent and self-assertive, more adventurous, and inclined towards nonconformity in religion. These characteristics were ascribed to generations of struggle against the Wealden clays and the absence of strong manorial control; he was less subservient to authority than the Downsman, who regularly touched his forelock to the local squire and, like 'the men of Kent', had been frequently the focus of radical dissent since the Middle Ages. The famous maxim of the Sussex working class – 'We won't be druv' – is almost certainly Wealden in origin. From the Weald came the saying about the Downlander: 'You see yon man, he cooms from the Hill [the Downs]. He sucked in silliness with his mother's milk and he's been silly ever since.' The foreigner's opinion of the downlanders was:

Sussex born and bred,
Thick in the arm
And weak in the head

'Old Wilson' deserves to join Meredith's literary representation of the hog-eating Sussex peasant, 'Andrew Hedger', who lived north of Steyning in the Sussex Weald. He was a reactionary who yearned for the days before railways when marryings were at Christmas and there were grand Harvest Suppers, but found solace by 'eating hog by the haur'.[12] The most vivid representation of the Sussex labourer comes from Rudyard Kipling's absorption of the Wealden past after he moved to Bateman's in 1902. His most famous creation is old Hobden, the poacher-hedger who symbolises the archetypal Sussex Wealdsman. It is doubtless on account of labourers like Hobden that the English peasant has never been denigrated as has the French peasant.

The literary characters were offered as a kind of moral base-line against which the worth and status of others such as the factory worker and 'city slicker' could be compared. Later writers contrasted the modern ways of work in mines and factories, with their minute sub-divisions of labour, with that of the old-time rural workman's skills. The latter not only made a thing, as distinct from adding an element to something being made in a factory, but could make various things besides. When John Halsham sketched his old countrymen near Lindfield, Ford Madox Ford discovered Old Wilson on the Kent and Sussex border, and Kipling sent Old Hobden round the world from Burwash, they represented them not as hodges and yokels, but as skilled and intelligent labourers, who made anything the local community wanted, often of very beautiful build. These writers thought factory work a cause of weariness, endurable only by pay, and noted how 'hands' rushed away from their place of work at the end of their shift to get some of the excitement their work had failed to yield. They claimed that a good

32   *The Reaper, a sculpture by La Thangue, 1890s.*

rural craftsman was, on the whole, happier than the average townsman and derived more satisfaction from his work.

POVERTY, UNREST AND HARDSHIP, 1830-50: THE LABOURERS' WAR

Cobbett's view was that a full belly to the labourer was the foundation of public morals and the only source of real peace, but in his day this was uncertain. It was for this reason that he wrote *Cottage Economy* (1821) at North Lodge, Worth, near Crawley, the practical approach to his goal of rural regeneration. Soon afterwards rural disturbances broke out in Kent and spread into East Sussex and thence westwards to the Chichester district. Cobbett's name for the unrest, which began in August 1830, was 'The Labourers' War'. The violence included the destruction of threshing machines, the burning of ricks and barns, attacks on overseers of the poor, and intimidation of farmers and landowners to force up wages. Cobbett had predicted that the burning and destruction would happen and that it would begin in Sussex and Kent, not on account of the discontent being greater there than elsewhere but because those farm labourers were the most radical, militant and vociferous and would rise earliest in protest. So it proved.

A primary cause of the revolts was the fall in agricultural prices from the end of the Napoleonic Wars in 1815. This led to poverty among farmers in the post-war depression, their reluctance to pay labourers a sustainable wage and resentment towards the clergy's tithes. Farmers also began to withdraw the traditional custom of gleaning after the corn harvest on which cottagers relied to help them through the winter. The year of the riots proved a bad season and it was followed by three more. Meanwhile, some of the overseers of the workhouses were acting harshly towards inmates. Poverty among labourers was compounded by the enclosure of commonlands, such as the 500 acres in Chiddingly by an Act of 1813, which denied the cottager the cow or two and the few sheep and geese he had put on the common. The violence of the rioters was exacerbated by smuggling, which had created an organisation among labourers resisting authority.

Beyond these circumstances was a deeper and newer malaise. The poorer agricultural districts, such as the Weald of Sussex, had a population which had increased beyond the means of farmers to employ them at a sustainable wage. Brede and Burwash, for example, reported in 1834 surplus labourers, mainly single men, for whom regular work could not be provided. The solution adopted at an increasing number of parishes was assisted emigration to New York or a British colony, the costs of removal reckoned less than the burden on the Poor Rate.[13]

The authorities made every effort to incriminate Cobbett with the revolts and he narrowly escaped imprisonment. Thomas Goodman of Battle, who was convicted of setting a barn on fire shortly after Cobbett's address there to labourers, was browbeaten into giving a false testimony against him. Cobbett was acquitted when the owner of the barn, and others at the meeting, testified to the libel. Cobbett's relief is evident from his reply to the people of Battle.[14]

The various strands contributing to the discontent can be illustrated from events at Brede, the first place in Sussex to experience insurgence, in November 1830. Initially the overseer of the poor was the target. The rioters put him in a little cart, which he had made for men to haul stone and gravel from a nearby wharf, and about 300 men subjected him to

33 *Ploughing with oxen on the South Downs.*

'rough music'. He was dragged by women to the borders of the parish and threatened with harm if he returned, but after an absence of some time he was reinstated in his position at the workhouse. Then wages came up for discussion and the men considered taxes and tithes responsible for the farmers' reluctance to pay better terms, so a storm broke over the head of the Rev. Hele, son-in-law of the owner of the advowson, the Bishop of Norwich. The leaders this time were farmers. On audit day 1830 a mob of many hundreds of men with their wives and children assembled at the parsonage. The rector refused to give in to intimidation, although the farmers claimed they might suffer injury from labourers if he did not accede to their demands, and after some delay his tithes were paid in full. The labourers found that a promise of extra wages was not being kept and turned on the the farmers. On 5 November a set of resolutions drawn up by them approving the removal of the overseer and an increase in wages was signed by the minister, six farmers and six labourers. One of the signatories was subsequently wounded while smuggling after his release from prison. Bufford, an arsonist who pleaded guilty, was executed, but so great was the feeling of the country in his favour that he was treated as a martyr, his corpse exhibited in his coffin and a subscription made for his family.[15]

In an incident at Robertsbridge a barn was destroyed by fire and the assistant overseer of the poor house bundled out of the parish by labourers who assembled *en masse*. Similar attacks on property were made at Westfield and the overseers carted away to more 'rough music'.[16]

The uprisings of the peasantry continued. In December they collected in considerable numbers at Mayfield, and going from farm to farm pressed all those they encountered into their ranks. Remonstrance and entreaty were in vain; farmers, tradespeople and labourers, all were obliged to congregate and accompany the multitude. They visited the Rev. Mr Kirby, whose tithes for a portion of the parish amounted to £1,100 or £1,200 a year, and demanded that he should immediately reduce them to £400. The rest should be remitted to farmers, to enable them to pay their labourers 2s. 3d. and 2s. 6d. a day, to which Mr Kirby reluctantly assented. They then went to the house of Lord Carrington's bailiff, so that it should be destroyed, but it was spared. His wife gave refreshment to the party, and they left to pursue other targets.[17]

Exhilarated by their success, the Mayfield peasants wrote to the Earl of Liverpool (Prime Minister 1812-27, and presumably resident at Buxted Park), stating that they intended dining with him in the course of the week. His lordship, hearing that they had assembled at Mayfield, rode to them and told them that he did not desire to be so far honoured but if, instead of calling on him, they would content themselves with entertainment at a Buxted public house, they should have plenty to eat and drink.

There was good feeling on both sides when a party of peasants paid a visit to Mr Courthope, of Whiligh near Wadhurst. Courthope was not at home and the insurgents demanded of his wife whether there was a threshing machine on the premises. On being answered in the negative they asked if there was a haying-machine, and being answered in the affirmative a consultation was held as to whether they should leave; which they did peaceably. At Ringmer peasants successfully won two shillings a day from local farmers, having hitherto received nine shillings a week, which farmers allowed was too little. The mob, augmented at every farm they visited, was between three and four hundred by the time it reached the Broyle, then an unenclosed space.

Eventually incendiarism extended into West Sussex, though it was never so prevalent. Some farmers at Storrington took the precaution of discontinuing the use of threshing machines. At a meeting held in Pulborough's vestry room, after labourers at Billingshurst and Wisborough Green had secured an increase in wages, a deputation of four labourers out of some 150 assembled, entered the room

> and said, in a tone which indicated strong feeling, 'Have you, gentlemen, a mind to give us two shillings a day? We are come here to-night for an answer, and an answer we must have before we go. We have been starving on potatoes long enough, and there must be an alteration; we have come here peaceably, and we wish to go away peaceably; but we must have 2s. a day for our labour.

The demand was assented to. Some of the men said, 'We know what they have done in Kent, but we don't wish to do the same, if we can help it.'

At their height the deeds of 'Captain Swing' caused panic and people spoke of closing the recently opened alehouses, where it was claimed most of the discontent was fomented, but there was little comprehension among the middle and upper classes of the appalling state of the half-starved labourer. An exception, who took the side of the labourers, was Gideon Mantell, the Lewes doctor and famed geologist and palaeontologist. He helped put out a fire caused by arson at the Priory Farm, Lewes, and wrote in his diary:

> 19 November 1830: No one can detect the perpetrators of this and other incidents of nightly occurrence; many suppose it is the work of some agents of a political party; perhaps in a few cases this may be so, but to me it appears more likely to be effected by the peasantry, who have for years been ground to the earth by their masters.
>
> 25 November 1830. Another fire – at Berwick. The public attention wholly engrossed by this alarming state of things, and yet the Landlords will not see the necessity of calling the farmers together and making arrangements for their paying the peasantry in an adequate manner!
>
> 31 December 1830. The Assizes terminated yesterday; two poor fellows are to be hung, and many to be transported, or imprisoned. It is all bad; our peasantry are in a state

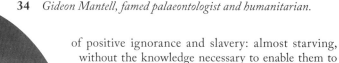

34 *Gideon Mantell, famed palaeontologist and humanitarian.*

of positive ignorance and slavery: almost starving, without the knowledge necessary to enable them to attempt obtaining redress without violence, without violating laws, which are made to oppress the poor and protect the rich![18]

[Insurgents went to] where a Mr Read was lodging who had hired of his lordship the other portion of the tithes, amounting to £700 a year. They demanded of this gentleman that he should forthwith saddle and bridle his horse; which being done, they ordered him to mount, which he also complied with. Two men then took the bridle, one each side, and accompanied with drum and fife, and followed by hundreds of the populace, he was escorted out of the parish; and having arrived at Mark Cross, they bade him good speed, demanding that he might never again be seen in the parish. Mr Read expressed his readiness to follow their instructions, and told them that they were welcome to share the corn on the premises amongst themselves.[19]

'THE HUNGRY FORTIES'

The poverty of labourers peaked in the 'Hungry Forties' before the Repeal of the Corn Laws in 1846 reduced the price of bread. In 1904, in response to a suggestion from Lord Rosebery, T. Fisher Unwin wrote to the national press inviting persons with memories of life in England before the Repeal of the Corn Laws to write down in simple language their recollections and experiences. Mrs Cobden Unwin, a descendant of Richard Cobden who had been a leading figure behind the Repeal, interviewed elderly persons living at Heyshott, Cobden's birthplace, and these simple unvarnished stories were given prominence in her book.

> Widow Sanders and her husband brought up eight children on nine shillings a week and bread at 2s. a loaf. 'Remember the old days! Law, bless yer, my dear. Why many's the night I've gone hungry, so the children might get me bit o' bread between 'em.' She had dreaded her husband flailing corn in the barn, afraid the strokes would stop, and her husband had dropped from the hard work and empty belly.

In similar vein, in broad Sussex, Charles Asridge recollected seeing children from Duck Lane come onto the streets of Midhurst to pick up bits of bread, and even potato peelings. Thomas Wrapson remarked that he had sneaked turnips from the fields and had them with a little bread for supper. When he first went out to work he earned a penny for carrying pails of water uphill and traipsed to Singleton and back, eight miles, on errands for medicines. For three pence he spread manure and picked stones in the meadow and for another three or four pence minded sheep for the day. He remembered 'leasin' (gleaning) the remains of the wheat harvest, a horn being blown to signify that the villagers could begin. The gains would be boiled with a little milk and slice or two of turnip, and each member of the family took a spoon and helped themselves. They thought themselves 'mighty lucky' with a herring or two. The best thing he could recall were allotments set out by Lord Leconfield.

> Yus, wages wor low the, but few 'ad the 'eart to leave Heyshott; they was afeared of them outlandish parts … But things changed, I can tell 'ee when Mr Cobden come … He paid me two shillings a day, 'e did … I never stole no turmuts after that.

George Pollard was born at Graffham but did not know his date of birth, other than that it was in Mr Manning's day (the future Cardinal Manning). He had done all sorts of work, including trips to London for grass mowing at Wimbledon and Wandsworth. If it was not for the hares and rabbits his family would have starved sometimes. His family could not afford tea; bread was toasted until it was black as coal before being put in the tea pot and served as tea. Time and again he had harvested in the Selsey district, carrying children on his back all the way from Singleton, sleeping at night in barns.

> Folks were rare sorry when Mr Cobden died: 'e did a power for Heyshott, 'e wor the best man what ever come here. We a'n't ever had such bad times since. Yus, I wear a cow-rock still, but I dunno as many o' my neighbours wear 'em.[20]

Unrest on the scale of the 1830s was never repeated. Landowners and tenant farmers experiencing the downturn in farming from the 1870s thought that the agricultural labourer had done best. On the big estates they were very well housed in decently repaired or newly built cottages with one-eighth of an acre for a garden. On the Petworth home farm of over

35 *A contemporary cottage scene from Cranbrook, Kent, by the local artists' colony.*

2,000 acres carters had been paid 16s. a week and ordinary labourers 14s. and the tenant farmers paid much the same. Men on task work could earn considerably more, but wages had generally fallen by 1881 owing to the farming depression. On the Downs men were generally paid higher wages. The able-bodied farm worker did comparatively well because he had harvest nearly the year round – the bark harvest in spring; the hay harvest followed; then much task work was available in hoeing; then came the wheat harvest and working on coppicing in the woods all winter. Alternatively, Wealdsmen, as at Rotherfield, could earn good money harvesting hay on the outskirts of London, then tackle the corn harvest on the 'Hill', before returning home for their own harvest about three weeks later. There was still the hop harvest to come. Lord Leconfield did not think labourers tackled heavy work as well as formerly. Women were no longer employed on farms, apart from tying at harvest from the 1850s.

An issue which escalated in the years before the Education Act, 1870, was that of boy labour. For generations children were regarded as indispensable to agriculture. In hop districts they became involved from infancy. In arable areas boys often began as bird scarers at the age of five and by age seven were waggoners' 'mates'; both boys and girls shaved hop-poles in winter. By the age of 11, and sometimes earlier, boys were strong enough to drive the plough of two, three or four horses over an estimated 8½ miles of furrow in a day's work, or to lead a horse hoeing in the hop gardens. Schools being set up unofficially before 1870 were much hampered by the irregular attendance of children taken from classes for farm work, the bark harvest in May and the acorn harvest in the autumn, and parents' reluctance to keep children at school after the age of 10, or to send them to night school, which in any case was generally impracticable for children caring for horses late in the day. Small farmers were particularly resistant to education in the Weald because with little capital they could generally work their farms only with the help of wife and children.[21]

Chapter 6

EARLY ACCESSIBILITY TO ARCADIA

ROADS

Outsiders' growing familiarity with Sussex, the principal cause of change in the county, was largely the result of improved communications from London. When Queen Elizabeth I was travelling near Uckfield in the 'wild of Sussex', Lord Burghley thought her journey more dangerous than in the Peak of Derbyshire, and 'Sousecks full of dyrt and myre' was a common impression of visitors to the county in the 17th century. Archbishop Leighton's nephew explained in October 1685 that boxes of books could not be dispatched back to Scotland from Horsted Keynes, near Lindfield, 'till the winter is over, for the wayes are already so deep, there is no removing of them without great damage'.[1]

Until the coming of the turnpikes in the 18th century, travel was notoriously bad. As Horace Walpole memorably remarked, 'Sussex is a great damper of curiosity' – a cry of despair made in August![2] Sussex roads in particular, on account of the depth of the clays and the steepness of the hills, were execrable. Elizabeth Montagu's carriage in 1738 had such frequent overturns when she made an excursion into Sussex from Tunbridge Wells that she thought a bone-setter a necessary part of the equipment for country visiting. Walpole's is the most eloquent condemnation of Sussex roads. He was visiting houses and abbeys in Sussex in 1752 and on the way to Bayham had difficulty hiring horses because the roads were so bad and decent inns lacking. A nervous traveller, he found the journey to Lamberhurst meant going up and down 'impracticable hills'. He appears to have been terrified at the descent of Silver Hill and appalled at the inn at Robertsbridge. Six miles further he declined another inn and at two o'clock in the morning put up with Excise Officers who had just shot a smuggler. Walpole had fared no better on a journey to Arundel three years earlier. The climb up Bury Hill finally exasperated him to cry out, 'If you love good roads, conveniences, good inns, plenty of postilions and horses, be so kind as never to go into Sussex … Coaches grow there no more than balm and spices.'[3]

The 18th-century novelist Mrs Radcliffe was no less frank about the dangers of road travel, but acknowledged the compensating scenery.[4] She set off from Capel in Surrey in 1800 and eventually reached the foot of Bury Hill but her horse was so tired after the toilsome journey through the clay it needed refreshment before mounting the hill. Shortly afterwards Mrs Radcliffe visited Alfriston from Seaford via the High and Over, 'over such a road as I never saw before; and travelling over such hills!' Two men helped the chaise down one of them but she was too frightened to ride on her return and chose to walk the greatest part of the way back to Seaford. Near Hastings her chaise was almost overturned and she walked the rest of the way.[5]

36 *Old Sussex highway in the Weald, a sketch by J.M.W. Turner, 1820s.*

William Cobbett was a critic of the roads. On his journey over the Low Weald towards Horsham he encountered the deepest clay he had ever experienced, covering only three miles on horseback in an hour and a half, finding what he called the 'real Weald' where the clay is bottomless.[6]

The Rev. J. Coker Egerton reported that when the local squire travelled near Burwash at night in the early 19th century his cavalcade consisted of four horses in his carriage, a man riding one of the leaders, a coachman and footman on the box and a 'Sussex moon', a man on horseback with a lantern strapped to his back, leading the way. Egerton had been taken to a wedding breakfast in a broad-wheeled wagon, any other vehicle being impractical, and noted that lime-wagons on the high road to Lewes could only be extricated in bad weather by placing faggots under the wheels. A man travelling along the road between Burwash and Ticehurst noticed a hat on the road, and retrieving it found a man's head underneath. Neighbours rescued not only the man but his horse who had fallen into the mire.[7]

From the mid-18th century private trusts were empowered to improve access between London and the main market towns and the coast. A French observer in 1821 sampling the coaches, coachmen in livery, postilions, the beautiful horses and the inns, together with the civil attention of everyone, pronounced that England was the first country in the world for these facilities.[8] The London to Brighton road was a tremendous boost to the resort, propelling Londoners to 'London-on-Sea' even though it took eight to ten hours to get there. The road, like the other turnpikes between London and the coast, not only stimulated new coastal resorts of the 'London sort' but opened up the interior of the county to wealthy incomers seeking country estates. The hard surfaces of these 'cockney highways' made them among the finest in Europe in the early 19th century. The speed of the traffic astonished continental visitors and brought country houses served by turnpikes within two or three hours travelling time from London.

Some of the wealthy newcomers in the hilly part of the Weald bore the costs of road-making themselves. The Horsham-Crawley turnpike, seven miles long, was constructed almost at the sole cost of Broadwood, the famed London piano manufacturer, who then built Holmbush, his country mansion. The owner of Mabledon, a fine new seat on the turnpike from Tunbridge Wells to East Grinstead, paid for the reduction of an incline where it passed through his estate. The brothers Burrell, with their fashionable residences of Knepp Castle and West Grinstead Park designed by John Nash, financed the part of the Worthing-Horsham turnpike which gave access to their seats. Towards the end of the 19th century the process of gentrification extended beyond the old turnpikes. As Ruskin explained, less wealthy newcomers would build a house on a former farm and then make themselves unpopular by compelling the parish to make up green lanes into hard roads, which accelerated the invasion of more *nouveaux riches*.[9]

John Cary's *New Itinerary* of 1817 reveals that 30 stage coaches ran daily to Brighton from 17 inns in London, mainly via Reigate, Crawley and Cuckfield, but also along the new road cut from Hickstead, which was shorter, and through Lewes and Dorking, the fastest coaches taking six to seven hours on a journey of 53 miles by the shortest route. A 'post coach' left London three times daily and some operators had two daily coaches on the Brighton route. The night coach to Cheapside left Brighton every evening at 10 p.m., arriving at 6 a.m. the next day and leaving again at 10 the same evening, to arrive in Brighton on the early morning of the following day. This was patronised mainly by commuting 'stockjobbers' and other City people, Cobbett's *bêtes noirs*, who by this means could spend daytime at the Exchange or their London office. Worthing's tally of daily coaches from London was nine. Although some were using the new cut, now the A24, to avoid Steyning, the 59-mile journey had slower coaches than Brighton's and took an average of nine or ten hours. Bognor and Hastings had four daily coaches from the capital, Littlehampton, three, and Lewes and Rye two each. The traveller from London to the latter, bound for Boulogne, spent 12 hours on his journey to the packet boat. Eastbourne, then a fledgling resort, made do with a summer service of one coach daily, and Shoreham had a direct link to London only on Saturdays.

Maude Egerton King, whose father was a famous Brighton coachman, noted that his first two-horse coaches at the beginning of the century took 12 hours to cover the distance between London and Brighton, with leisurely stops for lavish refreshment on the way at Sutton, the *Tangier* at Banstead, Reigate, Handcross and Staplefield Common. Twenty years later, *The Age* brought out a contingent of gazers each morning when it left the coach offices in Castle Square – 'a thing worth looking at, with its pole-chains of burnished steel, and its daintiest of ribbons and superb horses in silver-mounted harness, and horse-clothes embroidered with royal crowns in silver and gold'.[10]

The improved roads rapidly changed the character of the country they passed through. Farm rentals rose and many small farmers sold out or gave up tenancies, their lands being turned into landscape parks by new gentry. Farm labourers became gardeners and servants. New inns and attendant dwellings arrived. Cobbett noted in the 1820s that 'deep-lane country', unsuitable for carriages, continued to hold out against change, but beside the high roads landscape was being rearranged for aesthetic pleasure.[11] Travellers along the London to Brighton road encountered almost uninterrupted parks and ornamental farms in place of the old yeomen's working farmsteads, but unmanaged minor roads meant they were firmly anchored to a zone little more than a mile each side of the road.[12] The carriage wheels of

37 *Stage wagon at the* Talbot Inn *in the Borough,* London.

the wealthy travelled back and forth and wrought physical and social transformation along the turnpikes. Notable, too, would have been readier access to markets like Horsham, Heathfield, Hailsham and Farnham for farmers, increasing the opportunities of supplying the Wen of London and Brighton with chickens, hops and wood. The consequences of the great improvement of the roads on people's well-being generally are impossible to assess, but Lord Torrrington mused on this during his Sussex tour in 1788 and concluded that the new road system had introduced learning and arts into the county and removed wretched families 'who buried themselves in mud and ignorance', introducing instead the 'wit and gallantry in the parishes of Marylebone and St James's'. He thought particularly of how unimproved must have been the dull life of the sequestered females,

> miserably employed in reading, working, walking, oblig'd to rise early, go to bed early; sometimes to receive their neighbours, and relations, but never tasting (in those Gothic days), the dear, and eternal delights of flirtation; the midnight supper; the dance till daylight; fashion opposed to fashion; dress compared with dress; eating ices in January – and wearing roses in February.

He compared with their former existence the 'modern hands that never work, and limbs that never move but in a dance!'[13] Changes percolating into the yeomen's farms on account of improved transport may have included more hogsheads of port in the cellar and more reading matter, including newspapers. Cobbbett was horrified to find new-fangled parlours, bell-pushes, mahogany chairs, sofas, wine glasses, decanters, dinner breakfast sets with dessert knives and similar luxuries amid the traditional plain furnishings in solid oak.[14]

Yet roads, until the coming of the motor car, bore little traffic. Michael Fairless (Margaret Fairless Barber) throws light on the vehicular traffic passing the White Gate at her house at Mock Bridge, Shermanbury (now on the A271) at the end of the 19th century. The distant stamp of horse hoofs heralded a heavy flour-wagon going to and from the mill – 'with a team of four gentle horses, gay with brass trappings and scarlet caps' – the white-clad waggoner on the top of the piled sacks with reins looped over an inactive whip, for the horses knew the journey. Occasionally she took a lift on the wagon, flinging herself down on the empty flour bags and being soothed by the monotonous tramp of the great grey team and the music of the jangling harness. Whirls of white dust would signify the annual Cattle Fair. All day long beasts streamed in broken procession along her road, followed by a squadron of well-fed cart-horses and ponies and, finally, a long line of carts which had waited for the dust to subside brought pigs and fowls. When they had passed her road sank into silence again. Some days there were so few passers-by that her road was lonely, apart from the lamp-lighter who came nightly to the bridge. Barges on the river Adur in calm weather dropped 'slowly and sullenly down with the tide', sails half-furled. The river was heavy with hay-barges in early summer.[15]

Novelist Angela Thirkell describes the arduous climbs horses made between Brighton and Rottingdean at the beginning of the last century. It was always a sore point with her as a child to be told by her mother to get off and walk up the long hills when the horses slowed down. Another of her mother's 'amiable weaknesses' was to get her passengers in their private coach to sit well forward at a steep rise, throwing the weight as near to the front as possible.[16]

Most Sussex roads, such as that from Edburton to Poynings at the foot of the Downs, were no wider before the last century than a single wagon. But at distant intervals the hedges were curved backward to make a bay, 'lest so remarkable a thing could happen as two wagons desiring to pass each other'. A wagon's four horses each carried a frame of bells on their collars, to warn carters ahead they were coming. The road surface was repaired by tossing down flints and trusting the wheels to roll them in. A vivid picture of powerful horses on the road was provided by William Wood, who was saddened at the loss of the 'proudest music of all, that of the bell team'. Stepping with springing hocks, and high lifted bending knee, they set the bells going merrily with every shake of gaily carried head and flowing mane, a beautiful sight to send any countryman's heart beating with pride and happiness; they are gone; you must jump back into the hedge to escape the noisy, stinking motor lorry.[17]

One of the great sights of the road was 'The Ship of the Downs', the picturesque blue and red painted Sussex wagon occasionally seen on the terrace ways on the hills. Thurston Hopkins observed that a carter with a load of chalk could negotiate a precipitous road which did not appear wide enough for a wheel-barrow, but with a leisurely – almost contemptuous – way he nursed his horses and manoeuvred the wagon round dangerous corners and through difficult drive gates. The Sussex wagon was of immense size and would carry a load of three tons with ease. Three horses in line were generally allowed for a heavy load, but when the Weald was muddy four were often required. Many of the wagons were over a hundred years old, as one could tell from the ponderous wheels and exceptionally wide felloes. The horses understood every command spoken by the carter, and seldom did he find it necessary to guide one of the horses with a gentle tap with his long whip.[18]

Edward Johnston of Ditchling had been so struck by the sight of this, 'a kind of Fairy Ship for Beauty', that he still recalled it in wonder 42 years later. He thought that to describe all its locally shaped parts, including its little stop chamfered and the painted banisters, would need a vocabulary of its own of between 50 and 100 words. The empty wagon he saw could have carried a hay-rick and was drawn by six horses in pairs. They were slightly decked with coloured ribbons and wore historic shiny brass ornaments. Three carters, shouldering long whips, walked at their heads in a glorious procession. He was told by a man the right technical name for each horse according to its position in the team.[19]

The drove-road network criss-crossed the county bringing cattle and sheep eastwards as far as Kent from breeding grounds in Wales and the West Country. Highly skilled (and highly paid) drovers avoided as much as possible roads carrying human traffic on account of the tolls and damage to their animals' feet. Drove roads instead followed greenways over commons and heaths and other wild parts of country, across village greens and farm-tracks, the animals picking up mouthfuls of food on the way. Herds and flocks moved slowly, the drovers usually sleeping with their animals at night.

In wet weather, and nearly all winter, the country roads were covered with mud an inch or more in thickness, interspersed with small pools of water. It was customary for houses with stone and brick floors to be washed down with buckets of water and scrubbed with a long birch broom. Feet were kept dry with the patten, a flat piece of rough wood half an inch or more thick, shaped like the sole of a boot and with sides quite straight. To it was attached a band of iron, round or slightly oval, about half an inch broad and a quarter of an inch thick, by means of two upright pieces of iron fixed by screws, one to the heel and the other to the tread of the wood. A person standing on a patten would be about three inches from the ground, two little pieces of leather being nailed to the sides of the wood. 'The patten was not secured to the foot in any other way, and when women wished to put it on they simply stood behind it and put their toes through the space left above the wooden sole. It required almost an education to keep the pattens on, but women began to learn the art as children, and when it was acquired, could walk some distances, two or three miles, without difficulty.'[20]

RIVER NAVIGATION

Along with the improvement to roads went beneficial changes to water transport and the drainage of low-lying pasture. The lower reaches of the Ouse were in a deplorable state towards the end of the 18th century. The outfall, encumbered by sand and shingle at Newhaven, was accessible only to small, lightly-loaded ships, and so little water entered the river that tides were imperceptible at Lewes only nine miles upstream. The Brooks, as the meadows were called in the lower part of the valley were under water for as much as eight months in the year. This situation was dramatically improved from 1790 by new cuts to straighten the river, new sewers, a breakwater to stop the eastward movement of shingle, and the provision of 25 locks and a straightened course on 22 miles of the upper Ouse. Sheep-breeder John Ellman, in various capacities with the Commissioners of Sewers, contributed energy and enterprise to these projects, which Cobbett noted created rich grazings in the Brooks for downland farmers. Commercially the river navigation was never entirely successful, and it fell into disuse given competition from the growing number of branch railways. The once busy line of watermills have been largely converted into residences.

Canalisation of the Western Rother to Midhurst began in 1791, of the River Adur in 1806. The moist ambitious project was the Wey and Arun Canal with its extension to Chichester and Portsmouth, which provided a strategic inland water route to London when shipping in the Channel was preyed upon by the French during the Napoleonic Wars. The Newbridge-Pallingham Lock on the Arun Navigation, dug in 1787, is notable for the Lording's aqueduct over the River Arun at Lording's Lock, a water wheel lifting water from the river into the canal. Other impressive monuments are the tunnel to avoid a wide meander of the river near Pulborough and the Orfold Viaduct, now partly collapsed, which took barges on to the Thames. The most renowned instigator of such projects, and of agricultural improvement in general, was George O'Brien Wyndham, the 3rd Earl of Egremont, who financed the construction of the Rother Navigation to supply his estate. The river Adur was also substantially improved.

RAILWAYS

Paradoxically, one of the advantages to living in London was the ease of getting out of it. The turnpike roads had made the countryside within a radius of about fifteen to thirty miles from St Paul's conveniently accessible earlier, and by the 1870s the dense network of suburban and long distance railway routes running in and out of London termini, unmatched anywhere in the world, made travel from hot and sultry streets into cool woodland glades or open Downs easy.

The railways, mostly single-track, that 'opened up' the Weald, such as the lines from Eastbourne to Tunbridge Wells, from Brighton to Horsham and Guildford, and Lewes, East Grinstead, Uckfield and Robertsbridge to Headcorn, became crowded with friendly, talkative farmers, cottagers and market people. Sheila Kaye-Smith, in *The Weald of Kent and Sussex* (1953), remembered 'beating' by bicycle the slow train from Crowborough to East Grinstead, and the little wayside stations, often gay with flowers, with the stationmaster-cum-porter-cum-signalman. Her favourite railway was the Kent and East Sussex, which

38 *The railway viaduct over Lewes Road, Brighton, 1846.*

39 *Third-class excursionists travelling to Brighton, 1850s.*

followed the River Rother from Robertsbridge to Tenterden, where one could change for Dover or Hastings for five pence less than by the direct route which was four hours shorter. Road traffic at gateless level-crossings was warned by a porter with a red flag. The train jogged so slowly through the hop gardens 'that we can snuff the scented shadows of their aisles, or watch the gaily coloured groups of hop-pickers at their bins among the hop-poles, or admire the careful skill of the hop-tiers on their stilts'. She noted that 'East Grinstead was a great railway centre', with four lines converging on two stations on two different levels – the upper and the lower level – which belonged to two different companies.[21]

The single-track line from Pulborough via Petworth and Midhurst to Hampshire through the Western Rother valley was so friendly a service that regular travellers to London via Petersfield running late to the station would send children ahead to ask the driver to hold on a little.

On some trains comfort seems not to have altered since artist John Linnell's day. Philip Mairet travelled down to Hassocks on the London to Brighton line in February 1917 'behind one of its old yellow-canary locomotives stained with wartime dirt and neglect'. On a freezing day, the compartment windows were opaque with the travellers' breath; long metal boxes held hot water under the seats, which were cooled by the time the train got to Haywards Heath and were replaced with new ones too hot to touch.[22]

The Horsham to Brighton railway in the 1930s had a splendid historian in Philip Gosse. The 'real country', he wrote nostalgically, began at Dorking. The change into old-fashioned carriages at Horsham, before the train made its way to Steyning, was a marvellous introduction to 'Old Sussex':

> The train wound its way not too rapidly through meadows and freshly ploughed brown fields with the glowing South Downs always in the distance, and the black ring of Chanctonbury surmounting all. A plough, drawn by three stalwart horses, went slowly along with none of the noise of modern mechanism. The pleasant prospect on either side was unspoiled by ugly hoardings, which on the main roads shout aloud at you to buy their tooth-paste, petrol, or British lager beer … Here and there stood an old farm labourer's cottage. There were big woods and small spinneys in place of tall factory chimneys and mean bungalows. Wild flowers grew and bloomed, unpicked and untrampled, on the steep banks of the cutting where the train went through some slight incline. No women or children stood by the railway track as they do by the motor roads in the spring, with outstretched hands grasping tired bundles of pale primroses, lent lilies, drooping bluebells, or yellow cowslips, flowers torn from the meadows and woods where they belong. Brown men, brown like the mother earth where they were born and bred, and from which for generations they have won their living, moved slowly about their concerns.

As the train drew nearer to the Downs, it seemed to lose its way. Sometimes Chanctonbury Ring was seen through the right-hand window but a moment later it had disappeared, to reappear suddenly at the opposite side as the train veered across to serve a distant station. From time to time it stopped at small wayside stations where one or two country people with numerous parcels got in or out, moving slowly as is the countryman's way, with many welcomes and farewells to their fellow-travellers. At each station the guard discussed with the railway porter the hopes and fortunes of the local football team, so that by the time passengers reached their destination they had become authorities on the Brighton and Hove Football Club. Gathering hand-luggage, people were greeted by smiling friends and the stationmaster and porters on Steyning station. From Victoria Station in London it had taken two hours to travel fifty miles, a poor time compared with the Brighton express or a motor car but not a minute too long for retired doctor Philip Gosse, for he had seen the Sussex of a century ago, which he could never have done from the main railway lines or motor roads. Sheila Kaye-Smith was in agreement with him that the best way to see rural Sussex was by the little railways and not by motor.[23]

Yet it was the railway that began the transformation of the sleepy county. Brighton and the coastal towns burgeoned with middle-class patrons and working-class day-trippers arriving on excursion trains. As Virginia Woolf rightly remarked, much of the horror of the countryside before the Victorians was that people sat or rode behind stout sweating horses. By the 1880s the Pullman Express was travelling from London to Brighton once a day in 60 minutes, advertised as 'the most luxurious train in the world', and the boat-train to Paris headed for the cross-Channel embarkation port of Newhaven. From the mid-1930s the 'green electrics' of the Southern Railway, celebrated in verse by John Arlott, ran between Victoria Station and Brighton every hour and spread their speedy, clean and quiet tentacles over Sussex. They gave a boost to the custom of weekending which had originated with the steam railway.

Major cattle markets, fairs and large-scale brickworks moved to railway junctions such as Haywards Heath and expanded at towns served by railways, such as Lewes, Hailsham

40 *Haywards Heath mock-Tudor, designed by Harold Turner.*

and Steyning. In parts of the Weald the coming of the railway led to resuscitation. An example is the Heathfield poultry-breeding industry which spread into neighbouring parishes. Until the railway came in 1880 the district bore no marks of agricultural prosperity. There were some hops but the main crop on the rather poor soils was oats, the main cereal for man and beast in the Weald. The railway offered the opportunity to venture into 'higgling', the production of chicken for the London market, and this rapidly became the staple product of the district. Almost every small farm and smallholder raised poultry for fattening by 'higglers', leaving coops waiting on the wayside for collection, which gave a remarkable impression of prosperity.

Another direct result of the railway was the creation of Crowborough as a health and holiday resort, marketed by Charles Leeson Prince, a local doctor, after the railway arrived from London in 1868. His advocacy of the bracing air of the elevated district, absolutely free, he claimed, from the smoke and dirt of London, led the principal landowner, Lord Abergavenny, to lay out extensive tracts of land for hotels and villas on what had been a military training camp during the Napoleonic Wars. Numerous incomers were attracted to the town, notably Sir Arthur Conan Doyle, the town's leading citizen, and writer Lewis Lusk.

The most dramatic development arising from railways was the creation of Haywards Heath, Burgess Hill and Hassocks on the London to Brighton line. Haywards Heath and Burgess Hill began as 'urban villages' on commons enclosed by Parliamentary Act. The commons and wastes in the manor of Keymer were enclosed in 1828, the legal and other expenses defrayed by selling 200 acres to speculators. Villas sprang up along the turnpike from Cuckfield to Brighton. Settlement became rapid after the station opened in 1841, and industry was attracted. Haywards Heath grew around a lonely station opened to serve Cuckfield, the heath being enclosed in 1862 and turned over to building. M.A. Lower of Lewes called it a fine 'abode of civilisation' in 1870 and approved of the villas and pleasure residences which 'had grown up like magic'[24] but some, like Belloc and Halsham, condemned it as a sham and humbug way of living which was erasing the 'Old Sussex'.

'Londonisation' created specific forms of human habitation – Victorian and Edwardian villas, weekend cottages, rows of semi-detached houses, bungalows, plot-land shack communities, dormitory towns and villages and modernist Art Nouveau dwellings, together with golf courses, youth hostels and other leisure facilities, such as landscaped parks, 'wild gardens' and arboreta, model farms, estate villages, holiday camps, sanatoria, private schools, petrol stations, roadhouses and the rest – in effect, modern Sussex.

INNS

One of the most celebrated Sussex inns was the *Swan* at Fittleworth, which E.V. Lucas once described as probably the most ingeniously placed inn in the world.[25] The sign of the *Swan* (now sadly removed) was certainly as old as Queen Anne's reign and the building itself two centuries older than that. The old stables recall the stage coaches and post chaises which once visited. For centuries it was the haunt of fishermen, and after Constable came to Arundel in 1833, Victorian artists, both famous and forgotten, left their paintings on the panelling in the little lounge in lieu of payment for the hospitality. The picture room in the restaurant features paintings by Thomas Collier, George Cole, George Vicat Cole, A.W. Weeden, Philip Stretton and many others, and the Visitors Book has many distinguished names including that of Rudyard Kipling, who wrote, after one of his earliest journeys by motor car, in 1903, 'Thirty miles from R[ottingdean] in three hours.'

Another outstanding inn was the *White Hart* at Lewes. William Verrall's patrons in the 1760s were offered novel French cooking based on recipes he published in his *Cookery Book* in 1759, derived from menus of the French cook St Clouet. One of these was *Turbot à l'Italienne*, turbot marinaded in vinegar, white wine, salt and water, stewed with onions, bay leaves and mace and served with a delicious sauce. *Un Jambon aux Epinards* was another of his main courses. Verrall despised the 'English way' of soaking ham in brine and serving it 'hard as flint' with some greasy cabbage and followed the French technique of gently simmering it until tender and serving it with a suitable garnish.[26]

On his tour of Sussex in 1782 Lord Torrington stayed overnight at the *White Hart*. It was then run by Thomas Scrace, who 'begged leave to acquaint the Nobility, Gentry and Others that he has a Larder always well stored, likewise the best Wines of all sorts, also Brandy, Rum, Arrack, etc., neat as imported N.B. Neat Post-Chaises and able horses at the shortest notice.' Torrington and his companion do not mention French cooking and enjoyed brill fish and the good port and beer, but were so displeased with their accommodation up two pairs of stairs – and the bedroom door forced open by drunkards – that he concluded: 'There cannot be an inn of a worse description than is the *White Hart*, and the *Star* looks as badly; so if ever I shou'd come this way again, the *Bear* must be my trial.'

Lord Torrington's mixed fortunes on his Sussex tour are enlightening. He did well at the *Bells* in Northiam in the 1780s; the *George* at Rye was dirty and had a wretched stable but they found the *New Inn* at Winchelsea good despite the tough fowls the landlord recommended as they had been freshly killed. At Hastings the inn could supply no fish but they had an enjoyable meal including cooked wheatears plucked on the spot for their dinner-spit which had been caught to order by the shepherd at the castle. At Battle they chose an inn suggested by the landlord at Winchelsea which turned out a failure. At Herstmonceux they were happily accommodated and fed on mutton chops and broiled ham (the standard Sussex dish). The *Castle* at Brighton was an excellent tavern. The *Swan* at Forest Row turned out a gem; after a 'leg of mutton and turnips just boiled', a plum pie, good cheese and half a pint of brandy 'made me feel as full as an alderman'. All the inns at East Grinstead were pronounced vile but the *White Hart* at Godstone thankfully supplied their needs.[27]

41   *The* White Hart, *Lewes.*

Although Lord Torrington was unhappy at the *White Hart* (Lewes), William Wood, a farmer at Twineham, had nothing but praise for it in the late 19th and early 20th centuries. He went regularly to dine at the Farmers' Ordinaries of old and found that the inn, like inns generally in Sussex, provided every market day a good, solid, well-cooked meal,

> the like of which it is difficult to find today; tastes have altered, possibly the majority now prefer the imitation Italian restaurant menu now universal, but there may be a few who prefer the old style, and the only place in Sussex that I know of, where you may be sure of getting it, is at the *White Hart*, Lewes; no sideshows there, but plain well-cooked joints of the best Southdown mutton and Sussex beef – no imported meat permitted …
>
> When I first attended the Market Ordinary at the *White Hart*, over sixty years ago, there was always a choice of thick or clear soup, a choice of fish, joints of beef and mutton or port, always game when in season, and at other times chicken, duck, turkey or goose, and the price was 2s., but in those days nearly every man at the table had a bottle of wine, and before the proceedings were over sometimes found it desirable to have another.[28]

Farmers on market days certainly had big appetites. Wood tells a tale of the *Black Horse* in Horsham at which he was present.

> At this Ordinary there was no chairman, customers came in at their convenience; legs of mutton and rounds of boiled and roast beef were placed upon the table, and the man who chanced to be seated where the joints were placed carved and helped himself … An old Scotchman, named Young, came in and took the seat I had just left, in front of this leg of mutton, and with him came two big long-legged sons. The landlord came in behind the waiter who brought the leg of mutton, and as Mr Young began to carve it, in a very rough and ready way … stepped forward and said 'Excuse me, Sir, but I must ask you to carve that joint with a little more care, you must remember there are other customers who will presently want some of it.' The old farmer replied, 'Don't worry yourself about this leg of mutton and the people that are coming in presently; when me and my two boys have done with it there won't be any left worth troubling about.'[29]

Early ramblers were even less lucky with inns than 18th-century aristocrats. In his *Green Lanes and Field Paths* (1877) Louis Jennings advises walkers in the Downs to take a supply of provisions and camp out on the hills, for the villages at the foot of the hills offered no accommodation. At Cocking the author could get no accommodation in the village and so went to the *Bell*. There he was told there was no bed 'for love nor money' and nothing to offer by way of refreshment but bread and cheese. At the *White Horse* at Sutton, where labourers were boozing in the tap-room, the landlord said he could only provide accommodation if notice was given beforehand.[30]

Belloc tells of an inn at Bramber that offered so delightful an experience his companions in *The Four Men* (1912) refused to visit it again for fear of disappointment. The joy of eating and drinking on summer evenings in the gardens had been memorable, with bats flying overhead and the song of a nightingale.[31]

Chapter 7

DIALECT, FOLKLORE AND FOLK SONGS

One of the most striking changes in Sussex over the past 150 years has been the loss of country speech, the pronunciation of place-names and the high sing-song drawl of the countryman, which was basically Saxon in origin. Until the mid-19th century the traveller would have heard country people speaking a dialect which differed a little according to where the speaker was brought up, so that a native of Henfield, for example, might have different expressions and accent to one from East Sussex. A stranger to Sussex also noted differences in speech and habits compared with other counties. To Kent-minded Ford Madox Ford it seemed that the differences between his county and West Sussex were as great as with China. The change to modern speech was rapid. Dialect fell to the polish of the elementary schools from the 1870s, of the new grammar schools that first appeared in the early 1900s and to new influences such as the wireless from the 1920s. It is, however, the arrival of urban newcomers from outside which has been the principal cause of the sudden loss of Sussex speech, and with it Sussex folklore and customs. No one has made this point more clearly than Hilaire Belloc. He remarked that the traditional pronunciation of his nearest market town's name was 'Hors-ham', because Saxons had called it the 'horses-home', and wryly noted that newcomers mispronounced the place-name as 'Horsh-ham' but did not yet call a 'horse' a 'horsh'.[1] He went to extraordinary efforts to stop the ignorance, including bribing a train guard to call out the old name in the vernacular, but Londoners won the day. A Mr Pocock of Alciston, a village near Lewes, could not be identified in the mid-19th century by a lawyer who wanted to interview him because he called himself, in a broad Sussex burr, 'Master Palk of Ahson'.[2]

Many words were pure Saxon such as 'stade' (a landing place), 'barton' (a farmyard), and 'bly' (a likeness). Pronunciation was also broad Saxon. Barn was 'bearn', gate, 'ge-at', house, 'huss', laths were 'latts', yeast was 'yust', yes, 'yus', drive, 'druv', Mister and Mistress, 'Muster and Mistus'. The letters 'ea' were usually pronounced 'aw', so the real Sussexian called Haywards Heath 'Heward's Hawth'. A few elderly people still said 'hon-lye' for 'only' as late as 1900 and older people pronounced the double letter in 'the' or 'them' as 'D'; mice were 'meece', tallow, 'toller'. The old plural was used, i.e. 'nestes', 'postes' and 'ghostes' for nests, posts and ghosts, and users of this curious speech apparently sang 'Rocks of Ages' in church. Instead of 'soon', 'sooner' was said, and for grew, knew, etc., 'growd' and 'knowd' were substituted. Will was pronounced 'wool' and country people would say, 'let it be how t'wool', instead of 'be it as it may'. Wealdsmen called the Downs the 'Hill', Romney Marsh and the Pevensey Levels the 'Mesh' and their own lands the 'Wild'. Durrant Cooper also noted words of French origin pronounced in the French manner in the Rye district: Day was pronounced there 'dee', mercy as in French *merci*, bonnet as *bunnet*, Mermaid Street as Maremaid Street.

In the late 19th century differences in dialect were apparent in the speech of some of the old men compared with that of their sons. Beckett noted that the pure, picturesque, Sussex vernacular was slowly giving way under the influence of the elementary schools. One rarely met the man who pronounced the double letter in 'the' or 'them' as 'D'; the word 'mice' to the new generation was no longer 'meece', although one still heard 'tallow' called 'toller'. The curious old plural was still used by aged people. Sheila Kaye-Smith, author of novels based in East Sussex, was particularly interested in country speech and noted the different expressions of successive generations. 'Ask Grandfather if it will be a stormy day and he will tell you, "Surelye, fur de ships' tails is all to wind'ard." Father will answer, "Well, it may be, for the glass is low," while Sonny will reply, "Not half."' Parish's *Dialect Dictionary* includes many words formerly in common use which are now obsolete, such as 'spaddle', to bring mud from boots into the house.[3]

Ahson, Heffle, Linvul and Pidnoo were earlier pronunciations of Alciston, Heathfield, Lindfield and Piddinghoe. The sonorous long final -ly and -lye of so many names, such as West Hoathly, were dropped, and Ardingly and Chiddingly were clipped to Arn'ly and Chid'n'ly, and given a mincing equality. John Halsham in *Idlehurst* (1898) predicted correctly that in the next generation 'the last of the vernacular speech would have fallen before the all-absorbing pronunciations of Mayfair and the Old Kent Road'.[4]

The gradual loss of dialect led to collections of the dying country speech. One of the earliest publications on Sussex dialect was Richard Lower's of Chiddingly, who in *Stray Leaves* (1862) published Tom Cladpole's *Jurney to Lunnun*, which had appeared in pamphlet form. It recounts the many adventures met with:

> I think, says I, I'll take a trip
> To Lunnun – dat I wull,
> And see how things goo on a bit,
> Lest I should die a fool!
> For Sister Sal, five year agoo,
> Went up wud Squyer Brown;
> Housemaid, or summatt – dunnow what,
> To live in Lunnun town.

In the following specimen of genuine West Sussex speech of about 1900 an old cottage wife speaks to her husband:

> 'Tummas, it be time tur git the medsums; I be a-goin' ter go up around t'hill this mornin' ter get un. I wunt be 'ome till latish like; but as yer be goin' hayin', yer'll get yer bait [food and drink] in the fiel', an' I'll cook up a bite for 'ee whe 'ee gets 'ome; 'bout seven 'twill be I speckses.'
> 'That'll be all right, Ann; I rackons that'll be 'bout it; an' dunn'ee furgit some agermony for me liver. 'Ee bin a bit outer sorts o' late like.'

The old lady went across fields and collected some 'agermony', together with rest-harrow, from a hedge with which to brew a concoction to make a gargle and a cure for the toothache. She then called on an old friend who remarked:

> Well, I be danged, I warn't aspectin' ter see yer come along smarnin'; but I sees as you be a-findin medsums. I bin a-thinkin' 'bout that 'ere mesel. Now's the time, and the moon be 'bout right; on'y, as yer knows, me ole leg don't a-carry I ser well as 'un used ter do; but 'twer bettern 'twas now I've a-putt that ther sungreen 'intment on'un.

The visitor continued:

> I be glad ter 'ear that, surelye; but there, Jeane, I knowed as 'ow 'twud putten right. Afore I furgits it may I fetch along a bit o' that 'ere Tansy ginger [Tansy] yer got a-growin' in yer 'edge-side, as I wants ter make a little o' that 'ere stimmeglant; it'll do Sary's lad a sight o' good now 'ee be a-getting over they 'ere fevers.[5]

Nathaniel Blaker published a good specimen of mid-Sussex dialect of the late 19th century:

> Eh be gwene t' Henvul t'mor ter tolk at dem dere hogs. Dey say deirn be better dun ouern, eeh sey dey beant. Ouern be a godd lot o' shuts, and dey be middlin lusty. De trevlin's purty bad, and de brooks be out, but b'out-t-will eh shall goo, regn eh shall git dere somehow.

In translation this would read: 'I am going to Henfield tomorrow to look at them there hogs. They say theirs are better than ours. I say they are not. Ours are a good lot of shuts [half-grown pigs] and middling fat. The travelling is pretty bad, and the brooks are out, but be it how it will I shall go. I reckon I shall get there somehow.'[6]

A good example of early 20th-century East Sussex speech is the dialogue provided by Rudyard Kipling in *The Friendly Book* between two farmworkers skilfully making a stake-and-binder hedge in the Dudwell valley in Burwash. This has a flow and naturalness of which Kipling was a master and it is a good documentation of a place where weather and humanity meet. The brook was rising fast and threatening crops:

> 'Gor a-mighty Jesse', he bellers out to me, 'get that rubbish away all manners you can. Don't stop for no fagottin', but give the brook play or my wheat's past salvation. I can't lend you no help', he says, 'but work an' I'll pay ye.'
> 'You had him there', Jabez chuckled.
> 'Yes, I reckon I had ought to have drove my bargain, but the brook was backin' upon good bread-corn. So 'cardenly, I laid into the mess of it, workin' off the bank where the trees was drownin' themselves head-down into the roosh – just such weather as this – an' the brook creepin' up on me all the time.'
> Long before noon, Jim comes mowchin' along with his toppin' axe over his shoulder. 'Be you minded for an extra hand at your job', he says.
> 'Be you minded to turn to?', I ses, an' no more talk to it – Jim laid in alongside o' me. He's no bunger with a toppin' axe.[7]

Arthur Beckett thought that Amy Sawyer of Ditchling was the only author in the county who devoted her talents to the writing of local dramas. These are now invaluable for they preserve vestiges of dialect, idiom and customs which have since vanished. East Sussex speech was used by Sawyer, for example, in *The Brown Pot*, which has a contemporary kitchen scene:

> Scene: *A Sussex farmhouse about 1860. Sink, broken looking-glass, towel on nail, bucket, handbowl, plates, etc., on shelf. Two pots, one brown, one yellow, are cooking on hearth. Table, two chairs, one stool by fireplace.*
>
> Marse Pannett: Mis' Tester! Mis' Tester ! (*looking round*). She beänt here seemin'ly. (*He puts trug on table and takes out a potato.*) There be a nice lookin' tater now! Fair spoilt! All them darn ratses. And a fine takin ol' Tester 'ull be in when he sees 'em. Not one or two, mind 'ee, ate up clean, but a bit out here and a bit out there till the whole bilin be good for naun. As for that 'ere pison, 'tain't no manner o' use. They licks their lips and gets fat on it. Ah, I 'lows as us can show the finest, fattest, most contented set of ratses in the county. 'Fer'ts', that's what I says to him: 'fert's,' I says, 'an' a nice liddle dawg or two.' But bless us an' save us what he can't stand is the idee that we'd be enj'yin' ourselves. He be prapper contrary, be Mus Tester. An' a good rat hunt be a dish for a king, that it be.[8]

For dialect of the 1840s see pp.54-5.

CUSTOMS AND FOLKLORE

It is understandable that old-world beliefs and customs should have retained firm hold in Sussex until around the end of the 19th century, especially because many farming families had inhabited the same district for up to five centuries. The historian Lower gives an instance of a high sheriff who selected javelin-men from his own resident tenantry all bearing the name Botting. The persistence of the same family name over many years will arrest the attention of any visitor to a village churchyard, as it did Virginia Woolf at Rodmell, who wished they could come back.

Dr Andrew Allen's *Dictionary of Sussex Folk Medicine* (1995) gives many examples. He explains that the rural and urban poor would have adopted whatever healing lore was traditional to their family or community and that *in extremis* they tried out any remedy they had heard of. Usually there was in every village a 'healing woman' or mountebank to whom people turned for help. Such folklore was based on ideas from the Reformation and comprised inefficacious superstitious nonsense and remedies which appear to have actually cured people.

In the first category Allen puts a 'cure' for Ague – malaria endemic in Sussex marshes into the 1790s and later still in Pett and Guldeford Marshes – which required the swallowing of live spiders; a popular Sussex cure for receding hair involved massaging the fat from badgers into the scalp; a laxative tonic was made by heathmen from birch sap. A widespread Sussex custom was keeping a hot-cross bun baked on Good Friday in the house all the year as a protection against ill-luck and in the event of illness a fragment was powdered and used as a medicine. In the second category Allen put remedies which appear to have been successful, such as cobwebs and mouldy bread, used to heal wounds and treat burns and as a poultice in milk swabbed on skin infections. Portions of mouldy bread were left on beams on Good Friday, a practice evidently widespread in Europe. The mouldy foodstuff tended to become contaminated with a species of penicillin which evidently released a wide range of bacteriological antibiotics well known in ancient China and Greece. Scurvy, a deficiency of vitamin C, caused deaths in Sussex well into the 18th century. As Dr Allen remarks, it is is difficult to understand how rural people could fail to eat sufficient fruit and vegetables, but this appears to have been the case. The archetypal Sussex man and woman was apparently a carnivore – primarily a hog eater – and tackled puddings, cheeses, bread and sweetmeats of every kind with gusto, but had no liking for fresh vegetables.

A number of old customs persisted until relatively recently. 'Clemmening' was the old custom in East Sussex of going from house to house asking for apples and beer on St Clement's Day (22 July). Sussex blacksmiths commemorated their patron saint by firing their anvils with a loud explosion and keeping a half-holiday. At Burwash it was the custom to dress a figure with a wig and beard and pipe in his mouth and set it up over the door of the inn where the blacksmiths feasted on St Clement's Day.[9]

Another annual ceremony in a county that used to have many orchards was 'wassailing', in which people drank the health of their apple trees in the hope they would bear well. It often involved song and dance to drums, bells and whistles, and the beating of branches with sticks to wake the sleeping powers of fertility and to ward off evil influences. Cider was poured over the tree roots, or bread soaked in a 'wassailing bowl' was placed in the tree branches as an offering to the tree. The words of one song ran:

> Stand fast root, bear well top,
> Pray God send us a howling good crop.
> Every twig, apples big;
> Every bough, apples now.
> Hail to thee, old apple tree!
> From every bough
> Give us apples now;
> Hatsful, capsful,
> Bushel, bushel, sacksful,
> And our arms full, too.

Among the labourers and shepherds on the South Downs a belief in the existence of fairies, or as they called them 'Pharisees' ('fairiesees', a plural corruption of 'fairy'), had not died out. The 'hag-tracks', or circular growths of fungus which abounded on the uncultivated turf, were attributed to their agency. Lower, in his *Contributions to Literature*, recounts some curious narratives in connection with this subject. The poet Habberton Lulham learned from an old shepherd on the Downs near Ditchling how:

> Down the midnight's coombe's
> Green, winding hollows, still the little folk
> Go dancing 'neath the moon, and round their rings
> Sit in applauding circles.

Early 20th-century poets drew inspiration from places where people had long had contact with invisible and supernatural presences. Charles Dalmon refused to believe that Pan and every nymph and satyr had fled from Sussex:

O never say that Pan is dead!
But listen for his pipe instead
And listen, listen, till you hear
His merry music, sweet and clear.
It comes to all the faithful who
Still listen as men used to do.[10]

Chanctonbury Ring was the heartland of Sussex folklore and it is no coincidence that Nancy Price sought the Devil there (unsuccessfully) as late as 1956. But fairyland in general did not survive the Second World War – railways and the motor car, mass tourism, mechanisation, agri-business and noise and light pollution have seen to that. The *New Statesman* in 1938 alluded light-heartedly to the changing circumstances:

The hey for car and charabanc
And the sun-swept Downland scene,
By Saltdean, Withdean, East Dean and Woodingdean,
Roedean and Rottingdean!
And lightly on the Sussex earth
Where Romans laid their bones
Strew fag-ends, match-sticks, nut-shells, tin cans
Fruit skins and juice-cream cones!

FOLK SONGS

Sussex men and women would burst into song at the drop of a hat. The music and carollings were purely home-made, as were country dancing and games. Everyone sang a good repertoire of country melodies at convivial meetings and people were so fond of singing that labourers compiled folk songs, something inconceivable in today's south-east England. W.H. Hudson, in *Nature in Downland* (1900), thought you could hear Sussex singing best in the evening in the village public house, especially on a Saturday when wages had been paid. A succession of men would spontaneously sing rollicking songs with loud choruses in which all joined. The most curious and interesting point about Sussex singing was the love of high-pitched voices and a 'go-as-you-please tuneless tuneful manner', prolonging

some notes at random, which he thought resembled the most primitive kinds of vocal music surviving in Europe. One of his most remarkable experiences was hearing a woman shepherd between Stanmer and Westmeston singing in the sweetest, most musical voice Hudson had heard. In the thinner and purer atmosphere of the Downs it carried distinctly over an area of seven or eight square miles.[11]

42 *Shepherd's hut, Weald and Downland Museum.*

Sussex shared in the traditional songs of the South Country, which were first collected by the Rev. John Broadwood, of the family of pianoforte manufacturers with strong Sussex connections, when they were beginning to die out in the mid-19th century. *Old English Songs* was published in 1843. Many of the songs were sung in Broadwood's childhood at Christmas by the country people of the Surrey and Sussex Weald when they went about wassailing at neighbouring houses. He rescued them from oblivion to provide specimens of Old English melody. They were harmonised by Mr Dusart, organist of the chapel-at-ease at Worthing.

His work was continued by Lucy Broadwood, of the same family, who had a particular association with the Horsham folk-song tradition and published the foremost collection of English folk songs in 1889, followed by *English Traditional Songs and Carols* in 1908, which included 'The Sussex Mummers' Song'. One of her sources was Henry Burstow, a cobbler from Horsham who claimed to know 400 songs. The composer Ralph Vaughan Williams, who became fascinated by folk song and sought to preserve its traditions, described her as the 'greatest English folk-song scholar' and visited Horsham at her recommendation to record the singing of Henry Burstow. It was the song 'The Captain Cried All Hands', collected from Mr and Mrs Verrall of Monk's Gate, Horsham, which inspired Vaughan Williams' 'Monks Gate', now one of the most popular hymn tunes. Williams also wrote an unpublished piece for orchestra, *Fantasia on Sussex Folk Tunes*. The five songs on which it was based, collected by Lucy Broadwood from Henry Burstow in 1893, are still sung by members of the Horsham Folk Club, which celebrated its golden jubilee in 2008. Burstow's collection of folk songs was published in 1911. Williams was instrumental in getting Cecil Sharp a state pension for his work in discovering an immense amount of folk song.[12]

A number of the old Sussex songs were sung at sheep shearing and at Christmas. The first verse of a sheep-shearing song runs:

> Here the rose buds in June, and the violets are blowing,
> The small birds that warble from every green bough;
> Here's the pink and the lily and the daffydowndilly,
> To adorn and perfume the sweet meadows in June.
> 'Tis all before the plough the fat oxen go slow;
> But the lads and the lassies to the sheep shearing go.

and continued:

> Here stands our brown jug, and 'tis fill'd with good ale,
> Our table, our table shall increase and not fail;
> We'll joke and we'll sing and dance in a ring;
> Where the pink and the lily and the daffydowndilly [etc.]
> When the shepherding's over, and harvest draws nigh
> We'll prepare for the fields, our strength for to try;
> We'll reap and we'll mow; we'll plough and we'll sow.

On a sheep-shearing morning all the men met at the captain's cottage, where a feast called the 'White ram' was provided. Having breakfasted, the men arrived at a farm about seven a.m. and began their work. Once in the forenoon and twice in the afternoon their custom was 'to light up', as they termed it, ceasing work for a few minutes, drinking their beer and sharpening their shears, then setting to work again. Their dinner-hour was one, but this was not the great meal of the day, supper being the time of real enjoyment, and when this was over they would remain for several hours in the house, smoking their pipes and singing their sheep-shearing songs.

The great shrine of folk singing, apart from Horsham, was Rottingdean, the home of the Coppers, among the most important folksingers of their time. When the English Folk Dance and Song Society was founded in 1898, one of the first acts of its Honorary Secretary, Mrs Kate Lee, was to record songs from the mouths of members of the family, songs which in some cases were in manuscript or in print two or even three hundred years ago and had been handed down in the memory of farm labourers who could neither read nor write. Mrs Lee said she would never forget the pleasure that the two Messrs Copper gave her when singing the Sussex songs of which they were so proud. William was a former foreman of a farm and his brother Thomas was landlord of the *Plough Inn*, a very small public house. They thought they knew 'half a hundred' songs and you only had to mention the subject of a song and they would start at once: love songs, sea songs or plough songs. Kate Lee's 'copper-full of songs', published in 1899 in the first *Journal of the English Folk Song Society*, constituted a unique repository of song which is currently influencing England's folk song revival.

At least seven generations of Bob Copper's family had a passion for the music and poetry of traditional English songs. Bob's earliest memories were of winter evenings round the fire singing songs such as *The Banks of the Sweet Primroses*, *The Honest Labourer* and *The Brisk Young Ploughboy* with his grandfather James (b. 1845) and his father Jim (b. 1882). His grandfather recalled singing *The Shepherd of the Downs* with both his own grandfathers in the mid-19th century. It was the combined imagination and determination of James, Jim and Bob Copper that ensured dozens of traditional songs were saved – the words, the tunes and the ways of rendering them. From the 1950s they began to preserve the music, too, with sound recordings. James wrote down in 1922 the words of 22 songs. In 1936 Bob's father wrote down the words of another 47, and in 1950 he wrote to the BBC about the family folk-singing tradition. This led to the broadcast from the garden of the *Eight Bells Inn* at Jevington and from 1957 the BBC employed Bob to record folk songs and dialect in Hampshire and Sussex. This field collection formed the basis of Copper's book *Songs and Southern Breezes* and a LP of the same name. In 1963 was published *Songs from Rottingdean* and in 1971 *A Song for Every Season*. At the age of 80 Copper toured the United States with his family of singers. He received an honorary degree from the University of Sussex, the Gold Badge from the English Dance and Folk Song Society in 1978 and an MBE a few days before his death in 2004.

Hilaire Belloc loved singing and set the words of his verse to music, that for 'H'naker Mill' being in a high, plaintive melody. Belloc loved to hear his own songs sung chorally. His voice, a high tenor, was capable of tremendous power in the kind of song which required roaring, and he was particularly fond of the songs he had learnt in barrack rooms and on the march, accompanied by tunes heard long before. Whatever his mood, he would always sing anything anyone requested.

James Murray Allison, proprietor of newspapers and advertising manager of the *The Times* and later the *Daily Telegraph*, held parties at Hill Farm House in Rodmell in the 1920s where everyone sang continually, before meals, during meals and after meals. H.B. Morton remarked:

> We sang our own songs, Belloc's songs, and everybody else's songs, and the outburst was always completely spontaneous. As one starts a conversation in easy and familiar surroundings, so we would start a song. Often I watched the amazement of those who were unaccustomed to such riotous gaiety. Some would forget their shyness and join in, others would listen to the performance, and I remember one occasion of cold disapproval.[13]

Arthur Beckett was a great lover of traditional Sussex and contributed a Sussex song of his own which had much popularity, the 'Song o' the Sussex Men'. Each verse (in rich local dialect) commemorates a county 'worthy', beginning with the three saints, Wilfrid, Cuthman and Dunstan, and proceeding though Tom Paine (of *The Rights of Man*), Tipper (the inventor of the noted beer bearing his name), John Dudeney (a self-educated Downland shepherd who became a Lewes schoolmaster), the poet Shelley, and Free-Trader Cobden, to the final hero. The rousing climax and chorus was:

43   *Horses ploughing below the Downs, 1930s.*

> Now doänt you wish that you was born in Sussex
> by the Sea,
> Where every man's a famous man, as famous as
> can be?
> But the good comfort from the thought that 'neath
> the wide blue sky,
> You cannot choose a better place than in Sussex
> fur to die!
>
> CHORUS
> For it's good to live in Sussex, the land o' the
> brave and free
> Where men are bruff and honest – such men as
> you an' me –
> If you weren't born in Sussex, whoever you
> may be,
> Then come an' *die* in Sussex land, sweet Sussex
> by the Sea!

It is said the song became a sort of Sussex anthem and was sung regularly at the annual dinner of the Men of Sussex Society, now unhappily defunct. It is still sung at meetings of numerous Sussex organisations.[14]

Amy Sawyer was inspired by Cecil Sharp, at Ditchling in the 1920s, to explore the English folk song tradition in her plays, and Philip and Ethel Mairet sang at parties some of the songs collected by Cecil Sharp.[15]

DRINKING SONGS

Hilaire Belloc's *West Sussex Drinking Song* is the best-known of the genre:

> They sell good beer at Haslemere
> And under Guildford Hill,
> At little Cowfold as I've been told
> A beggar may drink his fill:
>
> They brew good ale in Amberley too,
> And by the bridge also;
> But the swipes they take in at Washington Inn
> Is the very best Beer I know.
>
> CHORUS   With my here it goes, there it goes,
> And all the fun's before us;
> The Tipple's aboard and the night is young,
> The door's ajar and the Barrel is sprung
> I am singing the best song ever was sung
> And it has a rousing chorus.[16]

Belloc's *The Four Men* (1912) has other drinking songs, including the Sailor's; his three companions help him with the chorus near the *Crabtree* near Leonardslee:

On Sussex hills where I was bred,
Where lanes in autumn rains are red,
Where Arun tumbles in his bed,
And busy great gusts go by;
When branch is bare in Burton Glen
And Bury Hill is a whitening then,
I drink strong ale with gentlemen;
Which nobody can deny, deny,
Deny, deny, deny, deny,
Which nobody can deny!

It was at the *Crabtree* that Grizzlebeard raised the question of what places men may sing at. Belloc explained that new regulations prevented them from singing in the *Crabtree* or in the open 'in our own dreadful time'. To him it was one of the clearest expressions of the 'Londonisation' which was to lead up to the banning of cocks' crows in the countryside and might go on, before long, to stop the pealing of church bells.

Charles Dalmon's drinking songs are among his best verses:

O, the tap-room in the Winter
When the ground is white with snow,
But the arbour in the summer
When the honeysuckles blow!
So, landlord, ice the cider,
And put rose-leaves in the beer;
And we'll drink with any fellow
Who will pay the frothing here!

(The Arbour)

The parson's rich, but we are poor;
And we are wrong, but he is right –
Who knows how much his cellar holds,
Or how he goes to bed at night?
But here's to Parson Herrick's Muse!
Drink to it, dear old comrades, please!
And, prithee, for my tombstone chose
A verse from his Hesperides.

(Parson Herrick's Muse)

The First World War produced the famous Sussex marching song, 'Sussex by the Sea', still sung at public meetings; the first stanzas of one version are:

Solo Voice (1st Verse):
Now is the time for marching,
Now let your hearts be gay,
Hark to the merry bugles
Sounding along our way,
So let your voices ring my boys,
And take your time from me,
And I'll sing you a song, as we march along,
Of Sussex by the Sea.

44   *Michael Blann, the best-remembered singing shepherd, c.1920s.*

Chorus, All:
    For we're the men from Sussex,
    Sussex by the Sea,
    We plough and sow, and reap and mow
    And right good men are we:
    And when you go to Sussex,
    Whoever you may be,
    Your may tell them all that we stand or fall
    For Sussex by the Sea.

And the conclusion:

    Oh, Sussex, Sussex by the Sea.
    Good old Sussex by the Sea,
    You may tell them all that we
                stand or fall,
    For Sussex by the Sea.[17]

Colin Andrew has collected about twenty complete folk songs of Michael Blann in the Barclay Wills Collection in Worthing Museum but unfortunately Blann left no indication, except in one instance, as to the tunes that he used.

Chapter 8

CHURCHES AND CLERGY

Sussex has over two hundred churches and chapels, although very few are really as exceptionally fine as those of Boxgrove, Shoreham, Steyning, Winchelsea or Alfriston, which Philip Webb, a founding member of the Society for the Protection of Ancient Buildings, thought had a spire set down on its tower with greater refinement than anywhere else.[1] There are more pre-Conquest buildings, or parts of buildings, in Sussex than any part of England; there are 21 screens from between *c.*1270-1370; 20 church chests of the 12th and 13th centuries; and mural paintings of the 11th and 12th centuries. The soaring lines and breathtaking perspectives of the Wagner churches in Brighton are extraordinary, world-renowned achievements.

The 18th and early 19th centuries were the high point of nonconformist chapel building. The main theme in the history of the Anglican Church in Sussex is its lack of spirituality at the beginning of the 19th century and the resultant changes brought about by such developments as the Oxford Movement from the 1850s, which led to controversial widespread church restoration and the building of the great Victorian churches. The Sussex seaside has both Classical and Gothic Revivalist churches, some associated with great names such as R.C. Carpenter, Sir Gilbert Scott, Sir Reginald Blomfield, J.L. Pearson and C.E. Kempe. The reintroduction of the Catholic faith from the mid-19th century was also notable in Sussex, although a population loss has occurred in many parishes in the Downs. Up Marden in the remote western Downs above Chichester had two to three hundred parishioners in 1871 but today it has barely thirty, and similar remarkable falls in number are general where loss of local employment has not been balanced by the migration of urban newcomers, as at Coombes, Botolphs and Arnington in the Adur valley, and the Arun valley group including the Stokes.

A tremendous change took place in the appreciation of church architecture from the early 20th century. It was customary to call all churches 'mean' that did not evince the matured styles of the 13th and 14th centuries. Thus the early Sussex historians Dallaway and Horsfield dubbed St Botolph's and Coombes 'small and uninteresting', remarks generally extended to all surviving small downland churches, such as Tarring Neville. These simple churches are now cherished for their own sake and some find them more moving than grander buildings. The little barn-like churches are among the oldest and simplest. Those dating from Saxon times or immediately afterwards are more numerous than anywhere else in England. The change in their perception is related to the hungering for 'Old Sussex' experienced by urban visitors escaping from industrialisation. In these simple churches the soul of 'Old Sussex' lived on most strongly, both in fabric and in wall paintings.

45 *Alfriston Church spire dominates the village and the common called the Tye and is a focus for the lower Cuckmere valley.*

46 *North Marden Church in the remote South Downs, north of Chichester.*

The best account of the impression made on visitors by the little churches is provided by Simon Jenkins:

> Romans, Saxons and Normans penetrated these Downs. They sowed, reaped and mostly starved. They also prayed, and did so in churches of the utmost simplicity. You can go to Iona or Jarrow, to Cornwall or the Welsh Marches, and you will not find a more moving witness to early Christianity than here in the uplands of West Sussex. Idsworth, North Marden, Up Marden, Didling, Hardham, Coombes and a dozen other churches feature in few guidebooks. They are too small, too undistinguished. No Dissenter chapel is more ascetic. A single space sufficed for the offices of the liturgy, one roof, one porch, one pulpit.

The historian Ian Nairn had directed him to Up Marden by writing in Pevsner's Sussex volume that it was among 'the loveliest interiors in England'. Jenkins found it sitting in its clearing amid yews and alders, down a farm lane off a road that went nowhere. He never met a soul near the place, though somebody walked through the woods each day to unlock it. 'Opening the creaking door you enter a simply plastered double chamber. There are no chamfered arcades, no corbel heads or Perpendicular windows. Up Marden has no aisles, no transepts, no window tracery. Norman masons did not drag Caen stone from their barges up into these hills.' Nairn declared that it moved him more than religion and Jenkins thought its atmosphere was due to slow, loving and gentle accretion, century by century; no carving, no art or architecture could account for its effect. It was a work not of architecture but of humanity, somewehre that moved the spirit more than a cathedral: 'The Downland churches that disturb us unbelievers'.[2]

John Marsh (1752-1828), one of the most distinguished residents of Chichester, has left a vivid account of the Chapter and choir of Chichester Cathedral when he first arrived in the city in 1787. The Bishop, Sir William Ashburnham, was over eighty and reckoned a fine preacher, though cold-hearted with respect to the poor and his own family. The Dean was Dr Harward, a headstrong and passionate man, much given to swearing, dealing out his oaths to the vergers when he had least cause of complaint. He was also very litigious and remarkably irreverent in church. The precentor was the brother of the Bishop, and so very nervous that at times he 'amounted to a species of mental derangement'. To some members of the Chapter the real Bishop was the precentor's wife, who was a very efficient woman with such great influence over the Bishop that young clergymen seeking preferment canvassed her first. Besides three canons residentiary, the choir consisted of only six badly taught boys and four singing men or lay vicars, who were dilatory in attending services and of whom two sang poorly.[3]

There was also a marked lack of spirituality. The Rev. Boys Ellman of Berwick observed that at the time the new turnpike road from Lewes to Eastbourne was made (1819), the only resident clergyman along the entire route was at Wilmington. A coachman had told him that as a young man he drove his master after morning service at Wilmington on a Sunday to Herstmonceux rectory, where four clergymen dined together between services. As it turned into a wet afternoon the four clergymen, instead of attending their various services, spent the whole afternoon in card playing. Ellman noted that when he was a boy the church services were very slovenly. Anything in the shape or form of ceremony was avoided as much as possible, and regarded as 'Popish'. The services were long, the sermons very 'dry' and, as a rule, above the understanding of the rural working classes, but Ellman detected, here and there, a deeper and more childlike faith than was to become common in the mid-19th century.[4]

Ellman had known long experience of poverty ever since his entry into the priesthood, and this must have been the case for many priests with pitiful livings:

> I had learnt to be very economical. I kept pigs and worked hard in my garden in my leisure hours, sending what I grew to the market at Lewes. I had started a Dame's school in a cottage, and Clothing and Coal Clubs, and all required money which I had to supply myself. It was seldom that I had any butcher's meat and my suit of clerical clothes lasted the four years before I could buy more. To make them last as long as possible, I wore the clothes I had had as layman when working in the garden. Newspapers and books were luxuries I could not afford.[5]

His priestly abilities overcame the limitations of the contemporary Church. During the summer of 1839 he took the fortnightly afternoon service at Lullington to help the incumbent, who was a poor man who had left the neighbourhood but did not want to resign the living till Michaelmas, every penny being important to him as the value of the living was only £20 and there was no house. So Ellman took his services and calculated that the internal measurement of the church was 16ft square, the present church being the chancel of the old one. But on one occasion he counted 40 heads inside the church and 30 more outside the open door even though the population of the parish was contained in one farmhouse and two cottages.

CHURCH RESTORATION

Numerous reports on churches describe dilapidated buildings before Victorian restoration. An account of Poynings parish church *c.*1880 is a vivid example of the neglect into which the church had fallen. Louis Jennings found the fine massive tower and lofty roof of the church striking the eye from afar, but within the building little was in any way satisfactory. Large patches of green mould disfigured the walls, and the lath and plaster of the ceiling was dropping in great lumps to the floor. 'I was obliged to sweep a lot up today', said an old woman who was cleaning for Sunday, 'and every week it keeps falling down.' When a bad patch was pointed out to her she said, 'That's the Government, sir. They've got to do that. That part of the Church is the Government's.' (The manor of Poynings was then in the hands of the Crown.) There was a bare and sorrowful appearance about the church, not attributable to the carelessness of the rector, who had written an exhaustive account of the edifice and the neighbourhood round about,[6] but to the inadequate means for putting so large a building in decent order. Jennings learned that it had been ill-used from time to time, even pillaged by common thieves, and now it would require a large sum to restore it properly. In the south transept 'the very graves have been violated by midnight marauders, and the floor left in broken masses'. Tombstones were torn away, brasses carried off, stained glass destroyed. The altar, like the rest of the church, had a mean and poverty-stricken appearance. The rude old table is not even covered.[7]

The merits of a church restoration were evaluated by Victorian congregations quite differently from the 'expert' opinion of the present. Pevsner and Nairn in the Sussex volume

47   *Berwick Church, restored by Edward Boys Ellman.*

of the *Buildings of England* series are unduly censorious and apply standards of architecture poular a generation or more later to earlier achievements in restoration. That at Patching is an example. It is noted as architecturally 'bad' by Ian Nairn, but a tablet placed on the piscina by a grateful congregation in 1835 reads:

> The inhabitants of the parish of Patching have erected this [tablet] as a slight but affectionate memorial of their gratitude to Sir Richard Hunter of Dulany Cottage, who at his own cost repaired and beautified this church in 1835. Blessed be the Lord God of our Fathers who hath put such a thing as this in his heart to beautify.

Similarly, the Pevsner entry for Berwick remarks that 'the church has suffered much at the hand of the restorer of 1856. The N arcade he put in is quite illiterate and clumsy on top. So is the chancel arch.' The 'restorer of 1856' was the renowned reformist the Rev. Edward Boys Ellman. In a watercolour of 1850 his church is shown with a collapsed north aisle, an unsafe east wall, a base of a spire that had been struck by lightning and not replaced, the wall of the south aisle in a tumble-down state and the eastern gable of the nave filled in with timber. In the absence of a wealthy patron, Ellman and his wife saved every penny for the church restoration and school building themelves. Ellman re-roofed the church and restored it amateurishly with his own funds, to the glory of the Church and himself, but not to the approval of Dr Pevsner.

His daughter described what happened and how the restoration was funded:

> The east chancel wall had at some time been moved inwards, shortening the chancel by several feet; the spire had been burnt down by lightning a hundred years before; the tower damaged; the north aisle had been entirely pulled down in the eighteenth century as it was then a tumble-down state – the walls were in places almost tumbling down; the roof was literally a rabbit warren and rotten: the earth came up nearly to the windows in the south aisle; the east window had been blocked up; the flooring was rotten, and altogether the church was in a shocking state. Ellman proposed that the villagers should levy a tax voluntarily for two years, according to their means, he himself being rated with the others, a plan that was cheerfully accepted without a dissentient voice. A few offerings came from relations and friends, and Ellman made up the rest of the money. His wife's mother sold her jewels to buy a chalice and paten, and to have the ancient church plate regilt. Together husband and wife designed and worked the carpet for the altar rails. On St Thomas' day 1856, Church service were once more held in the old church now restored to its old beauty. It was almost the first church restored in Sussex, and certainly the first in the neighbourhood and with its high new chancel screen, its reredos, and low open seats excited attention in the neighbourhood.[8]

The restoration of Sussex churches aroused the wrath of William Morris's Society for the Protection of Ancient Buildings founded in 1877, and some of the language used was hardly Christian. Winchelsea's fate was regarded as particularly disastrous since it was thought of as an 'incalculably precious piece of work'. In 1892 the church was threatened with 'restoration'. A representative sent to spy out its condition reported that the parson was a 'surly fellow' and suggested that the actress Ellen Terry, who lived nearby, 'might have some influence in the right direction'. But neither Ellen Terry's nor anyone else's influence prevailed and in 1904 architect Philip Webb, Morris' deputy, reported: 'Damn them, they are *improving* the wood carving in the Lady Chapel.' Probably in response to this news the society's representative again went over to Winchelsea and reported to Webb:

> We walked over to Winchelsea and found those glorious tombs being shamefully scraped; too late now to smash the head of either parson or architect against an angle of them. There is a race of hereditary parsons here called Patch, who will not be satisfied while there is any interesting thing remaining in that old fragment of a church.

Webb also thought Slaugham a lost cause in 1905: 'Slaugham is ravishing, but woe is me, has also been ravished, sickled over with a pale cast of idolatory', and he was severe in his criticism of changes at Worth church:

48 *Philip Webb, co-founder of the Society for the Protection of Ancient Buildings, who retired to Caxtons near Three Bridges.*

49   *Murals on Berwick church arch by Duncan Grant.*

> The transformation by the resurrectionist reformers has been lamentable. I always lose my
> temper when in church, for the example of 'soul in building' for historical reasons as well
> as vigour, was great, and has now been smalled down with the vengence of stupidity.

He was also distressed by the 'witless fiddling' at Burwash church, but he was delighted
with Etchingham church. This was the subject of a letter from him to William Morris:

> On Friday [June 1896] I was at Etchingham … the church just one of those placid
> fourteenth-century Sussex pieces of serious village building; a kind of happy sing-song
> of labour and unconscious feeling; which was as of picked up manna in the wilderness
> to me. The tracery part of all the nave and aisle windows is still holding untouched glass
> of its date – all masculine and of colour none better in the world. Damnation – touched
> all about it, but did not touch the glass except in one place. Date 1360. Three separate
> brasses of Etchingham leaders of sword folk; the earliest of the founder. Collegiate choir
> of eighteen stalls for monks with some ten or twelve mercy seats as could be in a simple
> way. One of them Reynard the Fox up to his tricks.[9]

Berwick church became well-known when just before the Second World War Bishop
Bell, Professor Reilly and others selected it to inaugurate what was hoped would become a
general redecoration of Sussex churches so that the public could see what a riot of colour and
ornament churches in the Middle Ages possessed. The task of redecoration was entrusted
to artists of the Bloomsbury Group, Duncan Grant, his partner Vanessa Bell, and Vanessa's
son Quentin. Their art is on canvas and is that of their own age, medieval only in spirit.
Above the chancel is Grant's 'Christ in Glory', adored by the Bishop, the Rector of Berwick
and a sailor, soldier and airman who had gone to fight for Christendom from Sussex homes

in the war. There is also the 'Annunciation' by Vanessa Bell, the 'Nativity' by Grant and the 'Parable of the Wise and Foolish Virgins' by Quentin Bell. The latter also decorated the pulpit.[10]

BRIGHTON

Paradoxically, Brighton the city of pleasure was also the city of religious revival and it is studded with magnificent churches. It is to the munificence of the family of the Rev. Henry Michell Wagner (d. 1870) that this is largely due. At his death Brighton was divided into various parishes, each with its church. St Martin's was built (1871-91) at the expense of the three sons of Wagner, in memory of their father. The Church of the Annunnciation followed (1864), this and three other churches – SS Mary and Mary Magdalen, St Bartholomew's and the Resurrection (since dismantled) – all being built at the sole cost of the Rev. Arthur Douglas Wagner, the Rev. Henry's son. He also built schools and gave large sums to maintain the churches. A crowd of aged and poor gathered on Saturday mornings at St Paul's to receive from the vicar's hands their weekly allowance. 'He never sought, and never obtained, any acknowledgment from high places, but he won what is far more precious – the undying love and veneration of thousands of priests and people all the country over', remarked his anonymous biographer.

There was extraordinary suspicion and opposition to the building of the 'Big Church' of St Bartholomew's as the walls grew higher and higher. The town council were also disturbed that the total height exceeded the approved plans and other variations were complained of. Eventually objections subsided and a huge parallelogram of nine bays was erected. Its great height – four feet more than the nave of Westminster Cathedral – and the great nave, 170ft long and 58ft wide, was the work of Edmund E. Scott, a local architect.[11]

A glimpse of the Church in Brighton immediately after the First World War is provided by author Ernest Raymond, who wrote of his time as one of the three curates at the parish church of St Nicholas in 1919. The vicar of Brighton was delighted to announce that stipends for juniors would be raised to £200 a year, a figure regarded by Raymond as hardly appropriate to five years in Orders, four of them as a chaplain in the army, and his exacting work as a curate, but it provided a living of sorts for a young man in 1919. This was the last time, he felt, the Church of England reigned in some assurance and power, especially over a preponderantly middle-class and residential parish like Brighton, which could provide as many as a thousand at Evensong on Sundays. As a junior curate he enjoyed cricket. Hove Cricket Ground was nearer to him than Lord's or the Oval, and he was often there – indeed many clerical collars would be dotted about the Pavilion, parsons being among the few who could steal weekdays off.[12]

DISSENTING CHAPELS AND OTHER CHURCHES

Nonconformist chapels pervaded the Weald and the old seaports in particular, and a variety of religious sects were established. Wealden nonconformity went back to the 14th century, when local peasants had been Lollard followers of John Wycliffe, and was sustained by the burning of martyrs in the Tudor period. At Cade Street chapel, near Heathfield, founded in 1769 by the followers of George Gilbert, popularly styled 'The Apostle of Sussex', is a cross in the graveyard commemorating those of the 17 martyrs burnt at the stake in Lewes who lived locally. The chapel has galleries on three sides and Gilbert's former cottage beside it. Numerous gravestones have terracotta relief plaques made by Jonathan Harman in the early 19th century. The Jireh Chapel at Lewes, a timber-framed building of 1805, contains the tomb of its founder, Calvinist William Huntington, and retains its original box and family pews as well as the 'Grand Pew' where the elders and deacons sat. Still remembered with awe are the sermons of its pastor John Vinall, which have recently been published in the United States. The Friends Meeting House at Ditchling is an 18th-century building in its own little tree-lined close with a relatively unchanged chapel, gallery and graveyard commemorating people who travelled long distances to attend. Gideon Mantell, the famed Lewes surgeon and palaeontologist, commemorated in verse those buried there early in the 19th century.

The Methodism of John Wesley took root in both urban and rural situations and other sects multiplied so that a town such as Shoreham-by-Sea contained, apart from the two parish churches and an Anglican church on Shoreham Beach, chapels of Methodists, Baptists, Congregationalists and the Henry Huntington fraternity. The first nonconformist chapel in Shoreham appears to have been of the Countess of Huntingdon's Connexion about 1800. John Wesley travelled from Fareham to Rottingdean in 1758 and doubtless gained adherents, but a chapel was not built until 1829 in New Road, largely financed by local grocer John Ratcliff. In 1831 the church had 12 members, including James Blake, their 'leader', a 'ship's smith' in his early twenties. During the next 40 years it became a lively church, with the local shipbuilding families of Suter and Stow among its members. The existing church dates from 1900.

One of the strangest religious sects, founded in West Sussex by evangelist John Sirgood in 1850, was called the 'Cokelers' or the Society of Dependents for their dependence on Christ. At Loxwood and the surrounding district near Wisborough Green they opened local stores as an alternative employment to domestic service for young women, who could then attend evening services and become a firmer part of the community. Their practice of agricultural co-operation, intended to cut out the middleman, was well in advance of its time. These were plain-living, honest people who valued poverty and denied themselves luxuries. As they eschewed marriage on religious grounds, their numbers fell off after Sirgood's death in 1916 and the sect is now extinct, but as recently as the Second World War Dependent women would have been seen in Loxwood walking in twos and threes, wearing tiny bonnets of black straw, black velvet shawls, black coats and black skirts reaching the ground, and accompanied by soberly dressed men with mutton-chop whiskers and little beards.[13]

The survival of the Roman Catholic faith on the estates of six noble families in Elizabeth I's reign led to the recusants sheltering Catholic priests in remote areas, notably West Sussex, throughout the 17th and 18th centuries. West Grinstead Park, owned by the Caryll family, who were repeatedly persecuted and fined, became a Roman Catholic mission receiving priests awaiting posting. John Caryll, the last of the family, was private secretary to Queen Mary of Modena and fled to France with her and her husband, King James II, in 1688. There is a portrait of him in the presbytery of West Grinstead, which contains priest holes and a secret chapel. On account of its being a stronghold of Catholicism, the estate became a focal point of the Catholic revival in the 19th century, and the present church of West Grinstead, built in 1876, has a special place in English Catholic life. Hilaire Belloc

(d. 1953), one of the greatest lay Catholic champions, lived nearby at Shipley and is buried in the churchyard. Mother Riccarda, whose parents were converted to the Roman Catholic faith at St Magdalen, Brighton in 1891, may be beatified shortly for hiding Jewish refugees in her Bridgetinne convent at Rome during the Second World War.

Numerous Catholic nunneries and other institutions were founded in Sussex during the late 19th century and subsequently. Notable is St Hugh's Charterhouse near Cowfold, the only Carthusian monastery in England, and Worth Abbey near Crawley. During sculptor Eric Gill's stay in Ditchling (1907-24) there was a considerable number of conversions to the Catholic faith by members of the handicraft Guild of St Joseph and St Dominic, strongly influenced by the Dominican Father McNabb. Worth Abbey is set on a ridge with glorious views to the South and North Downs. It was founded in 1930 as a daughter house of the Benedictine house of Downside in Somerset. Monks arrived in 1932 and were accommodated up to the 1970s in temporary buildings at the rear of Paddockhurst, a country house of the 1st Lord Cowdray. The site is now the largest Roman Catholic complex in Sussex, with the abbey, its church, a masterpiece of grandeur and simplicity by Francis Pollen, and Worth Abbey School, which occupies, with other buildings, the enormous country house and Victorian extension. The church of the English Martyrs, founded in a barn at Goring by Sea in 1937, is famed for its unique representation of the Sistine Chapel ceiling by Gary Bevans, in a new church built next to the old after the Second World War.

Chapter 9

THE CALL OF THE SEA

For generations, making a living from the sea, legally or not, was the main objective of Sussex people and the sea was the most precious of the county's resources. Coastwise shipping sailed the narrows of the English Channel and into the North Sea from a long line of ports on almost every creek and estuary on the Sussex coast. Wooden ships were built here in the days of sail and large amounts of timber were floated down rivers to the shipyards. Every port had its local fishermen and the 18th and early 19th centuries were the roughest of the smuggling days. Seamen, fishermen, shipbuilders, pirates, smugglers and coastguards brought fame and notoriety to the county. Until the second half of the 19th century Sussex ports were filled with the sailing cogs, luggers, ketches and hoys that entered and left harbours while engaged in the coastwise trade. More adventurous sailors crewed sturdy-hulled brigantines and three-masted schooners, glorified trampships – working girls and proud of it – that were built in Sussex shipyards to sail round the globe. It was a way of life shattered by the iron steamships launched on the coalfields and the coming of the railways and lorry transport. Local fishing declined, too, in competition with steam trawlers and drifters from Grimsby, Yarmouth and Lowestoft, and even from Aberdeen and Peterhead, with the advent of the railway.

Maritime towns were entirely dependent on coastwise trade for their merchandise before the arrival of regular freight train services in about the 1860s. All coal and most other goods came in by sea, as it had for centuries. If a sou'-wester blew for weeks together in winter, supplies would become scarce and there might be a troublesome delay in the arrival of fruit for Christmas puddings. At places lacking port facilities, such as Hastings and Brighton, the small vessels serving the town were beached at high tide, unloaded rapidly, and floated off again on the next tide.[1]

Shoreham's history as a port is illustrative of the ups and downs of Sussex's maritime story over the past 200 years. Between 1801 and 1811 the population of the town was declining and a relatively small huddle of houses existed around a large half-dismantled parish church and decaying shipyard and quays off the High Street. Rejuvenation occurred from 1816 when the new harbour entrance was constructed. The 'seaside villas' built on one site, looking as if they had strayed from Brighton and Worthing, probably represent a speculator's vision of the town as a seaside resort. Their views were later blotted out by the rapid industrial development due largely to the rise of Brighton. In 1833 the handsome Norfolk Bridge linked the towns of Brighton and Worthing and in 1840 the railway, the first in Sussex, arrived. In 1845 the railway was extended to Worthing over a wooden trestle bridge, of which some timber survives in Marlipins Museum. Meanwhile the ancient shipyard had been joined by another at the opposite end of the High Street and by a third at Kingston, on Shoreham's border.

50   *The Norfolk Bridge and quay in Shoreham High Street, c.1900. Sailing vessels moored in the heart of the town.*

In the 1840s and 1850s vessels of more than 400 tons burden were trading with the port and being built in the shipyards. James Britton Bally was launching 14 vessels a year in the 1840s and 1850s and was famed for his three-masted schooners. A notice in a local newspaper for 1841 reported: 'Launched from Bally's yard … Schooner named Shark. This 160 tons ship built to carry fruit and Mediterranean trade … for merchants in London.' After the eastern arm of the harbour was provided with a lock in 1855, larger vessels increasingly preferred the deeper, more secure and well-wharfed branch of the harbour in Southwick and Aldrington and this mainly explains the rapid rise of Southwick as a maritime town at the end of the 19th century.[2]

All sailings in and out of Shoreham were controlled by the weather. A notice in the local newspaper for December 1840 said 'Arrivals this week very limited on account of prevailing easterly winds, which prevent ships getting to sea from Northern ports, and ships arriving from western ports.' According to the same newspaper the port was importing, among other items, coal from Newcastle, railroad iron from South Wales and the North East, eggs and stone from Normandy, butter and cheese from Ireland, oysters from Jersey and stone from the Portland quarries. Outward sailings were mainly in ballast but included wheat, oak timber from the Weald and boulders from the shingle beach.[3]

But from the 1860s the building of wooden ships was declining, and it finally ended at Shoreham in 1882. Shoreham became a shabby little place, distinct from garish Brighton and newer resorts such as Worthing. The poet Swinburne thought Shoreham at this time the quaintest place he had ever seen: it still retained its great wharves and timber ponds (for preserving timber), its oyster beds, lakelets storing shell-fish before supplying London restaurants, and splendid ships moored up against the muddy banks of the Adur. He was amused to find that the Shoreham infant, boy or girl, assumed a natural swagger as soon as it could toddle, and its rolling walk as it strutted along the crown of the pavement he thought would upset the gravity of a judge or bishop.[4] Another reason for Shoreham's charm was its compactness. Novelist George Moore described it as 'all clamped closely together, its feet in the water's edge'.[5] The New Road had extended the town by a furlong in the 1820s and at the end of the 19th century a little row of villas extended from the railway station, but one could walk over the town in a few minutes. The hubs of the town were two shipyards at either end of the High Street, and Shoreham was a working place, in contrast with 'respectable' Hove and the Regency terraces of Brighton or the Victorian parades in Worthing. There were no less than a dozen dissenting chapels and over 20 public houses.

The rather run-down air of decay that had settled in when Swinburne arrived had an appeal to writers and artists. People like R. Thurston Hopkins, who liked old harbours, shipyards, creeks and piers, were drawn irresistibly to Shoreham.[6] Artists who came from Chelsea at weekends were themselves bohemian and at home in the untidiness of a working town. Shoreham was the residence of five artists in 1891, including Brooking Harrison, whose works are in the Marlipins Museum, and James Aumonier (1831-1911), a prolific exhibitor at the Royal Academy. Another was Charles Gogin, a regular exhibitor at the Royal Academy in the period 1889-93, who took a converted sail loft as a studio in the Old Shipyard in the High Street. He was a friend of Samuel Butler, the author of the *Way of all Flesh* and *Erewhon*, who visited Shoreham on several occasions. Another visitor to Shoreham in the 1890s for many short and sometimes long holidays was the naturalist W.H. Hudson, whose biographer Morley Roberts states that he was introduced to the town by Alfred Hartley, an etcher and aquatint artist from Chelsea. Together they would go and yarn with the men at Suter's Yard, the Old Shipyard. George Moore, author of *Esther*

51 *The Ferry, Shoreham, 1909, a painting by Edward Walker.*

52 *The Canal, Southwick, 1930s.*

Waters, a novel set in the town, Ernest Henley, poets Charles Dalmon and Arthur Bell, Hilaire Belloc, travel writer S.P.B. Mais and, among more recent authors, John Oxenham and Ted Walker are connected with Shoreham or its vicinity, and admired it.[7] The poet John Davidson, although styled 'the first of the moderns', disliked the town when he stayed after a breakdown in 1897-8, complaining that it was 'doleful' and deepened the misery and hypochondria that drove him out of London.[8] The shipyards survived, building yachts and small pleasure boats. As late as the Second World War Ted Walker, a Shoreham poet of distinction, gave a glimpse of the Shoreham artisan of the old type in the memorial to his uncle who worked at Suter's shipyard before being killed by a mine on Lancing Beach during the war:

> On pay-days at the shipyard you played Brag
> Around an oil-drum with a greasy pack.
> A week's wages slipped through. You'd borrow back
> Enough to stand a round of beer later.
> Down the Marlipins they say you were
> The sort that got offered a man's last fag.[9]

Belloc experienced all the exultation and pleasures of sail and, like any other Sussex sea-dog, a share of the dangers, anxieties, terror and salvation. His *Cruise of the Nona* (1925), an account of his voyage down the Irish Sea and up the English Channel to his home port of Shoreham, is a sea classic. He was fond of Shoreham and thought it a proud day when the *Nona* got back to her old moorings in 'Stinking Shoreham', which she had not seen for two years.[10]

Belloc supplied a rare account of a storm at sea:

> The [first abominable spill of wind] suffered was off Beachy Head by Birling Gap on Whit Tuesday 1902, a day ever to be remembered. For the air fell off Birling Gap just like water out of a bucket, and nearly blew the *Nona* flat upon her beam. I let go the sheet with a run, but as it was she dipped perhaps a third of her mainsail, and nearly broke her lover's heart with fear. It is so sometimes with these high lands. The wind does not run true. It blows over them, and curls through a depression upon their edges, and curves, splashing down solid, in a bolt, on to the deep below. For on that day by Beachy, all those years ago, the true wind was but just enough northerly to let me keep a course for Newhaven, hauled very close and saving every inch. But that gust came suddenly right on the weather beam, from far east to north, and nearly settled my then young craft and him that cherished and still cherishes her.[11]

John Cowper Powys has left a vivid description of Southwick, which had developed on the eastern arm of Shoreham Harbour, in around 1920:

> No two harbours could be more different [than Southwick and Weymouth]. For this one at Southwick – and oh how hard it was to row against its tide! – had neither ancient wharfs, nor antique houses, nor any old stone bridge. It was simply a terrific volume of salt water, entering at top speed a long narrow backwater between the road and the beach and retreating in its allotted hour as it came in. But Southwick *had* a harbour. It had also a backwater. I therefore decided that Southwick would be my home! There was a high-roofed, rather sorrowful-looking dissenting chapel in the middle of the main street, no very startling thoroughfare, and next door to the chapel was a grocer's shop with a bow window protruding from the upper floor. The name over the shop was 'Pollard'. In the dust and heat the place smelt of sardines; but I went in, was shown this upper room by Mr Pollard, and a small bedroom besides, and without any delay came to terms … O, how vividly does that view out of that window return to me now … the open sea, the harbour, the backwater, the boat-builder's yard and the unimposing little street.[12]
>
> The bigger ships, if I recall correctly, and there were quite a number of them, mostly Danish and Swedish and Dutch and Norwegian, used to anchor outside Southwick Harbour, and it was the affair of Mr Pollard to race out in a rowing-boat, contending with other grocers, in order to be the first to obtain each ship's business as it anchored. He was a small, lively, brown-eyed man with a pointed beard and something of a gipsy air. He was a kindly man, and considering he had me at his mercy, he was certainly no cheat. His bills were not exorbitant, and though everything I ate tasted strongly of the shop, I was pleasantly ensconced in that upper room.[13]

Shoreham's story was enacted all along the Sussex coast, at Littlehampton and at places where small brigs and schooners had been on the stocks, such as Hastings and Rye. The latter had declined through the silting of its channel in the 16th century and the old haven had become a field, but the traditions of the sea persisted. They still built small vessels in the town as late as the 1920s, despite Belloc's observation that 'Any man seeking Rye Haven must resign himself to the will of God … There is no man living that can ever tell you the deep into Rye harbour for it shifts with every wind, and at the best it is of the narrowest.'[14]

The decline of the once distinctive fishing communities was widely deplored. The Hastings men enthralled tourists. These burly and often handsome figures held themselves

53 *Shipyard, Shoreham High Street, 1880s.*   **54** *A Sussex coaster, 1950s.*

proudly aloof from the other inhabitants and despised matrimonial alliances with artisan land-lubbers. On Sunday afternoons knots of them attired in cleaned-up jerseys or sleeved waistcoats would slowly parade 'with the air of aristocrats'. Their ancient customs included traces of a Christianised paganism. When fishing for mackerel, a member of the crew would throw out a small barrel which acted as a float to the line to which the nets were attached and utter a sing-song incantation which ran rather like this:

> Watch, barrel! Watch,
> Mackerels for to catch;
> White may they be
> Like blossom on the tree.
> God send us hundreds,
> One, two and three!
> Some by the head,
> Some by the tail,
> God send them, never fail!
> Some by the cheek,
> Some by the chin,
> God send us two plarims in [to the holds in the boat].[15]

Brighton was the main fishing port and in the heyday of Britain's herring fishery there was a summer migration of Brighton men to the North Sea fishing grounds for fish which was salted at sea, an unloved mainstay of the urban diet before canning and freezing. The tradition lasted up to the 19th century and the long absence of men in summer is reflected in the infrequency of births in the early parish registers during the spring months. Lewes and surrounding villages were supplied by sellers called 'Juggs' who carried fresh fish on their backs. Fishing was the main occupation at Worthing in the 1850s and its danger is movingly demonstrated by a plaque in Broadwater church recording the death by drowning of 11 fishermen, which left 28 children fatherless. Six Worthing men were lost when their lugger sank off Ramsgate at the end of the 19th century. At Rye, the regular trade with London, the fish being conveyed in specially made carriages containing tanks of water, existed at least from the 17th century and continues in a modern form to this day. Apart from these larger fishing ports there were scores of little places along the coast where rowing boats were beached. A major source of wealth was the oyster fishery, which lasted from the discovery of beds in the Channel in 1835 until the inshore waters became polluted with sewage around 1900.

A new development was the cross-Channel ferry from Newhaven. When the boat-train from Victoria pulled in the port burst into activity. Police, customs officials, railway porters and newspaper sellers appeared from nowhere, and disappeared as rapidly when the ferry-boat sailed. The crossing to Dieppe by steamer reduced some Victorians to utter helplessness, the voyage lasted between seven and ten hours, or even more. Jennings' advice was to:

> Content yourself with an exciting trip to Hampton Court or a row on the Thames; go and eat shrimps at Gravesend or what they call whitebait at Greenwich; drive down to Richmond for a half-cold and expensive dinner, or try an afternoon at the Crystal Palace; do any other indiscreet thing you like, but never be induced to go to France by Newhaven and Dieppe.[16]

55 *Montague Dawson, 'The Height of the Storm'.*

56   *The Brighton fishing fleet, 1880s.*

57   *Rye on its hill top.*

58   *Sailors on a Shoreham Quay,* c.*1890.*

To Richard Wyndham the harbour at Newhaven had unexpected beauty. Against a background of tarred sheds were fishing-nets hung to dry, and in the creeks were moored great rusty dredgers, old packet-boats and ex-royal yachts that had waited for years to be broken up; the ebbing tide left wooden hulks half-swallowed in mud. When sailors and fishermen met for their evening drink you heard the patois of Normandy.[17]

As a visitor, Enid Bagnold thought Newhaven had two characters. When the boat-train had gone there was a good-tempered 'village' air about the place and little boys hung about asking questions of sleepy porters.

Smuggling

The economic backbone of the Cinque Ports – privateering and piracy – ended with the Napoleonic wars, and the only legitimate pursuit for those with a passion for the sea was now the fishery and a vanishing coastal trade. Hence, the people took readily to smuggling. The roughest of the smuggling days were over by the early 19th century but reckless incidents remained in peoples' memories. Repressive measures had compelled the smugglers to be more crafty, but never stopped their illicit traffic. A Hastings man said his elders used to tell of 'armed gangs of smugglers tyrannising over the villagers as they carried their barrels inland, "borrowing" farmers' horses by night while the farmers lay prudently in their beds, knowing they should find their horses in the accustomed places in the morning, with a keg or two among the straw as payment for the "loan"'. Smugglers were either carriers or bearers. The former were paid 5s. a night and upwards according to the number of barrels they secured. Bearers were so called from the local name 'bat', meaning a bludgeon. They were security guards, usually disguised and in possession of firearms in the 1820s and '30s, and could earn up to 20s. or more a night. Most, if not all, smugglers were also on parish relief. Small farmers who did not actually engage in smuggling connived at a practice which would otherwise have left men permanently on the parish. Even so, 'putting down smuggling is the ruin of the coast' was the general opinion of law-abiding contemporaries. It was widely assumed that smuggling contributed to the labourers' riots in 1830-1 as those involved had become accustomed to working in gangs at night in winter and offering resistance to authority and could not reconcile their high living to the modest earnings of lawful work. One of the leading rioters at Brede was wounded while smuggling following his release from prison.[18]

Few were ashamed of being known to smuggle or of using smuggled goods:

> One of the most distinguished medical men – a leading member of 'society' – was called up one night to visit a smuggler who had been badly shot in an affray with a coastguard and had been dragged by his mates into a lonely cottage among the cliffs. The medical man gave out that he had been to attend upon a woman in childbirth.

Although manners had changed by the end of the 19th century, and it was considered *infra dig* for a native of Hastings to drink brandy on which the duty had not been paid, the 'condemned hole', a kind of high-fenced pound on the beach in which smugglers' boats were broken up to be sold as old timber, and the smugglers' stories still retained a glamour or romance. Perhaps the latest memento of smuggling at Hastings was the sight, around the 1880s, of 'a hero of the old days' stumping along upon two wooden legs, having lost his own in one of his mad adventures.[19]

Maude Egerton King, a Brightonian who married an MP, observed of Brighton's smuggling that:

> lawlessness was such that there was nothing for it but for the excisemen to wink at it as often as possible, very occasionally make a show of resistance, and at the worst clamp a culprit into gaol for a few weeks by way of reminder that the law of Protection did yet exist, if only to be broken!

There was not, she believed, a housewife in all the town but knew where to get her tea and brandy without paying duty, nor a lady that had not learned the trick of considerably reducing the outlay of her pin-money on 'real French' fineries, nor an innkeeper that would not wink as he assured a customer he could not get such cognac as his at *that* price elsewhere!

59 *A 'Jack Tar' stealing a ham from a grocer's shop, Shoreham, 1880s.*

King also noted that every gipsy and pedlar-wife would boast in strictest confidence that she had the very pick of forbidden continental fruit stored away beneath her homely wares. She remembered an old woman who came round selling fowls, butter and eggs in a basket covered with a white cloth. 'She had glittering eyes and a tongue off which the lies and the blarney rolled as easily as rain off a tulip leaf.' When her mother spied her coming she invariably cried, with a little presence of vexation, 'Dear, dear, there's the poor creature come again! Are the spoons out of sight, Susan?' On entering she bent over her basket and lifted out a little flask of the best French brandy or some tobacco.

It was mainly 'ordinary' people who fostered the smugglers' trade but the 'great folk' were also in it up to the hilt. It was an open secret that every fine consignment from the Continent found its way first to the Pavilion, so that the Prince might skim the cream off the top, while in more than one instance the poor fellow who brought it over was fuming his heart out in Lewes gaol.

Mrs King's mother had grim and thrilling tales to tell of the smuggling of her day. When a rumour spread in the little village where she lived that on such a night a cargo was expected, and that the smugglers were to pass through the village at such and such o'clock, everyone went to bed a little earlier than usual, closed their windows and doors, drew their curtains and pretended to know nothing about it. To her it was the supreme terror of her childhood.

> There was no sleep for me those nights. I used to say the Lord's Prayer over and over, and then just lie and quake in my bed hour after hour. And then I would hear a kind of trampling, only very far off, that came up the leg of my bed into my ear; for in those days the smugglers rode on horseback and all armed, as many as forty together. And then the sound came nearer and nearer till I could hardly breathe, and when at last they came clattering up the street right under my very window, I fairly went under the bed-clothes.

The morning after, one neighbour would find a little parcel of tea on his threshold and another a chunk of tobacco, or flask of brandy, which was silently accepted as the fee for good faith and closed lips. This account might have been the source of Kipling's *Smugglers' Song* which has the refrain:

> Them that ask no questions isn't told a lie,
> Watch the wall, my darling, while the Gentlemen go by![20]

Chapter 10

SUSSEX BY THE SEA

Some early developments on the open coast of Sussex were connected with the military defence of England against France and the erection of coastguard stations in the battle against smugglers. These were most prominent along the shortest crossings to France. Along the Royal Military Canal, 25 miles long from Pett Level to Hythe, the sites of barracks and Martello towers are notable survivors. Also conspicuous, and a pleasing contribution to the present scene, are coastguard cottages erected between *c.*1800 and 1880. Between Rye and Hastings were as many as six stations, of which the Coastguard Square at Rye Harbour, with its black-boarded watchtower and inn, and two lines of cottages at Pett Level are the most attractive.

But the main change on the Sussex coast was its complete remodelling by the social fashion of sea-bathing for health which became popular among the wealthy in the second half of the 18th century. From slow but perceptible beginnings in the 1740s, when patrons began to desert inland spas like Tunbridge Wells, the fad created an entirely new kind of urban development that engulfed long stretches of the 70 miles of Sussex coastline. Adventurers studded the Sussex coast with microcosms of London. Brighton, partly because of its accessibility to the capital, became the very acme of the English bathing resort, described grandiloquently by Dr Wigan, one of its medical practitioners, as the 'great sanitarium [*sic*] of the largest and wealthiest city in the world'. The movement was propelled by the Londoner's obsessive need to escape from the city in the heat of summer, the contemporary Parisian happy to stew uncomplainingly in his garret, and of the Englishman's fondness for a change of scene. Brighton entered on an entirely new lease of life from that of the rather run-down fishing town which had suffered severe damage from storms. With similar, if less grand, developments multiplying all along the coast, Sussex's rapid urban growth had no parallel in England outside the history of some northern industrial towns.

This frenzy of building was brilliantly captured in Jane Austen's unfinished novel, *Sanditon* (1817), in which she has fun at the expense of the new fashion. Mr Heywood expresses surprise that every five years or so he hears of some new place or other starting up by the sea, and wonders how they could half-fill them, while Mr Parker's hyping of the proposed new resort of Sanditon and his running-down of Brimshore, a rival place, is delicious satire:

> Such a place as Sanditon, sir, I may say was wanted, was called for. Nature had marked it out, had spoken in the most indelible characters – the finest, purest, sea breeze on the coast … excellent bathing – no mud … one complete measured mile nearer London than Eastbourne … the attempts of two or three speculating people to raise that paltry hamlet of Brimshore can end in nothing but their own disappointment … What in the name of common sense is to recommend Brimshore?

60 *Shoreham Fort, built in the 1850s to defend the coast from threatened French invasion, c.1890s.*

The novel was one of the the earliest literary creations inspired by 'Sussex by the Sea'. Another was Thomas Hood's witty satire on Hastings, then enjoying a supremacy among Sussex resorts until displaced by Brighton:

> 'Twas August – Hastings every day was filling –
> Hastings, that 'greenest spot on memory's waste!' –
> With crowds of idlers willing or unwilling
> To be bedipped – be noticed – or be braced,
> And all things rose a penny in a shilling.
> Meanwhile, from window and from door, in haste
> 'Accommodation bills' kept coming down,
> Gladding 'the world of letters' in that town.
> Each day pour'd in new coach-fulls of new cits,
> Flying from London smoke and dust annoying,
> Unmarried Misses hoping to make hits,
> And new-wed couples fresh from Tunbridge toying.
> Lacemen and placemen, ministers and wits,
> And quakers of both sexes, much enjoying
> A morning's reading by the ocean's rim,
> That sect delighting in the sea's broad brim.
>
> *Hastings*, Thomas Hood[1]

One's reception at a hotel in the busy season depended on whether arrival was by private carriage or stage coach and how successful were negotiations with chambermaids whose practise it was to sell inferior bedrooms before better ones. Once suitably accommodated, the first thing was to inquire about the baths. A visitor would be accosted by a band of half-sailors and half-fishermen who pulled their forelocks and asked, 'Want a machine, sir?' Tickets would be obtained for several mornings bathing and the driver, in red-plush breeches and waterproof boots, provided towels before shutting his 'victim' inside. As the vehicle began to jolt over the foreshore, beginners felt like Jonah in the whale. The whip cracked and the horses went deeper into the sea.

61 *A view of early Hastings.*

62 *Early Hastings.*

> Kicking down the hood of the machine and clinging to a rope fastened to the outside, the hapless bather descends the steps, all but washed away by the waves. Getting bolder, the bather stands on the soft sand, staggering now and again against the cresting waves. When he has been slapped, splashed, braced and nerved, the sign was given to put the horse in again, and return to the shore – then with heart larger, chest expanded, eyes brighter, the bather departs to punish his breakfast.[2]

Richard Jefferies described how women fared at Brighton, noting with amusement how all ages and shapes, in dresses of every colour, disappeared from the bathing machine under the waves in a trice:

> An arm projected here, possibly a foot yonder, tresses floated on the surface like seaweed, but bodily they were gone. The whole rank from end to end was overthrown – more than that, overwhelmed, buried, interred in water like Pharoah's army in the Red Sea ... Down went each bather as if hit with a shot from a Catling gun.

Yet the women recovered immediately and picked their way back to the shore, preparing again to meet their inevitable fate. Jefferies thought that for such courage women deserved the franchise.[3]

Not everyone, of course, was swept away by the mania for sea bathing. The cult of the seaside at early Hastings did not command Charles Lamb's admiration:

> I love town, or country, but this detestable Cinque Port is neither. I hate these scrubbed shoots, thrusting out their starved foliage from between the horrid fissures of dusty innutritious rocks; which the amateur calls 'verdure at the edge of the sea'. I require woods, and they show me stunted coppices. I cry out for the water-brooks, and pant for fresh streams, and inland murmurs. I cannot stand all day on the naked beach, watching the capricious hues of the sea shifting like the colours of a dying mullet ... There is no home for me here. There is no sense of home at Hastings ... all is false and hollow pretension.

He reckoned that visitors became bored with wandering on the shingles collecting cockle shells and would have gladly exchanged their seaside rambles for a Sunday walk on the greensward of their accustomed Twickenham meadows. (There are hints in other works, however, that suggest Lamb grew to rather like Hastings.)[4]

The Development of Sussex Resorts

Watering places during late Georgian and Regency times tended to divide into three fairly well-defined types, each of which left its distinct imprint on the present scene. The townscapes of the largest resorts, notably Brighton and Hastings, bear traces of each and serve as a standard of comparison against which the progress of less successful resorts can be measured. In the embryonic stage of growth, speculators raised short rows of lodgings facing away from the sea (looking at the sea was not then fashionable) wherever there was a suitable beach and level ground. The type of dwelling favoured was a tall, narrow, terraced house, four or five storeys high, with bow windows to take advantage of the sun and provide a view of the social scene below. The buildings themselves were generally of flimsy construction, façades undistinguished and interiors very plain. Libraries, Assembly

Rooms, a promenade and other recreational facilities were provided in imitation of Bath and other inland spas. All these amenities were laid out without any conscious plan.

In the next stage of development came the creation of terraces, squares and crescents as single compositions by one architect and landlord, again in the manner of Bath. The majority fronted the sea and contained graceful, well-proportioned buildings reflecting the more successful resort's assurance. Brighton attained this stage when the Royal Crescent was built in 1798; Hastings and Worthing did not reach it for another 20 years; Eastbourne's growth was arrested at the first stage for half a century and Seaford never evolved from the initial stage at all.

A further stage was the comprehensive planning of estates on virgin ground to create integrated communities in the manner of John Nash's Regent's Park development. Brighton and Hastings entered this phase in the 1820s, but Worthing, Littlehampton and Bognor achieved little of this kind. Of particular interest are the traces in the landscape of ventures that proved failures, such as the little row of 'seaside villas' in Shoreham, hidden away by subsequent industrial development, and at Lancing, where bathing machines were publicised and two lodging houses existed but there was no hotel, library, or public rooms of any description. Similar failed speculations are traceable at Goring, Selsey and the Witterings. Worthing's townscape is notable in that it shows evidence of both rapid growth at The Steyne, Liverpool Place and Park Crescent, but also a long period of arrested development from the 1820s which left it for several decades with sporadically dispersed buildings amid farmland. The deadliest blow was the loss of the medical profession's approval, which appears to have been due to inadequate sanitation in its low-lying situation.

Architecturally, there were many variations on Classical themes at the early Sussex resorts. Initially Greek was the main inspiration, but there were sudden swings in fashions in both basic building style and embellishments such as ironwork and canopies. One of the more obvious ways of dating verandas is the contrast between the dainty exquisite ironwork of the Regency and the cumbrous, heavy, austere balconies of the early and later Victorian period. The Regency architecture of jollity, whimsy, fantasy and extravagance is the essence of the Sussex resort, and it is the Royal Pavilion at Brighton, Nash's sensational Indo-Chinese domed palace for the Prince Regent, that is the extreme embodiment of these qualities.

By the early 1930s the Sussex resorts had established their individual characters in the minds of patrons. Schofield connected Bognor with children; Littlehampton with sailors and sportsmen; Worthing with invalids; Hove with the wealthy; Brighton with the sporting and Eastbourne with the intellectual.[5] Although Brighton's 'mile after mile, its gay and fantastic front to the sea,' commanded most people's admiration, a number of the other bathing resorts were considered especially attractive. Theodore Hook, in his novel *Jack Bragg*, alludes handsomely to St Leonards, created from scratch from 1828 by the celebrated architects James and Decimus Burton. He thought, as did most early Victorians, that the elegance of its colonnaded terrace houses and Italianate villas afforded 'one of the most beautiful and wonderful proofs of individual taste, judgment and perseverance that our nation exhibits'. Decimus Burton and his supporters never hint that natural beauty is being irreparably damaged. On the contrary, the site of the town, where building in the 1920s would have created cries of outrage, was dismissed as a desert of barren cliffs fronting a sterile and shrubless ravine.

Dr A.B. Granville wrote even more admiringly:

> At St Leonards [Burton] has again given proof of this power of invention and love of the beautiful. We should look in vain on any other coast in England for such a range of buildings as those he has raised below St Leonards Cliff … None but the unrivalled crescents of Bath and Bristol is superior to the Marina of St Leonards … The whole of this varied region must be a little paradise for invalids; and the houses, whether those detached as Italian or Lombard villas with gardens, or those placed in rows like a series of Gothic cottages, are much sought after.

He considered that, in the sun of January and February, the Marina as a tranquil sea-bathing residence was preferable to the cold breezes on the cliffs of Brighton.[6]

Bognor was the earliest English seaside resort to be promoted by one man. Sir Richard Hotham recovered his health there and devoted the latter days of his life to making it a fashionable watering-place for those who wanted the luxury of Brighton but more seclusion. His showpiece was Hothamton Crescent (now occupied by Chichester University), of which the central residence, the Dome, has been described as 'the best example of late eighteenth-century work in any seaside town in Sussex'. After Hotham's death in 1799 Worthing gained ascendancy over the town. The *Sussex County Handbook* for 1912 stated that much booming had been done at Bognor and the town does its best to live up to it, with its hard sands, good bathing and well-kept promenade which stretched a mile along the sea front. The railway company kept faith in it by building one of the finest stations in the county.

Eastbourne is a massive monument to Victorian town-building under the aegis of the 7th Duke of Devonshire and the Gilbert family. The former's orgy of building, conceived in the grandest manner, was to win Eastbourne the title of 'The Empress of Watering Places'. As a single sustained piece of town-building, resulting from single ownership, it is unmatched in Sussex. Modern Bexhill was largely the creation of the 7th Earl De La Warr, who developed it when the agricultural value of his estate declined in the 1880s. From the beginning his intention was to create a resort of high-quality houses, hotels and entertainment, though all was spread in rather higgledy-piggledy fashion. The Earl's progressive views led to Bexhill being the first Sussex resort to permit mixed bathing.

The optimism of the Sussex seaside received a great boost from the master builders of '30s modernist architecture. One of the great achievements of the 9th Earl (d. 1976) was the De La Warr Pavilion, built in 1935 of a steel-frame and ferro-concrete construction to the design of German Erich Mendelssohn and Russian-born Serge Chermayeff and intended to be a 'crucible for creating a new model of culture provision in an English seaside town'. Its 1935 sun decks, free-flowing spaces, reading rooms and entertainment for all were inspired by Earl's ideal of a 'peoples' palace'. Although there was tremendous opposition locally, it was the first major welded steel-framed building in Britain and architectural critics were generally in its favour, a writer in *The Times* declaring that it was by far the most civilised building on the south coast since the Regency.

Further along the coast at St Leonards-on-Sea rose Marine Court, the highest residential building in England at the time, strongly influenced by Le Corbusier's analogy of the decks of an ocean liner, a fitting image for a seaside environment. On the sea front at Brighton

63   *Erich Mendelssohn's and Serge Chermayeff's*
De La Warr Pavilion, Bexhill, 1935.

Wells Coates created the nautical-looking
Embassy Court and its tubular furniture,
insensitively placed in relation to Regency
Brunswick Square. For the first time in the
history of the Sussex house, dwellings were
deliberately contrived to provide fresh air and
sunshine, the county's most enviable natural
resources.

Sea Lane House at Middleton-on-Sea,
built in 1936 by Marcel Bruer, the Bauhaus-
trained Hungarian architect and furniture
designer, in partnership with F.R.S. Yorke,
pioneered modernism in Britain and is one
of the finest examples of Bauhaus-inspired
architecture. It is an L-shaped, flat-roofed
villa offering views of the sea, its bedroom
wing raised on concrete columns. The living
rooms are fronted by a curved balcony,
supported by a single column. This feature
softens the cubic look of brick cavity walls
and reinforced concrete. The unimpeded sea
view was lost when a bungalow was built in
front of the house in the 1970s. The house

64   *The Coates building,*
Brighton.

was designed during Bruer's two-year stay in Britain before the Second World War. Sea Lane House is the only pre-1950s building left in Europe that can be credited mainly to Bruer. A dumb waiter ingeniously goes up to the floor above where it is concealed in a sideboard. The master bedroom is roomy and had views of the sea but the guest bedrooms are small as cabins and were furnished like a Cunard cruise liner. Across the road is a Wells Coates' Sun House.[7] Near Rye is Frank Scarlett's symmetrical white house, with a little pavilion attached for his chauffeur, while at Birdham in the Selsey peninsula is Peter Moro's Harbour Meadow, the last of its kind built in Sussex before the declaration of war. Moro was interned for a while but went on to design the interior of the Festival Hall.

Shanty Towns

A special feature of the later Sussex seaside was the sudden rise of bungalow colonies, notably at Camber Sands near Winchelsea, Rye, Shoreham, Felpham and Pagham. The 'bungaloafing' habit at these unconventional communities, which initially had no water, electricity, roads, police, sanitation or medical facilities, expressed the new spirit of pleasure and freedom among a generation intent on kicking over Victorian values and adopting a bohemian continentalism. The mood continued into the 'uproarious' Edwardian years and, after the First World War, into the 'naughty twenties'. London actors and actresses, music-hall stars, artists and writers, together with professional and business people, 'let their hair down' in ways they could not in more formal resorts. Mixed bathing was not allowed at Brighton and Worthing, for example, in the early 1900s, and there were rigid regulations at cooped-up and stuffy lodgings, not to mention the other conventionalities of 'respectable' life. The colonies provided pleasure for bohemians but were a nightmare for authorities, being wasteful of land, destructive of natural beauty, and lacking in every basic service.

The pioneer holiday makers sampling the joys of Bungalow Town on Shoreham Beach had a long line of shingle from Lancing to the mouth of the River Adur on which they built, with wild enthusiasm, a makeshift colony of shanties and railway carriages. In 1901 it was described in a local newspaper as 'one of the most romantically unconventional communities in England', and shortly afterwards it was described as a kind of no man's land:

65 *Bungalow Town, Shoreham, 1930s.*

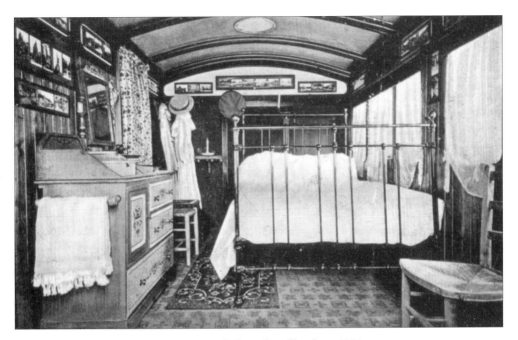

66   *Interior of a bungalow, Shoreham, 1920s.*

> Had you any idea before how delightful a sensation it is to wake up in the morning and find that a few yards of clean, tide-swept beach are between you and the sea? ... The sea air, the sunshine, and the glorious sense of freedom existing everywhere induce in you a glorious sense of happiness ... Shopping and making tea for six persons is exciting for people who have never had to 'do' for themselves and away from 'the weariness, the fever and the fret' of modern civilisation.[8]

Such media publicity brought a notoriety which escalated up to the Second World War and the 'booming' proved a godsend to the declining seaport of Shoreham.

Around the time of the First World War the famed Marie Loftus, the Sarah Bernhardt of the music halls, had taken over her big wooden house, Pavlova. She was married to Ben Brown, who had his own act with Mrs le Cerq who lived nearby. A few doors away was the comedian Will Evans, whose row of bungalows bore names of the characters he had played. Also nearby were members of the legendary Lupino family, the impresarios; the Le Freys, who had long been in the theatre; and F.L. Lyndhurst, the pioneer film producer, who had studios at both ends of Shoreham Beach in the early 1920s.[9] About the time of the Munich crisis Florrie Forde had rented a club here; Ramon Navarro, a famous silent film actor from Mexico, had a residence called Copper Turrets on what became a plot of rubble and wild flowers in the war; and stars Jack Buchanan, Carl Brissen and Fred Emery also relaxed in the same terraces. The only intact buildings after the war were bungalows used by soldiers and the little pebble-dashed Church of the Good Shepherd.[10]

Ted Walker, poet and writer, was brought up on the shingle at Lancing, before going up to Cambridge after the houses were razed to the ground in the war. He described Shoreham's Bungalow Town as a remarkable farrago of dwellings, 'very English in

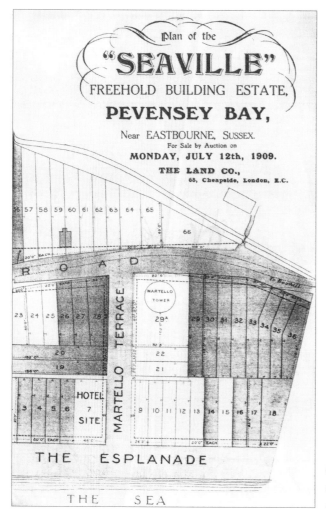

67   *Railway carriage dwellings,*
Felpham, 1982.

68   *Seaside dwelling at 'Seaville',*
a planned development in 1909 at
Pevensey Bay.

waywardness' and reminiscent in its unplanned clutter of the unpaved streets of Eel Pie Island at Twickenham before the last war.

> Many of the houses were converted railway carriages, off-loaded from lorries on to the salty grass with no more preparation than the kicking-away of the larger flint boulders. Some were scarcely the size of a garden shed, with openwork carapace of trellis and with comical little finials at the apex of their gables like the spikes of old German helmets.

Most were of wood, with asbestos partitions. Walker noted that nowadays such a development would never be countenanced, which he thought a shame, for the bizarre higgledy-piggledyness of that city of miniature homes, 'each a toy castle containing its liege-lord holding sway over ten square yards of England', had a character entirely

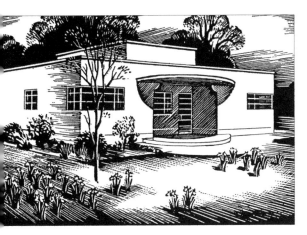

69   *Types of seaside dwellings, Pevensey Bay, 1930s.*

lacking in the post-war rebuilding. His home territory, become nondescript and lacking identity in the immediate post-war years, had been, in its own queer way, almost smart and fashionable.

> Preposterously unplanned, jerry-built, without style or charm, not twee enough to be comic, not blistered enough to be melancholy, a band of bricks between neglected fields and high water-mark, it was neither country, nor town, nor suburbia. *'God what a dump!'*, I had heard someone comment on my hub of the universe.[11]

In contrast to the unplanned Bungalow Town at Shoreham-by-Sea was the new seaside town of Beachland Estate at Pevensey Bay, designed as a weekend retreat by the sea by J. Maclaren Ross, with avenues, boulevards, closes, shopping centre, clubhouse, tennis courts and putting greens. It had its own bathing beach to keep away unwelcome

70 *Shoreham Beach, 1880s.*

trippers, and dwellings were fitted with special 'sunshine windows' and jointless flooring. A popular bungalow was of the 'Oyster' design, of Swedish origin, to give every advantage of sunlight. Such homes could be secured on the seafront from £375 freehold and from 1935 access was by electric train from Victoria. The brochure noted that one may bathe or wander about in beach pyjamas 'without courting the disapproval of the Local Authorities or Mother Grundy'.

71 *'Oyster' houses at Pevensey Bay.*

Chapter 11

BRIGHTON

> Farewell old Ocean's bauble, glittering Brighton.
>
> Horace and James Smith, *Horace in London* (1813).

Few places in the world have offered such an astonishing variety of experiences as Brighton – drugs, gay pride, heavy drinking, violence, architectural treasures, history, culture and high cuisine. Much of its appeal in the past was due to its intoxicatingly foreign atmosphere: to Victorians and Edwardians it was not only not Sussex, it was not even English. As Anthony Seldon, its erstwhile 'Master of Ceremonies', remarked, 'Brighton is the town to take one's family and also to take one's mistress, although not on the same weekend.' Keith Waterhouse once defined Brighton as a 'town which was helping the police in its enquiries', and William Plomer remarked that the 'siren Brighton was something between a mermaid and a barmaid', while its elegant rows of bow-windowed houses that are the architectural glory of the city demonstrate 'what wealth would do when it organized itself for the purpose of distraction', as Arnold Bennett noted in *Clayhanger* (1910).

Elizabeth Murray thought the sunshine and brilliance of the air freshened by the sea breezes had much to do with the reason of Brighton's charm. Then she mused on the parade of visitors who had succumbed to the lure of the place. Thackeray eulogised 'kind, merry, cheerful Dr Brighton' and put Becky Sharp in her bow-windowed Brighton lodging; Dickens sought repose in the *Bedford Hotel* where poor little Paul Dombey tried to read the message of the waves; London businessmen frequented the bohemian world which was the *Hotel Metropole*, among the shades of Henry Irving, Augustus Sala, or 'Dicky the Driver' and his coach and four; Edward VII alighted at the Sassoons' house, and diminutive Harry Preston was maestro of the Royal Albion.[1]

The Rev. Townsend's verses to the play *Charles the Second*, performed at Brighton in the 1820s, typically belittle the origin of the town so as to exaggerate the extent of its fame as a watering place:

> In days of yore, this gay and charming town
> Was a poor fishing cove, of no renown,
> No wit, no Fashion's charms adorn'd it then,
> No female Beauty, no accomplish'd men,
> But bleak and unfrequented was the scene
> In manners barbarous and in aspect mean …
> But mark, what changes since those days of old!
> What palaces! What wealth! What rank we own!
> With Fashion seated on her brightest Throne![2]

72   *Brunswick Town, c.1850s.*

In actuality, as Sue Berry has explained, Brighton was formerly a large, if rather shabby, fishing town before it became famous.[3] Horace Smith was the first to express in verse the joy of arrival at Brighton and the sadness of departure. And he also coined one of the most famous epithets of the city:

> The Cit foregoes his box at Turnham Green,
>   To pick up health and shells with Amprite
> Pleasure's frail daughters trip along the Steyne,
>   Led by the dame the Greeks call Aphrodite …
>
> Here with choice food earth smiles and ocean yawns,
>   Intent alike to please the London glutton;
> This for our breakfast proffers shrimps and prawns,
>   That for our dinner, Southdown lamb and mutton …
>
> Alas, how short the span of human pride!
>   Time flies, and hope's romantic schemes are undone;
> Crossweller's coach, that carries four inside,
>   Waits to take back th' unwilling bard to London.
>
> Ye circulating novelists, adieu!
>   Long envious cords my black portmanteau tighten;
> Billards, begon! Avaunt, illegal loo
>   Farewell, Old Ocean's bauble, glittering Brighton.

While Mortimer Collins told of the joys of Brighton in winter.

A glimpse of the luxury and elegance of the Kemp Town terraces is provided by an account of the reception by Kemp of the Comte de la Garde. He arrived after Kemp had been in residence for only one month in 1827 and there was only one other resident family, although 105 houses were in course of construction. The visitor was greeted by lines of servants in rich livery, stationed on the doorstep, who ran out to meet the carriage on its

73 *A plaque commemorating Dr Richard Russell.*

74 *Brighton Pavilion, east front.*

approach. Inside, another bunch of footmen filled the hall. The guest's name was taken at the door and passed four times from footman to footman before arriving at the drawing-room. The room was magnificently furnished with rich carpets, silk hangings and gilded fittings. A large crystal chandelier hung in the centre of the room. The walls were covered with pictures by the finest painters.[4]

Not all visitors were impressed by Brighton, Queen Victoria, every fibre of whose being was offended by contemporary Brighton, and the artist Constable being among them. To the latter it was the receptacle of the offscouring of fashionable London, the beach was Piccadilly at the seaside, and the din of coaches and flys annoyed him. Everyone he met appalled him: old bathing women swearing like men, the preventive service men with pistols, children's nursery maids, boys, fishermen, and above all the men and women bathers dressing and undressing. The Marine Parade he disliked because it was artificial. Even the fishing boats were not as picturesque as those at Hastings. In short there was nothing for him to paint but the breakers, the sky and the Chain Pier, which he did superbly.[5]

William Cobbett dealt out praise and censure in one breath. He was delighted with the general air of Brighton in 1832, considering it surpassing in beauty any other town in the world: 'Brighton is all beauty, whether it is in the streets, the buildings, the carriages, the horses, or the dresses of the people.' The neatest of carriages stood about the streets for you to step in to at your pleasure; for children there were beautiful chaises and coaches in miniature, drawn by goats elegantly harnessed, and attended by well-dressed and well-paid lads. Yet he poured scorn on the Royal Pavilion, calling it a Kremlin and describing it as a

75 *Advertisement for the* York Hotel, *Brighton,* c.*1920s.*

square box with a turnip in the middle, four smaller ones at the corners and bulbs placed promiscuously on top of the box. Nor could he forbear pointing out that the extravagance of Brighton's patrons in 'having a good time' was derived from their exploitation of the 'underclasses'. He had an array of derogatory epithets for these people, Jews, stock-jobbers and 'dirty-whiskered tax eaters' among them. He trembled to think what an unproductive set they were and how much harm they were doing to the economic and moral standing of England. He deplored the fact that Brighton was a place of no trade or commerce at all, and it had no harbour; he considered it a creation of the taxing and funding system, the valleys and hillsides being covered with elegant houses in place of corn-fields and sheep pasture.[6]

As a guide to early 19th-century Brighton, Thackeray can be as irresistibly entertaining as Brighton was itself, then filling with gilt-lettered hotels, four- to six-storeyed lodging houses and squares of palatial mansions. The burlesque was his particular love and its atmosphere, where no one is good and nothing is serious, has been the predominant flavour of the resort since its creation. His humour sprang from an accurate observation of the snobbishness and extravagance he found in Brighton and he depicted its people in comic vein: hard-drinking adventurers, army officers, match-making mothers, vulgar City magnates, seedy adventurers, and raffish upper-class bucks. Eating was of great importance in Thackeray's world and as a gourmandiser fond of passing a bottle of Madeira and puffing in cigar smoke, he found a surfeit of like-minded company in Brighton whose appetites had been raised by the celebrated air and whose constitution was being ruined by the excess.[7]

His enthusiasm overwhelms him in *The Newcomes*:

> Hail, thou purveyor of shrimps and honest prescriber of South Downs mutton! There is no mutton so good as Brighton mutton, no flys so pleasant as Brighton flys, nor any cliff so pleasant to ride on, no shops so beautiful to look at as the Brighton gimcrack shops, and the fruit shops and the market.

Although now an older man, he also is the ambassador for the Brighton of the early 1840s. He advised taking a ground-floor flat on the Cliff to examine the stream of humanity from London which passed by a league in length, pouring from Brunswick Town to Kemp Town and then back again, from three o'clock to dinner time. He was thrilled at the crowd of well-known London faces he saw there, their sallow countenances changed to pink under the administrations of Dr Brighton. He claimed to have seen in a single day 49 railway directors (who would have been in Baden-Baden but for the lines in progress), 13 barristers including the Solicitor-General himself, a Hebrew dentist in a curricle, and at least 12 famous actors and actresses, all breathing the fresh air an hour and a half from the City. Not to mention the tight-laced dragoons trotting up and down, with solemn, handsome, stupid faces and huge yellow mustachios.

> The crowd, sir, on the Cliff was perfectly frightful. It is my belief nobody goes abroad any more. Everybody is at Brighton. I met three hundred at least of our acquaintances in the course of a quarter of an hour, and before we could reach Brunswick Square I met dandies, City men, Members of Parliament. I met my tailor walking with his wife, with a geranium blooming in his wretched buttonhole, as if money wasn't tight in the City, and everybody had paid everything everybody owed him.[8]

After Thackeray's day middle-class crowds arrived by train in the summer season. Richard Jefferies, who visited the town in the 1880s, is usually thought of as a country writer but he was also particularly observant in towns. Brighton to him was the Piccadilly crowd transported to the seaside. He noted that the fashionable person ignored the beach, except when in a bathing machine, but promenaded twice a day, morning and afternoon, in the King's Road on the side of the shops. 'No one rows, very few sail; the sea is not "the thing" in Brighton, which is the least nautical of seaside places. There is more talk of horses,' he declared.[9]

And he had an eye for Brighton's pretty women, of whom there were more than anywhere else in the world. They all had the desirable plumpness and the glow and bloom of youth on their cheeks. The sea air and horse exercise on the Downs added a deeper glow to the face, like 'dew on a flower', which was admired by all when the girls paraded on the King's Road.[10]

'GOOD OLD BRIGHTON'

Late Victorian accounts of Brighton are usually full of genteel-looking and properly dressed strollers, equestrians and well-born or self-made carriage-folk promenading between the *Métropole* and *Grand Hotels* and the Marine Parade. A Ditchling landscape artist, J.C. Dollman, and his friend kept a series of sketch-book drawings of their holiday in Brighton in the spring of 1883 which gives a 'low-life' glimpse of the town. They begin in a cheap bed-sit and move on to a small commercial hotel, are almost blown away on the Marine Parade, meet the Salvation Army, and are attacked by a boatman's dog, each incident being spontaneously illustrated in the evening.

From the mid-19th to the early 20th centuries Brighton was the subject of verse published in local newspapers, often satirical in tone and invariably middle-class in flavour. Some of the earliest was Fred J. Walthew's *Poetical Satires* (1860). His King's Road was not the elegant concourse we learn of from other sources but an unpaved street of mud and muck after heavy rain. People splashed through the slush and mothers complained that it cost more to do the extra washing than keep the horses. Cleaners arrived casually and late, armed with hoes and a machine like a great iron comb, but merely moved pebbles and other

76 *'The Peoples Brighton', 1883, from a sketchbook of Ditchling artist J.C. Dollman, giving excursionists' impressions of the resort.*

muck to the sides. The poet wished his friend would help by telling the Corporation that things were better ordered abroad:

> You'd show them how Paris is daily swept clean,
> So that people may ride, and be fit to be seen,
> Without having blue and black turn'd
>   drab and green;
> But ah! I write nonsense, love, long will it be
> 'Ere Brighton, dear Paris, thus copies from thee.

He reported that people were growing taller in Brighton and in Kings Road found themselves constantly knocking against iron, wood, cord and canvas set at the height of the beams of a 16th-century cottage. A poetic campaign was devised to rid the town of the battery of guns that had not fired for fifty years and to remove the obstructing Brill's Baths, which had outstayed their fashionableness. On the matter of bathing, he thought it was conducted more modestly by foreigners than it was in Brighton. He noted with dismay that the Steine, shrubless and flowerless, had a dried-up fountain. At a *soirée* in the Pavilion, 'in a heavenly scene/of griffins sporting on their beds of green/and serpents coiling in the golden air', he encountered the innovations of the stereoscope, the electric telegraph and a display of electricity itself, none of which was completely successful.

When he says farewell in a grateful ode to the town he has known since boyhood, it is to a sandless shore and shipless sea, a Promenade where tradesmen mix with the well-born, a man calling out 'live boiled shrimps' or 'Nice day for a sail, sir', tuneless fiddlers and German bands, underworked customs men, the fish market, 'dear Mistress Gunn' (the famous bathing dipper of the Regency days) and the Pavilion, where citizens paid sixpence for admission. His greatest tribute is to the Marine Parade, which splendidly matched the best London architecture with what he loved most dearly:

> The boisterous, bounding billows,
>   white with foam,
> Sparkling and dancing as the
>   west winds moan.

In a lighter and more humorous vein were the verses of S.C.W. of the Edwardian period, originally published in the *Brighton Herald* and then in book form, with illustrations by W. Leigh Ridgewell showing loud-mouthed, boisterous young trippers upsetting 'respectables' on the promenade, or a policeman striding through the grimaces and cat-calls of local urchins. The year 1910 must have been fairly sunless as S.C.W. has a light lyric on his excitement at a gleam of sun, and he continues in *Summer Memories* of the same year to tell of the 'Sad limp nets in a rain-swept court', 'flannell'd fools 'neath the trees a-huddle', and

> Grumbling golfers and rain-warped caddies …
> Oil-skinn'd picnics and postponed paddies …
> Empty bandstands and chair rows dripping …

There was, however, another Brighton. Within 20 years of the appearance of the great crescents and terraces of Regency architecture, a squalid area of back streets and alleys had grown up in the vicinity of Edward Street, about which few Brightonians knew or cared. In 1858 a visitor threw down

77 *'On the Chain Pier at Brighton', 1883.*

the husks of gooseberries from his basket into the street and urchins pounced on them 'with all the avidity of a young pig eating apples after a windfall'. He followed them into dens in the district, including Pimlico, Gloucester Lane and Thomas Street, alleys where he stepped around night soil and other filth, and found dwellings 'unfit for cows to live in'. The air was sickly and damp and smelt of rottenness and vermin. This part of Brighton housed beggars, thieves, prostitutes, blacklegs and 'off scourings of humanity in their rages, squalid faces and debauched countenances'. The visitor compared the immense wealth of the most beautiful watering-place to be found in the world with the living standards of people who had not even the privileges of beasts in the fields.[11]

The slums were to be a running sore until they were cleared away between the two world wars, although not before Graham Greene had painted a horrific picture of them and of the violence of the racing gangs in *Brighton Rock* (1938). Eric Gill the sculptor, who had been brought up near the railway sidings, compared Brighton's formlessness with the planned little city of Chichester where he studied. It had never occurred to him before that a town could have a shape and as Brighton was not for him the Regency watering-place but Preston Park, the railway viaduct, the Seven Dials and the 'mass and mess of the unplanned slums round Edward Street' – 'a railway with a sort of encampment crowding round it' – he thought it 'meaningless' compared with the planned and ordered city.[12]

During the First World War, as Lady Asquith's Diaries show, the only signs of war were poor legless men. The bathing machines were full so she bathed off the pier.[13] It was at this time that Walter Sickert created one of the great images of transient pleasure on Brighton's sea front. On a summer's evening members of a pierrot troupe are going through their routine on a temporary stage. The sky is peach and violet, the artistes fluorescent under electric light. There are few people in the audience, most of the deckchairs being empty. The whole scene is rich in colour, complex in effect and supremely English in its 'the show-must-go-on stoicism'. ('Brighton Pierrots', 1915, in 'The Sussex Scene', an exhibition surveying 20th-century art in Sussex.)[14]

John Arlott experienced Brighton just before the Second World War and did not disguise the fact that it was in eclipse, an aura of vulgarity and seediness replacing some of the sparkle associated with its 'Regency ghosts'.

> All electric, down from London
> Every hour the green trains run,
> Bearing tribes of worshippers
> To the doubtful Brighton sun …
>
> Of an elegant Adam fireplace
> In a third-rate dancing club
> Forgotten print of the Regent
> In a dusty, smoke-fumed pub.
>
> Regency houses, row on row,
> In crescent, square and street,
> With pediment, pillar and portico,
> 'Bed and Breakfast' all complete.[15]

Brighton's Visitors

The earliest of Brighton's visitors resided in the 'smart' districts of west London. The railway brought tired masses choking from the pea-soupers of the East End, Hackney, Camberwell and Shepherds Bush. A.N. Wilson remarked that his parents at this time thought Brighton 'common' and did not go there, an experience which led to his loving the place. He thought many a middle-class father would note with approval the whelks and cockles, the paddling, huge sticks of pink and white candy, and the postcards of fat ladies in bathing costumes or girls with their skirts caught in the breeze, all showing that the old British working class was not dead.

Off-season Brighton appealed to John Betjeman when he was recovering from influenza. The street lamps shining on cobbled walls told him he was in Sussex but the fantasy of the Palace Pier at night looked rather like the royal residence of the Emperor of Abyssinia stretched on stilts into the English Channel. He loved the warm, almost empty, hotels, with old ladies discussing knitting patterns and retired colonial governors reading the *Spectator*. The pleasantness of staff in shops, hotels and restaurants and on public transport was singled out for praise and he found the sound of crashing waves and rattling shingle restful. In the morning, with sharp winter sun on a grey sea or reflected on creamy stucco terraces and squares, he visited second-hand book shops and antique shops in the Lanes, saw the Pavilion and Art Gallery and the great Victorian churches – St Bartholomew's, St Martin's, St Michael's and St Mary's – four of the grandest in England, rising like huge red battleships over the chimney pots. As he returned refreshed to London he congratulated the mayor, Corporation and officials for keeping the character of the town and making it so welcoming.[17]

Chapter 12

SOUTHDOWN SHEEP AND SHEPHERDS

Agriculturally speaking, Sussex has long been celebrated for its red Sussex cattle and, above all, for its short-woolled sheep, the renowned Southdowns, which at the hands of John Ellman of Glynde and others from about 1788 became the leading Downs breed of sheep in England, progressively ousting the local breeds of other counties and ultimately becoming internationally famous. They were bred especially to thrive on the nutrient-low turf on the bare chalk soil, widespread on the South Downs before 1940, and this explains their small size, hardiness and the agility with which they passed up and down the hills each day to graze. This achievement has proved one of the most successful developments in English agriculture. It brought immense fame to John Ellman, whose flock Arthur Young senior regarded as unquestionably the finest in the country. He was a Deputy Lieutenant of the county (as was his son, John Spencer Ellman, father of the Rev. Edward Boys Ellman of Berwick), and was showered with prizes and honours. Southdowns are lineal descendants of the sheep which grazed the Downs in the Neolithic period. As early as the 13th century the district had bigger flocks and finer wool than the western Downs beyond the Adur valley, which had fewer water-meadows and inferior natural herbage intermingled with woodland and deer parks. Simon of Senlis, steward to the Bishop of Chichester, confirmed this importance of sheep farming on the eastern Downs:

> I will, if you please, commit the custody of your manor of Bishopstone to Henry the sergeant of *Born* [Eastbourne], especially on account of the sheep which I keep in your hands, seeing that I believe the said Henry will devote himself well and ably to the matter … to Richard, whom Thomas of Cirencester sent you, I have committed the keeping of your manor of Preston [near Brighton] since I think he understands the cause of sheep.[1]

At the time Arthur Young was writing his *Annals of Agriculture*, in 1788, 200,000 ewes grazed the eastern Downs, producing more than 100,000 lambs annually, the highest stocking rate in the British Isles, which Young thought an amazing number and 'one of the most singular and curious circumstances in the husbandry of England'. Wool production was the main object of sheep farming and it is only since Ellman's death that the breed has been developed for the butcher.

Gilbert White's remarkably lucid account of Sussex sheep in *The Natural History and Antiquities of Selborne* (1788) is the best glimpse we have of Sussex sheep before Ellman improved them:

> One thing is remarkable as to the sheep; from the westward till you get to the river Adur all the flocks have horns, and smooth white faces, and white legs, and a hornless sheep

78 *John Ellman, the outstanding breeder of Southdown sheep.*

is never to be seen; but as soon as you pass the river eastward, and mount Beeding Hill all the flocks at once become hornless, or, as they call them, poll-sheep; and have moreover, black faces with a white tuft of wool on their foreheads and speckled and spotted legs; so that you would think that the flocks of Laban were pasturing on one side of the stream, and the variegated breed of his son-in-law Jacob were cantoned along on the other ... If you talk to the shepherds on this subject, they tell you that the case has been so from time immemorial; and smile at your simplicity if you ask them whether the situation of these two different breeds might not be reversed? ... The black-faced poll-sheep have the shortest legs and the finest wool.[2]

(The long-legged sheep on the western Downs were replaced by the improved Southdowns from the end of the 18th century.)

In 1829 the celebrated sheep breeder John Ellman retired. A massive and tastefully ornamented silver tureen, surmounted with the figure of a Southdown sheep and bearing the names of the 186 noblemen and gentlemen, was presented to Mr Ellman in August, and bears the following inscription:

To
John Ellman, of Glynde, Esq.,

On his retiring from the Farm
In which for more than half a century, he had devoted himself
TO THE INTERESTS OF AGRICULTURE
As a Token of their sincere regard, and a Tribute to his great merit,
Especially in improving and extending throughout
THE BRITISH EMPIRE
THE BREED OF SOUTH DOWN SHEEP
And his much admired conduct
TO HIS LABOURERS
This Piece of Plate is presented,
By a number of Agriculturists and Friends;
And to his Family,
A Portrait of Himself.[3]

Even in the days of reduced flocks at the beginning of the 20th century an idea of the enormous numbers of sheep that still grazed the Downs in the 1920s can be gauged from writings on Rottingdean by Bob Copper. He tells of the plaintive bleating heard from the surrounding hill country down in the village from dawn to dusk. The steep hillsides were ribbed with sheep tracks and sheep's wool clung to hedgerows and wire fences. The smell of sheep was borne on the downland breeze, and there were times when, if a street door were left open, sheep would enter one's parlour.

> When the shepherds were taking their flocks on to new grazing ground, and had to pass through the village to get there, a flood of woolly-backed invaders would come pouring down, threatening the entire village … The High Street would be so solid with sheep that you could have walked on their backs from wall to wall and cottage and shop doors alike would be hastily slammed. The dogs, in fact, did jump up and run about on the backs of the sheep, urging those in the forward ranks to move along a little faster.[4]

Sheep washing before shearing brought great flocks to springs or river banks. To the spring of pure water at the base of the Downs at Fulking came sheep from a wide radius. By means of a simple dam the water was raised to the required height. Men stood in the stream and were for several hours up to their waists in the cold water. When work was over they walked stiffly to the *Shepherd and Dog*, 'the water dripping from them and sprinkling the road like a shower of rain'. They suffered much from rheumatism in various forms and could only continue the work for a very few years. The sheep were penned across the road, blocking access, but two gates were supplied to let infrequent traffic through, little more than two or three carts in a day.[5]

The decrease in sheep numbers on the South Downs in the years just before the Second World War was mainly due to cheaper imported meat from Australia and New Zealand. After the war the natural herbage was largely ploughed up for arable, fed by artificial manures, and this led to the eclipse of the breed.

79 *Unimproved breed of Southdown sheep.*

80 *Improved breed of Southdown sheep.*

The South Downs Shepherd

'The man that really is Sussex is the shepherd,' said the 16th Duke of Norfolk as late as 1938 in Barclay Wills' book *Shepherds of Sussex*. The shepherd had been part and parcel of the Downs for six thousand years or more, and people assumed he would be there for thousands of years to come. In fact, without the shepherd no one could envisage a future for the Downs. Up to the early 1930s Sussex still had its own peculiar type of shepherd who did his job in much the same fashion as the shepherds of the Old Testament, tending sheep by day on the Downs, bringing them down in the evening to the fold and spending his nights with them during lambing time, despite the enormous changes that had taken place in the county since scriptural time. The Duke thought those experiencing the farming recession of the inter-war years should ensure the Downs be kept open against the day of the shepherd's return. Of course, the shepherd did not return, and in place of the shepherd and his sheep is unsustainable agri-business. Sussex lost at a stroke its reputation for being everything modern industrial society was not – ancient, slow-moving, cosy, spiritual, changeless – and became culturally poorer as a result.

Since Richard Lower wrote the first modern account of the shepherd, in *Stray Leaves* in 1862, writer after writer has been lured to portray this fascinating workman whose conditions of life were singularly different from others. The head shepherd was the most important person on the farm before changes in the late 19th century, for in addition to the shepherd's normal skills he judged with the farmer how many sheep the farm could support, how much 'keep' the sheep would need during the winter, and how to dispose the flock on the Downs season by season. He was so important that, generally speaking, he remained as a fixture when a farm changed hands. He had, therefore, to be a man of intelligence, responsibility and trustworthiness and the bearing of some shepherds made them indistinguishable to strangers from their employers.

Barclay Wills' portrait of the Sussex shepherd is infused with the townsman's fascination for his strange romance:

> Stand with an old shepherd on a hill-top on a fine summer day, and you will capture some of the beauty which has moulded his character and that of his ancestors. He is king of a beautiful and peaceful little kingdom. The purest breezes caress him. The music of his precious sheep-bells delight him … The flower-studded turf and the wild life around are more to him than any book. There are moments when you feel that his love for the hill-tops is beyond description in words, and in a vague way, that such a man is superior to the ordinary mortal whose life is full of trivial affairs … The poor old hill-shepherd may have given lifelong work for a meagre wages, but he is rich in many things that money cannot buy![6]

Tickner Edwardes of Burpham observed that the South Downs shepherd was not starving for companionship despite his lonely existence; any other farm worker would receive a visitor warmly, in order to pass the time of day, but the shepherd received him with the plainest and coolest unconcern. In the village pub he would sit and smoke a pipe and be the least communicative of the company. Edwardes noted that the shepherd's calling descended from father to son, generation after generation, and heredity may have evolved a special, self-sufficient man for this most solitary and exacting task. Edwardes also remarked on the fact that he spent his entire life amid the unceasing music of sheep bells and natural beauty and thought it surprising the shepherd has given us so few poets and imaginative writers.[7]

Numerous writers got into conversation with a shepherd. The one Louis Jenkins spoke to pronounced 'the' as 'de' and 'that' as 'dat', as would an African-American. He was a fine, tall man, with long black hair, somewhat grizzled by age, hanging down to the collar of his long, dark blue coat or half-cloak, such as one may see in the old

81   *A shepherd's hut, near Birling Gap.*

Derby figures of the shepherd and his dog. He had a rather handsome and intelligent face, and a Roman nose into the bargain, and looked as if he were descended from some prouder race than that which in these days bears the crook. Jennings thought he might have been descended from a higher social class, for the Tuppins and the Scraces, once the owners of broad domains but now gone from the records of the gentry, were still to be found in the cottages of the peasantry. Tuppin, or Tupyn, was a well-known shepherd name, and one of the family with whom Jennings had a slight acquaintance would instantly attract attention in any drawing-room by his manly appearance and bearing. Christopher Passmore of Applesham Farm near Shoreham relates that his father's shepherd was often mistaken for a prosperous farmer on Sundays when in the local inn, and shepherds on the Goodwood Estate had a most dignified bearing.[8]

Just after the Second World War Nancy Price had an agreeable encounter with a shepherd who had a hat of remarkable individuality and longevity, the result of wind and weather. Under the remarkable covering was a kindly weather-beaten face, the colour and texture of a russet apple, and two rather small but piercing blue eyes. He said, 'Yes, I remember when these Downs looked very different. Sheep as kep' smooth be disappearin'; no sheep croppin' this long while.' 'Sheep be scarce now.' 'And shepherds, too, I'm afraid.' She watched

him disappear with his flock and wondered if she would ever again see that picture of the Downs of which he made so essential a part.[9]

John Dudeney was the most famous of the South Downs shepherds. He was born at Rottingdean in 1792, a descendant of a long line of shepherds. When he was eight he began to follow the sheep in summer and sometimes drove the plough. At about the age of ten Mr Dunvan, author of *Lee's History of Lewes*, gave him a *History of*

82   *Shepherd in the lambing pen, 1930s.*

125

England and *Robinson Crusoe*. From then on he spent what he could afford on books at fairs. As he had little opportunity to read at home, he took his books in his shepherd's coat pocket and pursued his studies by the side of his flock on Newmarket Hill when they were quiet. He dug a hole in the turf to store his books and slate and placed a large flintstone over it. Up on the Downs he studied arithmetic, algebra, geometry, etc. Dudeney was then under-shepherd of a flock of 1,400 sheep at Kingston. He became head shepherd for Mr Ingram at Rottingdean but in 1804 gave up the flocks altogether and became a schoolmaster at his own school in Lewes. To use his own words, he hoped it would justly be said of him that 'he had been of some little use in his day, and to the generation and place in which he lived'. Another remarkably intelligent shepherd was Stephen Blackmore, whom the novelist George Gissing came across on Beachy Head about 1890. He read on archaeological topics and through his collection of flint arrow-heads was known to Sir John Lubbock.[10] Other shepherds were acquainted with Habberton Lulham, a close friend of Barclay Wills, and included Tim Rusbridge and Jim Fowler. They are recollected in Lulham's chapter, 'Stray Memories', in Barclay Wills' *Shepherds in Sussex* (1933-4) and in the photographs Lulham took of the shepherds which appear as illustrations in the book, splendidly capturing the mood of the inter-war Downs.

Dewponds, circular depressions to which flocks of sheep periodically descended for a mile or more to slake their thirst, have been the subject of much discussion. Gilbert White of Selborne was fascinated by the ponds on the summits of the Downs which never went dry, even in summer, despite the fact that rainfall was absorbed by the chalk. The most impressive book on the subject was that of Arthur and George Hubbard, who lived on the South Downs in the Jack windmill. They convincingly argued that the circular hollows that dot the Downs were in many cases prehistoric man-made ponds designed to collect water even on dry days. A local expert had looked around for a suitable site, and scooped out the earth to a depth of a few feet, leaving a floor of chalky rubble. Then, with well-chosen clay, he carefully puddled the bottom of the hollow and left it to dry. Perhaps a few stones were placed over the clay coat. If the ramming was well done the pond soon filled, and if the floor was kept intact the pond would fill, rain or no rain, for the dewpond was kept in water primarily by the condensation of mist and fog which are such a feature of the Downs in the early hours of the morning. Locals stated that a tree, preferably a hawthorn, facilitated the deposition of mist, especially if planted at the south-west side of the pond.[11]

One of the loveliest sounds connected with shepherding was that of sheep-bells. To Tickner Edwardes the sound of 'one rich, wavering peal of this music drifting over the wind-washed hills' brought a glow to his cheek,[12] and R. Thurston Hopkins has written enthusiastically of the bells, which recalled the Downs most strongly to him, a music rarefied by the silence and openness. He loved to drowse on the side of a hill with a dozen sheep-bells making their sleepy lullaby. His preference was for big brass and copper bells with their muffled, sonorous notes. When a shepherd changed his job he took his bells with him. A shepherd explained to Hopkins that their purpose was to detect straying sheep in mist and fog, a change of jangling in the fold telling of some harm befalling the flock.[13]

Chapter 13

COUNTRY HOUSES: HISTORIC AND NEW

Sussex was formerly divided into great estates on which lived families who had owned the same land, or occupied the same houses, for generations. They ranged from the great estates at Arundel, Goodwood and Petworth and included Wiston, the home of the Gorings, owned for 200 years in 1913 by just three male successors in direct line. The Barttelots had, according to tradition, been at Stopham since the Conquest, and the Ashburnhams of Ashburnham Place were also of Norman origin. Then there were many other great landed families, such as the Zouches of Parham, the Blunts at Crabbet and Newbuildings, and the Fetherstonhaughs at Uppark. In East Sussex were the Gages of Firle, the Hampdens of Glynde, the Frewens at Brickwall and the Abergavennys at Eridge. In addition there were innumerable lesser houses of the established squirearchy. Like old-established landed owners generally, these Sussex grandees were rooted in customs they were determined to maintain and the congenial country house atmosphere prevailed.

These were survivors among a new breed of owner, the rich migrants who invaded the countryside to play their lives in the style of the *grand homme*, whom Hilaire Belloc considered 'alien to the Sussex tradition' and to whom the old-established families sold their estates. Retired colonials, financiers, businessmen, professionals and other rich people arrived from the late 19th century up to the eve of the Second World War and erected new mansions and 'gentlemen's residences'. None had knowledge of the history or traditions of Sussex and most had little sympathy with it. In this revolution in estate ownership we can trace the seeds of the transformed Sussex of the present day. The social and economic changes wrought by the rich 'cockney' incomers were in many instances good. Armies of gardeners, chauffeurs and servants were employed in formerly impoverished and declining rural areas; shopkeepers and inns multiplied in nearby villages; building contractors, blacksmiths and saddlers, architects and tcarpenters, all flourished. Nor were the arts of agriculture entirely lost, for the newly wealthy bred pedigree livestock and splendid horses. One of the greatest gains to rural employment was that provided by the growing number of fox and deer hunts, which increasingly drew their active membership from the new estate owners.

One can trace in old directories and Ordnance Survey maps the country houses present at, say, 1900, the peak of their existence, and note the ones 'lost' since. In parish after parish of the Sussex Weald are six or more large mansions, most of them no longer in private occupation. Sales catalogues of the period 1875 to 1939 have the same persistent refrains – 'ripe for development', 'sites of eligible mansions and gentlemen's residence which do not detract from the amenities of the main estate', 'several sites for mansions, worthy of the attention of capitalists', 'valuable frontage to main roads'.

The most sought after pieces of real estate among prospective buyers in the early 19th century were elevated districts on sandrock or some other 'healthy' soil, not clay or marsh, which local doctors affirmed as salubrious. Variegated and extensive panoramas were also deemed indispensable. The first country house built with these criteria had been Uppark, erected in 1685-90 high on the Downs above a steep hill and provided with deep wells into the chalk. By mid-century a site within three miles of a 'first-class' railway station was also a prerequisite. This explains the rash of new mansions in the High Weald north of Haywards Heath, with easy access to the main London to Brighton railway line, and the spate of mansions built after the opening of the railway from Charing Cross to Hastings through the Forest Ridge and High Weald in the vicinity of Etchingham station. The society in the proposed area was also critical. Country house owners wanted similar country houses accessible for practical visiting. To tempt prospective owners to buy sites for mansions in the East Grinstead district no fewer than 12 existing 'Country Seats' or 'Gentlemen's Residences' were enumerated nearby – Hammerwood, Ashdown House, Oakleigh, Shovelstrode Lodge, East Court, Holtye Corner, Pixton House, Bramblehurst, Brambletye, Ashurst Wood, Barton St Mary and Wilderwick (some of these surviving as private houses today). If local society were right the next question asked would be, 'What about the hunting?' In the final stage of country house building, before the war, the motor car extended the search to rural areas not reached hitherto, along the summit of the Forest Ridge between railway lines, for example, and new factors became important, such as the provision of reputable private schools, which were proliferating in 'good-class' areas.

An entertaining account of an Edwardian and Georgian country house is centred on the Hornungs of West Grinstead Park, near Horsham. Hornung's grandfather was a Hungarian; his father a steel manufacturer at Middlesbrough. Hornung went wild in youth and, after extraordinary adventures abroad, married a Portuguese lady and became a highly successful sugar planter on his father-in-law's estate in Mozambique. He was a splendid sportsman and kept a fine stud at West Grinstead. West Grinstead Park, so coveted and so greatly loved by Hornung, had been part of the Burrell estates from the late 18th century. Park House, the home of Hornung, and Knepp Castle, still the home of the Burrells, were designed early in the 19th century by the famous Regency architect John Nash for the two brothers Burrell. Nash left Park House a small and compact 'Gothick' castle; it replaced an earlier house, nearer the centre of the Park, which had been occupied by the Catholic Carylls. After Walter Burrell's 'improvements' in 1860 it was neither one thing nor the other. The main rooms looked across the long low range of the Downs to Chanctonbury Ring where the deer were said to be descendants of the fallow herd enclosed with the park in Elizabethan times. In the middle distance, 'shining, like strips of looking glass', were narrow ponds known as 'The Stews', where deer drank in the evening, set about with three immensely tall elms, thought to be about 400 years old in 1913. A rising knoll to the left of the Stews was crowned by a clump of trees, in the front of which was an ancient oak, its vast trunk encircled by a wooden seat. It was known as 'Pope's Oak', tradition claiming the poet drafted the 'Rape of the Lock' under its spreading branches while staying with his friends the Carylls.

After Walter Burrell made his alterations, the most arresting feature became the vast church-like room built onto the library, the last of the three Nash reception rooms, though

Nash had obviously meant the crenellated round tower to be the chief feature of the house. Designed as a dining room, it had a wine cellar below, with windows overlooking the park. Nash had taken special trouble about the decoration of the rooms which occupied its ground floor and had personally designed the circular carpet, 24ft in diameter, and even the steel grate, fender and fire-irons.[1]

A similar story would be repeated all over Sussex, not everyone being delighted by the arrival of the *nouveaux riches*. To William Morris and Philip Webb, the gentility 'besmirched' the landscape with the arrogance of their houses, everyone 'proclaiming pocket'. The country houses remodelled the face of the county and transformed the character of rural Sussex, incurred complaints that the county had 'too many carriage folk'.[2]

HUNTING FOR MEDIEVAL CASTLES

From the mid-18th century a new class of tourist entered Sussex, the hunter of medieval antiquities. Foremost of the pioneers was Horace Walpole, who gave lively and informative accounts of his visits to Arundel, Bayham Abbey and Herstmonceux Castle in 1749 and 1752. The travel journals written up in village inns by the Hon. John Byng, 5th Lord Torrington, are such invaluable guides to the England of the day that he has justly been called 'the author of the *Rural Rides* of the eighteenth century'. On his Sussex tour in 1788 he found himself such a pioneer in the new Romantic Movement that it was almost impossible to get particulars of any of the county's antiquities; on account of the ignorance and want of curiosity of the natives, enquiries were usually unsuccessful. He noted ruefully, 'I always

83   *The interior of Ashdown House.*

wonder that an owner of a real antiquity does not print a short account of his possessions; which all visitors wou'd purchase with grateful avidity.'[3]

Torrington is excellent value as an observer of the general neglect of antiquities in his day. Coming across a tottering spire that was not a church, or a barn-like building with ancient mullions, the answer to his enquiries was invariably that it was 'an auncient old place'. Turning down a woody lane near East Grinstead he came upon Brambletye, a venerable deserted mansion, with two stone lodges, coped with stone to the top and difficult to demolish, the inside entirely 'pluck'd out'; a neighbouring cottager told Torrington it had been abandoned about 40 years earlier.[4]

Soon after his departure from Horsebridge, he turned up the Uckfield road and, on arrival at Park Pale, got a key of admission into Halland Park, one of the many grand old seats of the prime minister the Duke of Newcastle, who there 'display'd his folly, and prodigal hospitality, to the freeholders of Sussex'. But in 1788 the park of great extent and a forest of wood had been nearly felled and the old house was in process of being demolished, together with its avenue of trees.[5]

At Bodiam Castle, owner Sir Godfrey Webster had locked up the gate leading into the interior of the square and did not allow anyone a key, leaving Torrington to meditate

that a proper inhabitant would secure and preserve it and get a livelihood (or at least much support) from such castle hunters as himself.[6] He later entered the Battle Abbey remains, also in the ownership of the Webster family, and although they commanded pleasing views he found 'no care, taste, or cleanliness'. All the habitable part of the building was meanly and modernly glazed; the stables were under old arches, and above them the prodigious grand hall was full of 'shameful rubbish'. The southern side of the building was a fine ruin, but neglected too. He was told that Sir Godfrey yearned to pull down two remaining towers when he inherited the property from his mother, which Torrington thought would have signalled the end of Battle Abbey.[6]

Ashburnham Park, his next venue, lay in an immaculate park and was being entirely re-cased. Shown the house, with its elegant accommodation and handsome furniture,

84 *Bodiam Castle, described as the 'most fairy of English Castles' by its restorer, Marquis Curzon, whose monograph* Bodiam Castle *(1926) records his efforts to conserve the building.*

but few family pictures or old masters, Torrington thought it bespoke a 'nobleman of taste and splendour'. In a chest in the church were preserved a watch 'with a curiously enamel'd dial plate, given by King Charles Ist, in his last moments, to his friend John Ashburnham; and also the shirt worn by the King at the block, much stained on one sleeve with blood'.[7]

Torrington's comment on his next venue, Herstmonceux Castle and its Park, is of special interest because the desecration done there at the end of the 18th century rankles among lovers of English heritage to this day. He found the former deer park, four miles in extent, had been disparked and deforested by Mr Hare Naylor, whose family had acquired Herstmonceux from the Lords Dacre in 1708.[8] Augustus Hare gave a revealing account of the Park in the 1870s when he noted that avenues of tall Spanish chestnuts had once crossed it in every direction, but now there was only a line of chestnuts near the house and a few mutilated beeches, recent plantations, scanty turf and thickets of furze.[12] Some of the chestnuts survive on the edge of the moat. Others, which Richard Gilbert described as the most noble Spanish chestnuts to be found in Sussex, 'enormous veterans with spirally-furrowed trunks and huge limbs, like the arms of Atlas', line the Chestnut Walk, which was formerly continuous with the trees near the moat.[9]

Worse was to come. The castle which Horace Walpole regarded as the earliest large brick building in England, a valuable specimen of the transition from fortification to manor house, which overlooked the Pevensey Levels and the wall of the South Downs, was de-roofed and the interior gutted. Nothing remained but the great shell and the kitchen gardens, into neither of which, being locked up, could Torrington enter. By the side of the moat he reflected on the destruction of what had been of great interest to the antiquary, paintings, carved work, wainscoting, magnificent chimney-pieces, tapestry, etc. He thought it had all been sold as lumber and long since burnt, though sometimes a curiosity was to be found in a neighbouring cottage, such as a bedstead or an old panel-painting nailed over a hole.[10] This is broadly true but, according to Augustus Hare, the staircase, floors, handsome doors, window-frames and some timbers were re-used in the new Herstmonceux Place which the Naylor-Hares built on the hill above.[11] The destruction occurred in 1777 when Henrietta Naylor, the Rev. Robert Hare's second wife, decided to destroy the interior of the castle, which was entailed upon the eldest son of her husband's first marriage, and build another house on a higher site in the park which could be settled upon herself and the children of her earlier marriage. To justify this she claimed that Samuel Wyatt, the architect of the new house, had declared the castle to be in a hopeless state of dilapidation, although another expert affirmed that its condition was relatively good. It is said that in old age she repented and wandered round and round the ruins of the castle exclaiming, 'Who could have done this wicked thing?' The sorrow and indignation at the premature decay of the castle reverberates through Victorian literature.[12] Grose's prints reveal the grandeur, elegance and architecture of this ancient building. The mansion was restored by Claude Lowther from 1913, and by his successor Paul Latham, and is now an annex of the University of Kingston in Ontario.

Penns in the Rocks near Withyham was described by W.B. Yeats as 'the perfect country house where the green of July brought out the red of the bricks'. The little façade of the late 17th-century house which William Penn, founder of Pennsylvania, acquired through marriage to the heiress, faces huge sandstone rocks out of which trees grow so that their roots

85 *Interior of Herstmonceux Castle before demolition in 1776, from a watercolour by Lambert.*

twist and twine over the stones. The outcrop leads on to Rocks Wood, where more massive rocks obtrude. Vita Sackville-West described the scene as 'absolutely fantastic, a mixture of the most absurdly romantic age, and Shakespearean scenery, especially a Midsummer's Night's Dream, and Walter de la Mare, and Piranesi, and Mrs Anne Radcliffe'.[13] For Dorothy Wellesley, separated from Gerald, Duke of Wellington, it was a consoling place to return to after vagabondage abroad, and it was here that she lived a lesbian life and wrote imaginative nature poetry. Some of it was inspired by Penns and discovered by Yeats when he was editing his *Oxford Anthology of Modern Verse*. Visitors included Lady Ottoline Morrell, Ethel Smyth, Virginia Woolf, Sir William Rothenstein, Rex Whistler and John Sparrow.[14]

86 *Balcombe Place, former music and ball room.*

THE NEW COUNTRY HOUSES

The new breed of country houses built between *c*.1860 and 1939 included some of the most sumptuous and luxurious in England, entirely remodelling the Weald. Dinner parties were full-scale theatrical productions demanding large dining rooms with elaborate ornamentation. An extensive ballroom that could also serve as a music room was *de rigeur*, as was a billiard room. Kitchens were incorporated into a wing of the house, whereas traditionally they had been detached because of fire risks. This required careful ventilation, and the large scale of the entertaining necessitated practical design, innovative cooking, and cleaning equipment manufactured at factories in the Midlands. To carry this out invisibly, inaudibly, odourlessly and with an illusion of effortlessness, the 'downstairs' part of the mansion was segregated and, to an extent, hidden.

In 1944 Drewitt's in Warninglid contained ten bedrooms, including 'the Queen Anne' bedroom with antique furniture, three housekeeper's rooms, a handsome dining room and a library furnished with mahogany Sheraton and Chippendale. Colwood, also at Warninglid, was said to be unmatched in the vicinity, with old gables and superb views. Gravenhurst in Bolney had 35 bedrooms, 10 bathrooms and a great hall or music room. Lydhurst had a 'cheery entrance hall', nine bedrooms and four servant's bedrooms, 'a cosy study', large drawing room, magnificent library and 'full-sized' billiard room. The servants' hall, which had a separate approach, included two menservant's bedrooms, and 'effectually shut off from the residential part of the house' were the housekeeper's quarters and the butler's pantry and bedroom. Crabbet Park, near Crawley, was extensively rebuilt by Wilfrid and Anne Blunt with the aid of a family friend, John Pollen, from 1872 in a neo-Queen Anne style with a Horsham stone roof and dressings of Portland stone. Both the Blunts were amateur artists and had acquired some building knowledge, and Pollen was an assistant keeper of the South Kensington Museum. Crabbet had an impressively high reception hall, a ballroom with a semi-circular bayed extension and many large and airy rooms. Upstairs were high-ceilinged bedrooms. An impressive orangery with a semi-circular, open-columned portico was originally built to house real tennis. The estate became the centre for the Blunts' breeding of Arabian horses.

A good example of a mid-Victorian country house is Balcombe Place, built in 1856 in the 'Tudor Gothic style'. This lies in a considerable estate and has magnificent views to the South Downs across the wooded Weald. A music room with organ was a later addition. The house came into the possession of Lady Denman, the daughter of the 1st Lord Cowdray, who was largely instrumental in building the village hall, with murals by Neville Lytton commemorating the dead of the First World War. Lady Denman was associated with many charitable causes and was head of the Women's Land Army in the Second World War. Horsted Place, now a country house hotel, near Uckfield, was designed in 1851 for London businessman Francis Barchard by Samuel Dawkes in Gothic Revivalist style, and the interior includes Augustus Pugin's splendid staircase, fireplaces, linen-fold panelling, ceilings, door-cases and furniture.

Fairlight Hall near Hastings is a mid-19th-century 'Tudor Gothic' mansion that was acquired by Sir James Roberts (1848-1935), prominent in the Yorkshire wool industry. He was the son of a Haworth farmer and, having known the Brontë family, donated the old Parsonage to the Brontë Trust. He was also one of the rescuers of Sir Titus Salt's

87 *Fairlight Hall near Hastings, newly built in the 1850s.*

factories at Saltaire where he erected a statue in Salt's memory, and he endowed a Chair in Russian at Leeds University. He acquired a sporting estate in Perthshire but in later life was one of a number of northern industrialists who removed to Sussex. He is buried in Fairlight churchyard.[15]

A place illustrating the social effects of the country house movement is Cuckfield. The toy town itself still looks the way it did when stagecoaches passed through it but the surrounding district is full of country houses and smart villas which multiplied with improvements to roads. This led to advertisements for an 'eligible site for the erection of mansions' in a district with good shooting and two packs of fox hounds. The heavily Victorianised church, with its impressive ceiling and Charles Eamer Kempe stained glass, has walls lined with monuments of the gentry that transformed this part of the Weald from a rough-hewn and malign backwater into the congenial and prosperous-looking place it is today.

88 *Horsted Place, notable for its staircase and other interior features by Augustus Pugin. False shelves in the library providing access to the kitchen were added by Lord Snowdon when week-ending with Princess Margaret.*

'LOST' COUNTRY HOUSES

Increasingly, country houses proved uneconomical to maintain or adapt and were demolished or turned into commercial or institutional premises. John Harris was among the first to make the affecting discovery of ruined great houses after the Second World War. They had not long been left abandoned but furniture, paintings, and other traces of the inmates remained. He was led to investigate the site of Michelgrove, an ancient place in a fold of the Downs below Blackpatch, famed for its neolithic flint mines, by the discovery of a watercolour by Michael Angelo Rooker in the 1780s. This showed Sir William Shelley's romantic house of the 1580s, with Batty Langley Gothick porches and brick pedimented and pilastered stables 'that wouldn't have looked out of place in seventeenth-century Holland', which was demolished by the Duke of Norfolk in 1832. He discovered a timeless park redolent of antiquity. Only the turfed foundations of the house remained, but the stables were just as they had been depicted by Rooker, 'to the right of the house and as Anglo-Dutch as anything can be. The building was of brick, with stone dressings and comprised a temple-like pedimented and pilastered façade of the sort to be seen on canals in Holland or in Dutch topographical paintings.' (The Shelleys lived at Michelgrove for more than 250 years and their memorials are in Clapham church.)

Harris then went on to Slindon House (now a boarding school), then empty and requisitioned. First visited was St Richard's Roman Catholic church with its exquisite – and rare, for England – monument by Thorwaldsen of the Earl of Newburgh, who died in 1814. Further along the street was the 15th-century lodge, appropriately castellated as befitted what was once a palace of the Archbishops of Canterbury. The Gothic gates were padlocked but Harris and his companion got in behind the church through a hole in the fence. Later it was learned that this attractive old seat had been wrecked in 1921 by Mervyn Macartney, a graceless architect. There were still traces of the palace that Archbishop Cranmer exchanged with Henry VIII in 1539, but not many. The hunters found themselves on a lawn with a dried-up fountain. An open window beckoned them into a library of white-painted woodwork, the bookcases with cupboards below, of maybe Edwardian or Macartney Georgian revival. The shelves were empty except for a large number of copies of *London Illustrated Magazine*. One range of cupboards was locked; the others were empty, but a key fitted them all. When opened they disclosed precious porcelain wrapped in newspaper. The pair, astonished at this extraordinary find, felt inexplicably guilty and wanted to leave quickly, before some accusatory hand should appear.

They also visited West Grinstead Park, formerly the home of the Hornungs, sometime before 1949. They could hardly believe that the elegance of the Gothic rooms (designed by John Nash) was soon to be destroyed. The circular dining room was filled with sacks of potatoes. Despite a feasible plan to reduce the house to two ranges, down it came in 1965.[16]

The Crabbet Park mansion mentioned earlier was sold in 1957 on the death of Lady Wentworth, the Blunts' daughter. The M23 Crawley by-pass has severed the main driveway to Worth, and Forest House, Blunt's retreat, has been obliterated by the Maidenbower reservoir. The house survives as commercial offices and the fireplaces remain virtually undisturbed, as do the surrounding grounds and parkland with neglected Wellingtonia, eucalyptus and Lebanon cedar. Nearby Worth Park and Tilgate Park have been demolished; the latter is now a municipal leisure park with golf course. The Buchan Hill estate is also

89 *'One Servant', indicating the shortage after the First World War.*

municipally owned but the mansion and its grand tree-lined drive is now a school. Paddockhurst, a former home of the 1st Lord Cowdray, is an imitation Tudor house designed by Salvin (1869-72) and expanded by Sir Aston Webb in 1897, which is now Worth Abbey and Worth Abbey School. One of the largest country houses was Wykehurst, demolished in 1965.[17]

A Sussex Rectory

A country rectory was a particular form of country house but Herstmonceux Rectory, built between the 1830s and '50s, is remarkable for two reasons. One is the character of such interesting persons as Archdeacon Julius Hare, the grandson of Bishop Hare of Chichester, who was born in Italy and compared the view from his windows across the great sweep of the Pevensey Levels to the Downs and the sea with the Roman Campagna as it fell to the marshes of Ostia. The ruins of Herstmonceux Castle reminded him, in a small way, of the Baths of Caracalla in Rome. A renowned scholar, especially of German philosophy and theology, he also cherished paintings he brought back from Italy. He extended the rectory, a solid square building like a farmhouse, and added a tasteful conservatory between two main living rooms. He was no pastor, his long and repetitive sermons sending his wife, curate and the whole congregation off to sleep. He knew full well they would not understand a word of them. Villagers reported that, when visiting the sick, he would lay gentle hands on the invalid but 'say nowt'. He was devoted to his sister-in-law, who in her widowhood lived nearby at Lime, but terrified the wits out of her adopted son Augustus; with his wife's connivance he locked the frightened boy in Herstmonceux church during services and whipped him freely. One of Hare's wisest actions was to appoint John Sperling his curate. This remarkable early Victorian personality is the subject of biographies by Hare and by his friend Thomas Carlyle.

The whole house was a library, 14,000 books overflowing from the study and main book room (which still survives with its furnishings almost intact) and lining every other room, passage and conceivable (and inconceivable) space on crowded bookshelves ranged from floor to ceiling. People recalled him walking from room to room, book in hand, engaged in earnest study on publications now housed at the British Library.[18]

90 *Paddockhurst, formerly the home of the 1st Lord Cowdray.*

Chapter 14

Landscaped Parks and Gardens

In the mid-18th century the landscapers of Sussex were the established aristocracy and gentry who reshaped their estates in the manner of William Kent and 'Capability' Brown. Then followed the wave of *nouveaux riches* settling in the corridors along the turnpikes, gardening in the more eclectic style of Humphry Repton and his imitators. With the coming of railways, late Victorian capitalists expended their wealth in further landscape parks and gardens, and the comfortably-off inhabitants of rectories and vicarages, retired service officers and cottagers also caught the bug.

These rich 19th-century migrants turned parts of the High Weald into virtually a pleasure garden. The new estates had home farms, and some had model farms, but commercial farming largely ceased. Moreover, during the 19th and early 20th centuries many country landowners advanced the visual arts not only by laying out gardens and parks but by creating wider landscapes wherein the park was the focal point of their estate, or at least of the agricultural land visible from the house, as advocated by J.C. Loudon.[1] The principal populariser of landscaping farms in this way was William Robinson, the Sussex landscape gardener, in *Gravetye Manor* (1909) and *Home Landscapes* (1914), and there are still traces in the present landscape of these prospects. Blunt's Newbuildings estate at Shipley, near Horsham, where fields are still surrounded by thick hedgerows and shaws, and William Robinson's Gravetye are outstanding examples.

Apart from this 'park scenery' there were also ornamental cottages and their grounds, 'pleasure farms', and other forms of embellishment such as 'wild gardens' and collections of trees and shrubs from all over the temperate world. *Fermes ornées*, which were laid out with a view to utility as well as beauty, for 'picturesque farming' as it was termed, multiplied in the second half of the 18th century along main roads to or near the new coastal resorts, the classical Roman villa being the source of inspiration.

Typically, these were toy estates, new and whimsical residences of the gentleman farmer and bedecked with French windows, verandahs and other features to attract the eye of passers-by, 'bosom'd high in towering trees' with the surrounding woodland opened up by wide rides to give glimpses of neat farm cottages and well-bred livestock. Gilbert White of Selborne longed for someone to complete such an ornamental farm.[2] The term *ferme ornée* gradually dropped out of use in the 19th century and late Victorian gentry spoke of a 'pleasure farm' instead. This was generally a renovated and half-timbered, or stone- or brick-built, yeoman's farmhouse, but sometimes a new villa in the revivalist vernacular style was built. Such farmsteads on heavy land of mediocre quality were coming cheaply on to the market with the rising imports of grain and meat from overseas and the growth of trans-Wealden railways. The new owners planted up the hedgerows and the tail-ends

91 *Gardens at Herstmonceux Castle, initially designed by Walter Godfrey for Paul Latham.*

of fields, creating an illusion viewed from afar of continuous woodland. Many shaws, or belts of woodland around fields, were also thickened with hedgerows at this time. On the eve of the Second World War Robert Homewood's Wealden landlord 'did not value land for its own sake, but as a playground, a place where he could wander at will to admire the scenery ... to him [his estate] was a picture to be looked at'.[3]

The spread of this parkland over almost the entire county, following years of agricultural decline, was a distinguishing mark on the face of Sussex. Christopher Hussey, who was brought up at Scotney Castle and eventually inherited it, described it as 'a vast created landscape, natural enough to our eyes, but in reality managed as much for picturesque appearances as for economic returns'.[4] The 18th- and 19th-century landscape of parks and gardens survives in places, and includes some of the best examples of its kind.

Unsurprisingly, Sussex has more ancient trees than any other county. The Herstmonceux Castle estate, to which the public has ready access, is a good example of the ancient woodland and veteran trees common on land which had been medieval deer park, commercial forest and ornamental landscape. The age of these trees has not been determined by dendrochronology. Most Spanish chestnuts appear to be some 400 or so years old but one group is thought to be even older. The Knepp Castle estate, Eridge, Parham and many others are enhanced by the presence of numerous ancient trees, including oaks as old as the Tudors, thanks largely to their existence as former hunting grounds.

At the other end of the scale, the mid-19th-century rector of Bolney was so practical as to record details of his plantings in the parish registers. Three of his 'Bhutan pines', sown from seed obtained from a local director of the East India Company, survive, as do most of his Luccombe oaks and the 200 'fine tellers' he planted in the glebe hedgerows of the main London to Brighton road.[5] The Sales Catalogue of 1925 for Roffey House, near Horsham, speaks lyrically of the charm of the pleasure grounds, and the stained-glass designer Charles Eamer Kempe at Old Place, Lindfield embellished his grounds with statues and extended an avenue into the adjacent meadows, lawns and flower beds, in which he built a turreted ornamental pavilion as a workshop and design studio. It was supplied by water from a donkey well in the grounds which pumped water to one of his turrets. The White House, Isfield, was described as a 'bijou country house' in 1914. It was prettily clad in climbers and creepers, its dormer windows overlooking choice tree-planted grounds.

This landscaping was due in part to the natural beauty of the county and to the heavy, moisture-retaining soils of the Weald, their acidic leaf-mould an excellent medium for trees and all Ericaceous plants, including those introduced from the Americas, Australia, New Zealand and the Far East. Landscape designer Humphry Repton said that in Sussex every berry became a bush and every bush a tree. In relation to his art he thought, 'that it is only a matter of whether you do not spoil nature's work'.

Not everyone welcomed the mania for designed landscapes. The 5th Lord Torrington was one critic. In the course of his tour of Sussex he passed the 'parkish grounds' of a house owned by a member of the Evelyn family near East Grinstead and was not inspired by this standard example of current landscape design:

92 *Scotney Castle, Kent, the home of the Hussey family, devotees of the Picturesque.*

93 *Chestnut Walk,*
Herstmonceux
old park.

> He, like all other modern planners, and according to that general taste now prevalent,
> must stock up hedges, and lay wide, and waste; and then grow these lawns ill suiting the
> business of farming, which are obliged to be divided again by filthy rails and hurdles.
> Our ancestors were happy to ride from field to field, from wood to wood; but now all
> is to be lawn'd, to be clump'd; all to be seen at once! Surely modest nature should make
> but partial discoveries; to eager the eye, to indulge in the imagination; and not start all
> the charms in one display.[6]

A later critic of 'ornamental gardening' by the *nouveaux riches* was John Halsham. In his
Idlehurst, a valuable sketch of social and landscape change in mid-Sussex at the end of the
19th century, he tells of a Mrs Latimer of Blackpatch who for 'inscrutable' reasons built a
flamboyant mansion surmounting a lonely hill, 'all red gables and chimneys', with sweeps
of bare gravel drive and groves of 18-inch laurustinus and arborvitae. 'Now, of course,'
remarked this lady, 'We had to make all the garden out of fields ... we really beat you in
the view ... It only wants a few more good houses on the best sites to be really perfect.'
Halsham thought the hill-top villa and its clump of trees had become the typical landmark
for half the county.[7]

The ostentation of gentlemanly residences was too smug to be borne by William Morris
and his group, by George Meredith, who deplored the 'hectoring of lovely open country in
Surrey, Sussex and Hampshire', and by art critic Roger Fry.[8] But most visitors to Sussex were
enchanted by the spread of parks in the style of 'Capability' Brown or Humphry Repton.
French observers were captivated by them. Pichot in 1825 wrote, 'From every knoll the
eye surveys parkland which stretches from hillsides to valleys and from valleys to hillsides,
over meadows of a delicious green and gentle wandering streams ... Far and wide reigns
an air of security, prosperity and even happiness.'[9] The Comte de la Garde's impressions
travelling along the London to Brighton road in 1834 were of a garden-like landscape, in

which woods, lakes, meadows and rocky outcrops formed the setting for shoals of country retreats ('*Maisons de Plaisance*'), rose-bedecked thatched cottages and neat hamlets and hop fields, all radiating an air of ease and well-being.

> We roll along a smooth sandy road as if in a garden; on every side we are ravished with enchanting views. Here the immense parks have a lushness and variety due to the genius of successors of Kent and Brown. These clever imitators of Nature have had the talent to re-unite in an intricate tracery widely scattered outcrops, gushing springs, and winding streams, sometimes turning into azure lakes which flow through wide expanses of meadowland covered with flocks of sheep, and assorted breeds of cows, roebuck and fallow deer; all seems to unite beauty with the useful.[10]

Scotney Castle's medieval round tower reflected in lily-covered waters was the inspiration for the garden-making of the Husseys. In 1837-43 Edward Hussey III built a new Elizabethan-style house of grey and golden sandstone quarried in the grounds to face the ruins of the medieval moated castle. This was a collaboration with William Sawrey Gilpin, nephew of the Rev. William Gilpin, pioneer of the Picturesque aesthetic. The ruins were created by demolishing much of the 17th-century moated house, and a series of brilliantly contrived scenes was created by planting trees and shrubs in what is regarded as an outstanding example of the Picturesque. Two decades have healed the scars created by the uprooting of mature trees during the Great Storm of 1987.[11]

Garden and park making continued throughout the 19th century as businessmen bought up traditional estates and embellished them in the current styles. Kipling, for example, refers to the desire of the *nouveaux riches* to empark in Sussex:

> Perhaps you'll park it? … turn it into a fine new park … It was four farms, and Mr Sangres made a fine park of them, with a herd of fallow deer … How did Mr Sangres make his money? … It was pepper and spices, or it may ha' been gloves. No, Gloves was Sir Reginald Liss at Marley End. Spices was Mr Sangres. He's a Brazilian gentleman.[12]

A special feature of imparking in the triangle between Horsham, East Grinstead and Haywards Heath was the collections of exotic trees and shrubs. Some of the most spectacular gardens have survived and are open to the public, but these represent a fraction of the properties in this district which once had enviable stocks of trees and shrubs. Lydhurst at Warninglid was described in 1897 as having one of the most varied collections of shrubs in Britain, including over 400 Japanese varieties, and was famed for its avenue of *Cupressus lawsoniana 'Erecta viridis'*. Wykehurst in Bolney was said to be the most luxurious house of its age with splendid matching park and pleasure grounds.

The origin of the rhododendron that invaded huge parts of the Weald at the expense of the native flora was Valewood House, below Blackdown on the Surrey-Sussex border, where Harry Mangles hybridised it, advised by Sir William Hooker who gave him pollen from Sikkim seedlings from Kew around 1859. From then until his death in 1894 Mangles never ceased to create improved varieties of rhododendron as the 'high priest of the rhododendron cult'.[13]

The most chronicled Sussex garden is William Robinson's at Gravetye Manor, near West Hoathly, the setting for an Elizabethan stone mansion of broad mullioned windows and tall dormers built for Richard Infield, an ironmaster, and his wife Katharine in 1598. The spandrels on the west door bear the initials of the married couple, R I and K I, and in the hall is a cast-iron fireback of 1598 bearing the same letters. When he bought Gravetye, Robinson had already written *The Wild Garden* (1870), which railed against the bedding-out system and reproductions of Italian scenery characteristic of the first half of the 19th century, and had launched gardening periodicals advocating new fashions with large readerships. Robinson claimed to be an originator but in some respects, such as the naturalising of bulbs, he was indebted to Gertrude Jekyll's work at Munstead Wood. In reality, both Jekyll and Robinson imitated nature's work, drawing inspiration from the semi-vestigial wildness of the Weald itself and the traditional, unpretentious, English cottage garden. Robinson was explicit on this point: 'I am never concerned with Claude, but seek the best expression I can secure of our English rural landscapes, which are far finer than Claude's.'[14]

On taking possession of his neglected country estate in 1884 and a number of small farms, Robinson decided to keep a record of work done and, as a rule, the reason for it. His inspiration came in particular from the Forest Ridge. He explored inter-relationships within the diversity of nature and taught that its underlying patterns should be reproduced on every scale, however small.

> Fate gave me a piece of land in which all had to be done – every field, every wood, every cottage, every farmhouse, every road, and every fence had to be overhauled. The roads which had sufficed for the Tudor days when people rode horses more than they do now, were in grade quite useless for modern use … Everything was done with regard to landscape beauty, whether roadside fence, plantation, covert, all was done with that in view. The sloping ground round the house made the terracing necessary, and like all work of that kind, it gave rise to much labour, but it was a mere fraction of what arose when all the garden ground round the house was finished.[15]

Robinson took the then unfashionable decision of dispensing with a landscaped park:

> The question of park or farm was several times raised in arranging the place. My friend, Mr Marnock, the landscape gardener, thought that the best thing to do was to make most of the fields into a park. After some consideration I came to think that the divisions of fields necessary for the working of the place as a farm was the best and prettiest way. The divisions and copses or 'shaws' have much use as shelter, and for a place of its size I feel sure its present plan as a manor is far better than any approach to the more pretentious park. At one time I thought of opening the whole of these high fields into one park-like expanse, but now see that the place would not be improved by such a change. There is no way so certain of making a place bald and limited than removing objects and dividing lines which give distance, and a park without great breadth and dignity of great old trees is not beautiful.[16]

Instead Robinson's creative artistry at Gravetye was expended on the farms and fields he successively acquired, amounting eventually to some 4,000 acres. 'Almost every field was dealt with, beauty was never lost sight of, nothing from the making of a road to forming a fence was done without considering its effect on the landscape from every point of view.'[17]

In his *Home Landscapes* (1917) Robinson outlined with copious photographs what he had done on the numerous farms he bought at Gravetye: clearing out obstacles hiding lovely prospects, improving the surrounds of his lakes, and revealing groups of rocks on the sides of valleys. Each year's work on his estate was recorded in *Gravetye Manor* (1909). The following is a sample:

1890   In February planted 27,000 Larch in Marl Pit Field, near Birch Farm. Grubbed shrubs and scrub to reveal rocks in Rock Field, Mill Place. Propose to plant 15,000 Corsican Pine in Old Mead field. Several thousands of Red Dogwood Sloe planted. Several thousand broom planted. 5,000 Sweetbriar and much Holly put in hedges. Planted Calabrian Pine in Warren's Field from the estate of Les Vaux, Salbris, Loire-et-Cher, France. 120,000 trees planted in all. Began the Heath Garden. Stone Farm purchased for the sake of a fine group of rocks in Upper Rocks Field.

1891   Planted the upper part of Warren's Field with Scotch Firs. Planted about a thousand trees of new Canadian Poplar in Tile Barn Shaw. More Holly in.

1892   Planted 1000 Cedar of Lebanon, 1000 Riga Pine, 1000 Austrian Pine, 1000 Corsican Pine, and a few thousand Larch.

1893   Raised a wood of Oaks from acorns. Many water-lilies sent by M. Latour-Marliac and M. Maurice de Vilmorin.

1894   Sowed many seeds of shrubs, including Almond, Medlar, Wild Plum, Greengage, Cherry, Clematis. Planted about 80,000 Narcissus, mainly round the Lower Lake. Sowed Coneyburrow Field with forest Pines of Europe.

1897   Planted the best cider apples known to French growers.[20]

(Gravetye Manor became one of the earliest country house hotels; the grounds have been maintained according to Robinson's precepts by the first owner, Peter Herbert.)

Robinson's ideas of estate beauty were shared by Stephenson Clarke, who began to plant at Borde Hill near Haywards Heath in the 1890s, and placed on record his first attempts at shutting out unsightly views and improving the landscape generally.[18] Another who greatly changed the appearance of his estate on the same lines was Coventry Patmore, the late Victorian poet and writer who has described his joy when working with axe and saw on the edge of Ashdown Forest at Heron's Ghyll, 'releasing into the blue distance' prospects which had long been shut in by dense trees. He recorded his schemes for planting, draining and damming.[19]

Of the origin of Nyman's Garden near Handcross, developed by Leonard Messel and now owned by the National Trust, William Robinson wrote:

Living in a cool forest district with too many dark days [Messel] tried many trees and shrubs from New Zealand, Australia and America with the result that we saw them thriving on the Forest Ridge of Sussex. These trials of shrubs and rare trees were in what was once an old paddock near the house, protected by walls from north and east sides, and there one had the most instructive and in many ways most beautiful results I have seen in a garden. On a May day it was a joy to see the Indian rhododendrons and many a choice shrub flowered, and there for the first time one saw the fine *Eucryphia cordifolia* and *Davidia Involucrata* in bloom. One of the first to enjoy the charms of a garden of all the

94 *Leonardslee, the great garden of the Loder family.*

heaths hardy in our country, he formed a very good one, varied here and there with groups of cyclamens and many of the choice rock plants. He thought little of going to distant lands like New Zealand for his enquiries, and held that it was only fair to give them a good start as weakly plants from heated houses often failed, and it was found that a true test of hardiness could only be from robust plants grown cool.[21]

Leonardslee, the famous garden planted by Sir Edmund Loder from the 1890s, has an incomparable situation. Among wooded hillsides, flower-crowded valleys, lily-margined lakes, long, winding paths and running streams, plants and trees imported from America, Asia, Africa and Australia have been acclimatised without losing the native woodland character of the setting. Especially famed were Loder's scented strains of the Loderi rhododendron hybrids, planted about 1900, which still grow where originally planted. In the early part of the last century the garden was also famed for its kangaroos, eland, hartebeest, beavers, prairie dogs, ostriches and emus, which bred happily here.

The garden celebrated a centenary of public viewing in 2007. Anthony Noel wrote that when he first visited the place he was struck by its darkness. Returning recently, his impression was entirely different. The great storm of October 1987 blew away the gloom dramatically, and in fact saved the garden, which had been too thickly planted. In its new guise Leonardslee remains an earthly paradise.[22]

An expert in gardencraft was Walter H. Godfrey, the architect who later became influential in Lewes. He practised for patrons who did not wish to subscribe to Robinson's 'Wild Garden' style or to the Victorian fashions which preceded it. Godfrey drew attention to the architectural planning of George Devey's formal garden revival at Brickwall, Northiam, and used the style in his own work at Stanmer House, Brighton, for the Earl and Countess of Chichester, and for the Duckworths of Dallingridge Place, the Lawrences at Ashdown House, Walter Monington of Little Lodge, Newick, Arthur Edwards of Rymans,

Appledram, and Mrs Illingworth Illingworth of West Wittering. Paved walks, pergolas, terraces, courtyards, rectilinear boundaries, such as walls and hedges, and bowling alleys were designed in the manner of the formal 17th-century gardens that had been swept away by 'Capability' Brown and Humphry Repton. In the 1930s Christopher Tunnard began his Modernist-style gardens as a reaction against the notion of garden as 'fairyland'. Bentley Wood near Halland was a prototype of functionality and clean lines, bounded by a high wall and featuring a Henry Moore sculpture. 'Large glass sliding doors to the concrete terrace gave the impression that outside was inside, and vice versa.'[23]

The late 18th- or early 19th-century Holmhurst on the Ridge at St Leonard's was extended at the end of the 19th century by travel writer and biographer Augustus Hare, whose many illustrations in his *Memories of My Life* reveal that he incorporated into the interior fittings and souvenirs brought from Italy, his birthplace, and from Indian mosques, as well as ceiling beams from Baynards, Surrey. Using proceeds from his travel books Hare set the house in an extensive Italianate garden copied largely from the Villa Lante at Viterbo, with some detail drawn from the Villa Arson at Nice. A double stone terrace, with vases, obelisks and a well head from Italy, has a double staircase. The Arson Steps are curved to represent waves and are paved with Sussex pebbles in different designs, though the top step is inlaid with bits of marble from the Roman Palace of the Caesars and mosaics from the Temple Juno at Gabii and the Palace of Commodus on the Appian Way. At the staircase at the end of the terrace the imposing Ave Vale gateway still stands intact.

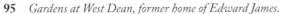

95   *Gardens at West Dean, former home of Edward James.*

The focal point of the garden was the huge marble statue of Queen Anne and her four attendant ladies – Britannia, Ireland, the American Colonies and France – which had stood outside St Paul's Cathedral. Hare learned that the statue, weighing 23 tons, was awaiting sale as stone in a mason's yard in south London and had it removed to Holmhurst by specially designed railway wagons and four trucks driven by 16 men and 28 horses. A new pedestal and the cost of removal came to £400, and the queen's railway ticket was £50. Hare sold the property to St Mary's Anglican Convent and School but it recently came into the hands of a building developer who sold off land to build the Conquest Hospital. He divided the mansion into apartments and built houses in the grounds. The larger part of the garden, listed Grade II*, is now as lost as was Heligan and is desperately in need of restoration, the Queen Anne statue just visible in dense woodland beyond the boundary.[24]

Chapter 15

NEW FORMS OF TRANSPORT

It beats me what they be adoin' on rushin' past like they doos, an' then rushin' back agen like they doos. There doan't seem to be no stoppin' nor no lookin', nor no doin', nawthin, just rushin' and tearin'. I think if I was Almighty watchin' I'd smile at this scurrin' to an' fro, an' fur nauthin' partic'lar.

Nancy Price, *The Heart of a Vagabond* (1955), describing the Findon by-pass in the 1930s.

The growth in car and motor-cycle ownership during the 1920s and 1930s had more consequence for Sussex than any other non-metropolitan county. Swathes of 'Old Sussex' were put within reach for the first time. Anyone could go in search of unexplored countryside, and a flurry of books with titles such as Donald Maxwell's *Undiscovered Weald*, and national newspapers and journals, tapped a market fed, if not created, by the motor car. Sussex's ancient towns and villages became accessible, and consequently visited, as never before; the South Downs rose to become an icon of England; the seaside was thronged with tourists, and omnibuses brought ramblers out of town streets.

A small two-speed motor-cycle took steep hills, and was wonderfully inexpensive on a long trip to Rye, although Mr and Mrs Average usually bought a 4 h.p. model with a pillion. The young, suburban Adonis, with well-brushed hair, tennis flannels, cigarette holder and eye for the girls, plumped for a 10 h.p. disc-heeled monster 'with exhaust pipes as fat as an anaconda and a bellow like a hungry mastodon' and, on pulling up, would cry to bystanders, 'Have a weed, old bean!' The low running costs of motor-cycles made them popular. Girls learnt one the greatest joys of the open road, pillion riding, a sensation thought more delightful than early flying. The sheer excitement at travelling down the Brighton road with a pillion passenger is best captured by A.P. Herbert's *A Peach on a Pillion* (1923):

> Ride on, pretty Percy! I'm clinging, I'm clinging!
>> I've needles and pins
>> From my skull to my shins,
> There's dust in my eyes, but I'm singing, I'm singing.
> I'm Helen, or someone, and you are my knight,
>> You've a peach on the pillion,
>> A girl in a million,
>> I'm clinging, I'm clinging,
>> And Brighton's in sight!
> Ride on brave Percy! I'm aching, I'm breaking,
>> I haven't a bone
>> That feels quite like my own,
> I've broken a suspender, my stocking is shocking –

> I wonder what that old gentleman said?
> > My Hector, my hero,
> > My Notting Hill hero.
> > I'm lashed to the saddle,
> > And Brighton's ahead!
>
> Ride on pretty Percy! Go faster, go faster!
> > Look round, do you mind?
> > To make sure I'm behind,
> But quicker!, the quicker, the slicker the Vicar
> He's waving, he's raving, the funny old dear!
> > Your face is vermilion
> > But I'm on the pillion,
> > I'm clinging, I'm clinging,
> > And Brighton is near!

Access to Sussex led to buildings, paving, kerbstones and lampposts replacing old ways of life along the coastal strip between Seaford and Bognor. But such thoughts were far from the minds of those 'sold' on the new invention, who found no exhilaration greater than that of travelling at up to 20 miles per hour on rises that horses had to walk up. Among the pioneers was Rudyard Kipling, who 25 years later was to bemoan the influx of people arriving by motor in the Sussex countryside in his verses *Very Many People*. Motoring not only became one of the passions of his life but inspired him to start a genre of motoring adventures which were later imitated by such successors as Dornford Yates and Ian Fleming and were the precursors of a flood of travel books on 'unknown' England, such as H.V. Morton's *In Search of England*. In a letter to his friend Filston Young in 1904, Kipling explained that his love affair with the motor car had begun in 1897 when 6 h.p. was a fair limit for a touring car; about 'fifteen miles an hour was something to talk about'. He could now live apart from towns (he had moved to Burwash) and, as a free agent, he could catch a train anywhere within fifteen miles 'and not when Jenny's hind leg or Jack's cough is better', and that he was rid of the whole tribe of coachmen, saddlers, corn-dealers, smiths and vets.

But his real joy in motoring was the 'exploration of the amazing England'. To him, an expatriate, it was 'a land of stupefying marvels and mysteries'. He cited a run through Sussex he had taken in six hours which had a literary and historical flavour. He went from the land of *Ingoldsby Legends* (north Kent), by way of the Norman Conquest (Battle) and the Baron's War (Lewes), into Richard Jefferies' country (Ditchling Beacon), and so through the Regency (Brighton), one of Arthur Young's lesser known works (probably on Goodwood) and Celia's Arbour (Portsmouth) into Gilbert White's territory. He noted that horses, after all, were only horses, but the car was a time machine on which one could slide from one century to another 'at no more trouble than the pushing forward of a lever!' He thought it miraculous that if he wanted petrol in a hurry he must pass either the place where Sir John Lade lived, or the garden where Jack Cade was killed.[1]

Shortly afterwards he hired from a Brighton agency, for three and a half guineas a week with chauffeur, a 'Victoria-hooded, carriage-sprung, carriage-braked, single-cyclinder, belt-drive, fixed-ignition Egbryo', which could cover eight miles an hour, and travelled the 60 miles to Arundel and back in the same 10-hour day. In this he witnessed, like his fellow

96   *Early motor cars at the* Old Ship Hotel, *Brighton.*

97   *A cyclist in London's countryside, 1891.*

98   *Rock Lane, Balcombe, singled out for London-based ramblers in 1844.*

149

99 *The English village according to* Punch *magazine, 1910.*

pioneers, the first shock of public outrage opinion. 'Earls stood up in their belted barouches and cursed us. Gipsies, governess-carts, brewery wagons – the world except the poor patient horses who would have been quite quiet if left alone, joined in the commination service, and *The Times* leaders on "motorcars" were Eolithic in outlook.' He then bought a steam-car called a 'Locomobile' which brought him to Bateman's in 1902 and drew on it for a tale called 'Steam Tactics': 'She reduced us to the limits of fatigue and hysteria, all up and down Sussex.' Next came the earliest Lanchester, whose springing, even at the time, was perfect, but no one knew how to maintain it. In response to furious telegrams, the manufacturer sent mechanics to Bateman's, who speculated on what had done what.[2]

Virginia and Leonard Woolf's decision to buy a Singer opened up their lives. Virginia realised it might imperil the complete privacy on which she set great store, but at the same time shared Kipling's view that it would expand that curious thing, the map of the world in one's mind, and hoped it would demolish loneliness. Three weeks later a little trip to Falmer and thence to Rottingdean and Seaford, with a call at Charleston and return to tea, 'all as light and easy as a hawk in the air', made her think being without a motor car had been like living in caves. Travel inspired her famous essay on Sussex, 'Reflections in a Motorcar'. (Lightheartedly, she told an audience she became a novelist to obtain a car, saying it was a very strange thing but people gave you a motor car if you told them a story.)[3]

Owing to the diversity of Sussex geology, the road surface changed colour as it passed over different rocks, from a strong red over sandstone to white on the chalk. Now, with the motor car, it became 'black as cinders and smooth as oil-cloth', corners being straightened and bordering hedges grubbed up for widening roads which, according to Virginia Woolf, were 'a mere racing track for the convenience of a population seemingly in perpetual haste not to be late for dinner'.[4]

Scawen Blunt of Newbuildings, Shipley, was involved in an early motoring accident which was instrumental in his battle to check joy-riding from towns at weekends; this seemed to him to be 'an invasion of the enemy in our peaceful Sussex Weald'. A young girl, the daughter of a local landowner's wood-reeve, had been run over and killed by a motor car at Buck Barn crossroads on the A24 near Southwater. He attended an inquest at the spot where the accident happened and found there a score of people, neighbouring farmers and the like, whom the parish policeman was showing the exact spot where the collision took place, the marks of the girl's blood still being visible on the road. The coroner then drove up, and out of a smart motor car came the three young men who had caused the death; everyone went into the barn close by, where the inquest was held:

> The scene inside when the court assembled was a curious one. It was a good old threshing floor with oak timbers, and on each side of the wide floor sat the twelve jurymen on forms, the coroner and one or two others at the far end of the table. The jurors were local people, farmers and labourers, with the Shipley parson, Sir Arthur Merrick's coachman and Captain Turner, a close neighbour. There was something medieval about the thing, a fine survival from the days of the Heptarchy, which seemed very real when the coroner explained that we were assembled under authority of the King to inquire into the cause of the death of one of his Majesty's lieges, to wit, Mabel Denman of this parish. Then the jury, having been sworn, they were instructed to cross the road and view the corpse, and I went to the cottage with them where the girl's body lay. Our proceedings were made all the more impressive from the intermittent roar of holiday motors passing in quick succession outside along the Worthing road, joy-riders, without slackening speed, or knowledge of or care of what had happened, or was happening. Light-hearted Londoners concerned with nothing but their own pleasure, and the thought of in how many minutes they could make the run from one point to another or their outing to Worthing.

The defendant, a young bank clerk from Balham, was eventually sentenced to two months' imprisonment.[6]

In the early days of motoring, before the invention of traffic lights, towns gradually learnt how to control motor traffic. The chief constable explained in 1927 that he had tried placing a policeman on a pedestal at the bottom of West Street in Brighton but drivers of small and enclosed cars had not seen his signals. He now proposed to adopt a semaphore system. A policeman would stand on point duty at the spot and operate levers connecting with signal arms. Gongs would be sounded during the day, and the signals be illuminated at night, an innovation which won the attention of *The Times*.[7]

From the early 1800s arose a passion for getting to Brighton quicker than any predecessor, whether by horse, motor, cycle, on foot, etc. One of the most interesting of many stirring records is that of Mr Arthur Newson, aged 42, who ran the 52 miles between the two towns in 1924 in six hours 11 minutes. One of the most famous annual events on the Brighton Road is

100 *The motor car age, 1930s.*

'The London to Brighton Run', which celebrates the Locomotives on the Highway Act on 14 November 1896, which abolished the requirement that a vehicle had to be preceded by a man on foot with a red flag and raised the speed limit for cars from four to 14 m.p.h. This historic Run, which has been held almost every year since 1927, ended initially at the *Old Ship Hotel* and the *Metropole* and attracts spectators all along the Brighton Road from Hyde Park.

Walter Wilkinson's vivid account of the effects of Sussex motoring in the early 1930s describes the subsequent concern for the countryside. Leaving the *Red Lion* at Angmering, still recognisably a village with gabled cottages and a green, his Punch and Judy wagon encountered motorists dashing through lovely country past Patching Pond as quickly as they could, 'victims of their own cleverness'. 'At one moment Sussex presented the slowly unfolding panorama of the sunny county, the eternal fields and hills, and the next minute the cars and lorries, like dominating invaders from another world, inundated the composed and lovely scene with all the racket of a dozen towns.' He thought everything worth living for had disappeared with his first steps on that busy road. He brightened up on finding villages where inhabitants were still engaged in disappearing crafts and gave modern things scornful glares.[8]

The speed and rush of the inter-war motorist inspired E.V. Lucas's 'Song Against Speed':

> Of speed the savour and the sting
> None but the weak deride;
> But ah, the joy of lingering
> About the countryside!
> The swiftest wheel, the conquering run,
> We count no privilege
> Beside acquiring in the sun
> The secret of the hedge.[9]

By the early 1920s conservationists had entered the fray, headed by Patrick Abercrombie, later a famed town planner, the first secretary of the Council for the Preservation of Rural England:

> We speak eloquently of the need to preserve and save from destruction the ancient monuments of this land, the visible signs of our history, but we are apt to forget that the greatest historical monument we possess, the most essential thing which is England, is the countryside, the market towns, the villages, the hedgerow trees, the lanes, the copses, the streams and farmsteads. In no country in the world has man fashioned the landscape so successfully to his own conception of beauty … No wonder that the innovations which came in with the motor age have been so bitterly resented by the country lover.[10]

Hilaire Belloc defended the county after 'London broke out like a bursting reservoir' with its 'evil modern machinery'. His anxiety that something endearingly and recognisably English was fading out of existence was first voiced in *Four Men* and returned to in his *Sussex* (1936), where the reader is repeatedly reminded that he is seeing only what is left of the county and only something inconceivable can save it. He asks himself, 'Can Sussex endure?' and reveals his own grief in his answer:

101   *Shell Petrol Company's advertisement depicting the Long Man of Wilmington, 1930s.*

02   *The new terminal building, Shoreham Airport, mid-'30s.*

103   *An aircraft flying over Lancing College Chapel.*

> Which of us could have thought, when we wandered years ago, in the full peace of the summer Weald, or through the sublime void of the high Downs, that the things upon which we had been nourished since first we could take joy in the world would be thus rapidly destroyed in our own time, dying even before we ourselves should die?

Unlike Wordsworth, who had denounced the adverse changes in his vulnerable Lake District a century earlier, Belloc did not make any constructive suggestions (apart from a belief in small-holdings) for a programme of countryside preservation that might have protected Sussex from further 'rash and ignorant assault'.[11]

The invention of the safety cycle in 1894 also had momentous consequences for recreation and the discovery of the countryside. The bicycle was the most romantic of machines, bringing an inexpensive sense of adventure and freedom to places motor cars could not reach. Cyclists restored some of their former glory to inns and country towns when a generation of city clerks and shopmen spent Sundays learning to read landscape through the eye, something made possible by the shortening of working hours. H.G. Wells caught the new fashion in *Wheels of Chance* (1896), in which young linen draper Hoopdriver sets off astride his temperamental machine, dressed in a new brown cycling suit, to explore the wider world of villages and market towns opening up before him. Countless readers of Wells' book must have been induced to discover London's countryside and to become 'a bit of a drawer' of buildings and scenery. Some took up cycle camping, carrying a simple tent and some provisions with them. One appears to have been Malcolm Muggeridge's father, who aroused in his sons such enthusiasm for the landscape on the outskirts of London that Muggeridge himself considered it a turning point in his life.[12] Cycling clubs multiplied. One of the annual outings of the Eastbourne Cycling Club, joined by local businessmen, was to the Litlington Pleasure Grounds, where they bathed, then had a high tea followed by a Strawberry Feast and entertainments into the evening.[13] Perhaps it is cycling which did more than anything else to make known to ordinary Englishmen the ordinary English landscape.

Shoreham Airport, created in 1910, is the oldest municipal airport in the country and has a remarkable place in the early history of aviation, though it never fulfilled its early promise. The airport's owners, initially the municipal authorities of Brighton, Hove and Worthing, envisaged it would become a key element in the growing tourist ambitions of the seaside resorts and this is symbolised by the Art Deco Grade II listed terminal designed in 1936. Periodic flooding of the grass runway, however, precluded regular passenger flights, which were restricted to France and the Channel Islands.

Shoreham Flying Club was founded soon after Brooklands at Weybridge opened in 1909. It was quickly developed into a pioneer flying school by the brothers Cecil and Eric Pashley. Cecil had taught himself to fly at Brooklands and flew most of the early airplanes of that era, including the Bleriot monoplane, the Bristol biplane and, his favourite, the Farman biplane. When the First World War broke out the two brothers were developing a high-powered 100 h.p. machine. Eric died in the war but Cecil became host to flying clubs and the leading local aeronaut. Other pioneer flyers associated with the airport were Amy Johnson and Charles Lindbergh. Shoreham Airport is a rich source of pioneer flying, but a persistent story which may be a myth is that of trainee pilots from Lancing College finding it necessary to force land at Roedean.[14]

After the First World War light aircraft were designed at the airport by brothers Fred and George Miles of Portslade, and Cecil Pashley renewed his training clubs. The railway station serving the airport and Bungalow Town never re-opened after the Second World War.

In the summer of 1930 there were early experiments in gliding at Beacon Hill in South Harting and on the flanks of Firle Beacon. Herr Kronfield, an Austrian, taught trainees at the former; the wonder of a 'lovely creature, moving almost motionless like a seagull over the cornfields in the valley, rippling in the wind like the waves of the sea' was witnessed at the latter.[15]

Chapter 16

DOUBLE LIVES: WEEKENDING AND COMMUTING

The Train!
The twelve o'clock for paradise.
Hurry, or it will try to creep away.
Out in the Country everybody is wise.
We can be only wise on Saturday.
There you are waiting, little friendly house;
Those are your chimney stacks with you between,
Surrounded by old trees, and strolling cows
Staring through all your windows at the green.
Your homely floor is creaking for our tread,
The smiling teapot with contented spout
Thinks of the boiling water and the bread
Longs for the butter ...

Pack up the house, and close the creaking door.
The fields are dull this morning in the rain.
It's difficult to leave that homely floor,
Wave a light hand: we will return again.
(What was that bird?) Goodbye, ecstatic tree,
Floating, bursting, and breathing on the air.
The lonely farm is wondering that we
Can leave. How every window seems to stare!
The bag is heavy. Share it for a bit ...
It is over ... Now we sit
Reading the morning paper in the sound
Of the debilitating heavy train ...
London again, again, London again.

'Weekend' in Aida Monro (ed.), *Collected Poems of Harold Monro* (1933), p.213

Rural cottages had been coveted for a good many years before Jane Austen wrote about them or Marie Antoinette made famous her Hammeau as a toy for a sunny day. The advent of bijou residences, known as *cottages ornées*, along the Brighton road from the late 18th century testify to this.[1] Yet it was not until the mid-1930s, Southern Electrics and the motor car that the cottage craze turned into a mania.

The sheer joy of a weekend break from London resounds through Sussex literature, even in those who loved the capital.

> Home is the hunter, home from the hill, and the Woolves are back from Monks House. And much refreshed into the bargain. Three solitary nights. Think of that! Was there ever such a miracle. Not a voice, not a telephone. Only the owl calling; perhaps a clap of thunder, the horses going down to the brooks and Mr Botten calling with the milk in the morning.

So Virginia Woolf wrote in her Diary under 28 June 1937 on her return to Tavistock Square from a long weekend at Rodmell, her Sussex refuge. She was at work, writing again before noon, hoping to drive her pen the harder after her restful holiday. She wrote on 20 October 1931, 'Oh, it's blue again over my skylight and please God it is always blue over our weekend, the blessed Rodmell week', and on 2 October 1932:

104 *Cottage, Ardingly.*

> I am backed by the downs; the country; how happy I and L[eonard] are at Rodmell; what
> a free life that is – sweeping 30 or 40 miles; coming in when and how we like; sleeping
> in the empty house; dealing triumphantly with interruptions; and diving daily into that
> distinct loveliness – always some walk; and the gulls on the purple plough; or going over
> to Tarring Neville – these are the flights I most love now – in the wide, the indifferent
> air. Not being jerked, teased, tugged.

Author and poet William Plomer, writing in the 1920s and '30s, anchored to London
on his return from abroad but with a peripatetic knowledge of southern England, also
expressed the 'healing and renewing' power of short breaks in the countryside. He thought
those who enabled him to take short breaks in the country were more than friends, they were
life-givers. Nothing was sweeter in London than the leaving of it, and the 'grassy silence',
a temporary interruption to his life which fell on his ears like a blow, was a therapeutic
shock. He wondered why anyone not under compulsion or supposed necessity would go
on living in London.

Plomer recalled his weekend visits to Sussex gardens such as West Dean ('more like
a secret entry into Nepal than a garden'), and Stern's Chalk Garden at Worthing. At
short stays with the Woolfs at Rodmell, the fig trees in late summer were 'expansively
southern', and there were 'pear trees weighted in abundance, the zinnias glowing in pure
scarlet, yellow and magenta, a heat haze over the valley of the Ouse at mid-day, an evening
opalescence backed by the silhouette of Mount Caburn in autumn and Virginia Woolf
writing in her workroom in the garden overlooked, rather incongruously, by the tower of
Rodmell Church'.[2]

Gerard Young, who tenanted a country cottage at Flansham near Bognor before the
last war, thought that everyone in towns wanted the chance to live with oil lamps, burn
logs on an open fire, smell honeysuckle on the porch and collect milk from the farm across
the fields. He proudly paraded about the 'estate' on Sunday mornings after arriving on
Saturday nights.[3]

The socialist journalist Robert Blatchford, who moved from Horsham to a farm near Slinfold in 1916, did not share these ideals. He warned 'elderly city-dwellers bent on emigration to England' to find a small town within an hour's travelling distance from London so that they could run up and down to town occasionally just to remind themselves how much they hated it, rather than move into deep clay country with no pump water or drainage, a day's march to the nearest grocer's and enduring boredom in winter.[4]

But his advice went unheeded. Every village within 40 miles of London and the larger towns had weekenders, many middle-class Londoners choosing to spend part of the year in a town house and moving out to a cottage or farmhouse for the rest. Everyone who could afford it left the city for a time in summer and became what the native villagers called 'comers and goers' or 'fly-by-nights'. The old cottages were, in their unobtrusive way, the principal feature of the beauty of the countryside. Now dazzling additions to the scene were provided by Modernist architecture. The Sun House on the borders of Ashdown Forest at Chelwood Gate was designed by Colin and Ralph Lucas as an overflow for weekend guests from a nearby house owned by Ralph's father. Objections by the local authority to the flat roof were eventually overcome by asserting it was needed to give sun baths to London children. Serge Chermayeff successfully won an appeal for a flat roof at his own home at Bentley Wood at Halland, but had to clad the concrete walls in cedar. The box-like house at Woodmancote, built for a Brighton dentist, was designed by Connell, Ward and Lucas.

To the weekending London businessman there was something reassuring about a very old cottage inhabited for many generations by ordinary, unrecorded and unrenowned, country folk, 'whom the city never called'. It gave an immediate sense of retreat, privacy and security. Above all, as Stella Bowen noted of Ford Madox Ford's cottage at Red Ford, it offered 'an escape from money and the money world – that is its message and value'.[5]

To a great extent, these cottages and cottage gardens, perceived by incomers as peculiarly English, had been provided by landlords for their agricultural labourers. The

105 *Ford Madox Ford's cottage at Cooper's, Bedham, near Pulborough.*

well-filled cottage gardens the labourers had made for themselves were furnished with vegetables, flowers, shrubs, fruit trees and bee-hives. In the 1820s Cobbett had noticed in them a neatness without formality. Landowners had built more cottages after the Swing Riots of 1830, endowing them with ample gardens, and it was the simple beauty and grace of cottage gardens, vacated by working people swept up in the rural exodus or made available by the decline in agriculture, that made them so popular with weekenders, writers and artists. Charles Dalmon knew something of the loveliness of the remaining cottage gardens at Washington as a boy:

> Trim gardens full of gillyflowers,
> With peaches at the wall,
> And filberts slipping from their shucks,
> With mulberries on the fall.
>
> And orchards where the boughs hang low
> With juicy Green-gage plums,
> And Blenheim Orange apples, and
> The pears called Bishop's Thumbs.[6]

Here the newcomers found the sense of order and comfort and the neighbourly feelings which they considered missing in the 'blocks' of Bethnal Green and Shoreditch.

In his valedictory poems, *Kettle Songs* (1922), Habberton Lulham retires to his cottage home at the foot of the South Downs and, sitting by the deep hearth of an inglenook in a firelit room, is cheered by the warmth and laughter of good-natured people who gossip light-heartedly about their memories and the little things happening in the village. The book conveyed the quiet persons's idea of the heart-warming peace and security Sussex offered to the retired.

The newcomers, with their cocktails and striped umbrellas, regarded cottages as Kate Greenaway exteriors, beautiful shells to be gutted. In came bottle-glass, antique panes from cathedral shops, copper warming-pans, fake oak furniture, orange chintzes, willow-pattern plates and 'old pewter', straight from the stage-set of Ben Travers' *Rookery Nook* (1926). Flower beds took the place of manure heaps, milking sheds were used for storing apples and garden tools or even a study.

Famous weekending parties hosted by Dick Wyndham at Tickerage Mill near Uckfield were attended by Tom Driberg, Peter Quennell, Stephen Spender, Cyril Connolly and numerous others. The latter thought visits there were the best cure for angst but noted that Wyndham was always fleeing the place as if it were the scene of a crime.[7]

One of the most remarkable of all weekenders was Bertrand Russell, whose unorthodox cottage, Telegraph House on the high Downs above the village of South Harting, had originally been built for the officer in charge of the 'semaphore' service to the Admiralty. Russell bought it for use at weekends and holidays but eventually enlarged it and turned it into his chief residence. Here he lived on and off for 30 years with three successive mistresses. When George Santayana first went there no road existed in the grounds and not a house was in sight around it. At Russell's death his brother ran a 'progressive' school there.

The *Week-end Book* (first number 1924), edited by Vera Mendel and Francis Meynell of the Meynell family of Greatham near Pulborough, aimed to while away weekenders' time with good and bad poetry, puzzles, songs, games, recipes, and quips. It bore on the frontispiece Monro's opening stanza from his poem 'Week-End'.

Books such as J.W. Robertson Scott's *How to Build or Buy a Country Cottage and Fit it Up* became bestsellers. Halsham also wrote *A Handyman's Guide* (1934) for those brought up in the ways of town life who might find themselves 'lost' in their new environment. He explained the responsibilities of the countryman, envisaging the reader as a cottager or owner of a detached house with garden, some out-buildings and a paddock or two, capable of being worked by the owner with the help of a gardener-chauffeur, and a handyman or boy.

This new society both undermined the remains of the old rural communities and at the same time strove to preserve the face of the countryside by writing to *The Times* and joining such organisations as the Society of Sussex Downsmen and the CPRE. The problem was that temporary residents lived in a place but were never really part of it. Locals reckoned they did not belong and would be leaving in a few years without understanding the country. Dr Joad, the leading critic of weekending, remarked that a leading barrister had turned three former cottages occupied by labourers into a large detached house for his wife, children, maids and nurses at weekends or occasional weeks in summer. He considered that they were camping in a thatched house and reckoned they knew nothing of the country, were ignorant of farming and took no interest in it and, although they subscribed to village cricket and football clubs, took no part in the life of the community. They employed quite a number of people living locally, but did not know them except as employees, nor did they know the other 'gentry' who were their neighbours. They did not gossip in the local pub and, although they admired the views and took frequent excursions in their car, did not walk in the surrounding country. 'Their roots and interests were in London; from London come their friends at weekends; from London their drinks, and from London their food. They spent their time playing tennis and playing bridge, motoring, drinking, cocktailing and lying about in bathing dresses in the garden altering the colour of their skins', occupations which, Joad thought, with the possible exception of the last, could be carried on just as well – perhaps better – in London. In fact, he argued, they were not living in the country at all; they were doing rather inconveniently in the country some of the things that people do very much better in the towns.

Joad considered the family representative of weekenders living all over the southern counties.

> In their red-tiled, eight-roomed houses, little family groups pursue the meaningless round of their isolated existence. The group is entirely detached from the community to which it should belong; it knows no spiritual centre in the church, no secular centre in meeting or assembly; it has no roots in the land; it takes no part in local government. It is interested only in itself. It has no concern for the climate and the soil; it hardly notices the change of seasons, except in so far as they entail a change of game. For it the trees go into leaf, the flowers blossom, the birds make nests, the hay is cut and the corn gathered, the mists come and the fruit, the smoke of bonfires rises and the golden glory of autumn is diffused about the land, in vain.[8]

Joad was not the only critic of weekending; Reginald Bray, lord of the manor of Shere in Surrey, enjoyed the intellectual companionship of those that ran down on Saturdays

106 *The Bogardes' cottage at Lullington, a drawing by Dirk Bogarde.*

and he rejoiced at the musical scores, books, journalism and paintings brought by his temporary guests, but he came to realise that the welfare of local people was being prejudiced by weekending in a number of respects. Visitors paid such large sums for country cottages that tenants were forced out and then new facilities were demanded. They also had a different awareness of the environment to local people. For example, the 'blossoming gorse' of the Londoner was a fuel regularly cut and burnt on local brick kilns. Various niggling differences between the rich suburban 'fly-by-nights' and the villagers led to friction and resentment.[9]

COMMUTING

The earliest commuters between Sussex and London used stage or private carriages for their transport and these needed the turnpikes; William Cobbett mentions Brighton members of the Stock Exchange making regular journeys to the capital in the 1820s. But it was the railway network which made commuting possible on a more general scale. After the electrification of the Brighton line and its links along the

107 *A traditional song for weekend parties, a page from the* Week-end Book *(1925).*

west and east coast of Sussex using the third rail system from the 1930s, the Southern Railway encouraged commuting between London and the coast by offering relatively cheap season tickets on the longer routes and improved facilities, with corridors and buffet and restaurant cars.

One of the first recorded commuters to take advantage of railway transport, albeit only the cheaper and most uncomfortable services, was artist John Linnell, a portrait painter in Bayswater who intended to paint landscape *en plein air*. His selection of Balcombe, a remote village in the Sussex Weald about 35 miles from London, may have been due to John Thorne's *Guide to Walkers in Sussex* (1844), which prescribed a walk from Balcombe Station in the introduction and extolled the beauties of trees and rocks, Linnell's principal interest as a newly fledged landscape painter. Extracts from his Diary for 1848 include:

July
13   To Reigate and Three Bridges. Thence by one-horse cab to Balcombe where I hired lodgings at Kennys Cottage.
22   At the Rock at Chillingly [Chiddingly] with Mary [his daughter], and Thomas in cart (Mr Marchant's, the Baker's). To Bayswater by the 7 o'clock. Lizzy [his wife] weak and ill.
23   Returned to Balcombe by 6 o'clock train in the evening.
24   Returned to Bayswater with Mrs Linnell and Elizabeth. Returned to Balcombe with the same persons by the 6 o'clock.
29   To Balcombe and returned to London by Third Class train.

August
5   To Balcombe with Hannah [his daughter, wife of Samuel Palmer] and their son Thomas More Palmer. Thence to Brighton, returning to Balcombe in the evening.
8   To Ardingly in van with all the family at Balcombe [presumably to sketch the rocks].
9   To Bayswater by early train.
12   John returned to Balcombe.
15   To Balcombe again by 6 o'clock evening train from London.
16   Made drawing in pen and ink of trees at Balcombe.
30   To Balcombe.
31   To Horsham.

September
1   To Uckfield, applied at the house of Streetfield Esq., and obtained a card of admission to walk over the grounds to see the rocks.
2   To Bayswater with Hannah and son.
7   To Balcombe by evening train.
8   To Penn's Rocks with William Marchant's cart.
9   Study of trees under shade at Balcombe.
11   To Penn's Rocks and with another horse to Harrison's Rocks.
16   To London. Returned to Balcombe in the evening. Sketching from nature to the end of the month.

October
2   To London. Third Class morning train. Returned in the evening. Studies from nature at Balcombe until the 8th.

    9   To town by Parliamentary train in evening.
10   To Balcombe, studies from nature 11-17 October.
19   To Balcombe.
23   Returned home with the children in the evening by Parliamentary. Cab from London Bridge to Bayswater.[10]

This double life in both London and the Sussex countryside placed Linnell among the first artists to turn the Weald into commuter country, thereby reversing the townward drift to the cities. His portrait painting in Bayswater ceased in 1847. Redstone at Redhill was bought in 1850 and more than thirty forceful years in landscape painting were ahead of him.

Commuting often led to a change in a person's personality between leaving a countryside railway station in the morning and arriving in the city. It was noted of Cyril Connolly, who paid a peppercorn rent on a farmhouse in Firle before moving to Eastbourne, that his was a nicely balanced double life. He shuttled between Sussex and London, changing his persona *en route* from the quiet family man with a young son to the adventurous man-of-the-world as he approached Victoria Station. Angst overtook him as the train passed under the North Downs.[11]

Chapter 17

SPORT

HUNTING

Sussex has always been a hunting and shooting county. The aristocracy and gentry were invariably keen sportsmen and so, usually, was the farmer, while the farm labourer was an inveterate poacher. Originally the main quarry was deer and wild boar, and medieval deer parks saved many a tree from the forester's axe. Mighty oaks abound in deer parks such as Old Eridge, recorded in Domesday Book, Sheffield Park, one of the best survivals, and Knepp.

From the 18th century Sussex became one of the fashionable fox-hunting counties of southern England and the aristocracy, squirearchy and *nouveaux riches*, and it was said that generations of hunting families opened first in the morning any letter from their huntsman. Still in favour up to the late 18th century was the old type of foxhound which had disappeared earlier from most parts of England. It was heavily built and adapted to the heavy soil of the Wealden woodland. Eventually, as horses galloped faster, the modern type of hound was introduced from Midland Hunts to keep up with them.

A letter from the 2nd Duke of Richmond to the Prime Minister, the Duke of Newcastle, dated 1738, vividly conveys the writer's passion for hunting and his commitment to the famous Charlton Hunt (the spelling has been modernised):

> On Wednesday I received the favour of your Grace's letter and I do assure you that if I could be of the least service to you I would attend you with pleasure. You know very well that before long I must go to London where besides duty I have some business and I hope to contrive to do them at the same time the week after next and to be back again in about a fortnight, when I shall certainly quit my hounds no more till a week before the meeting of the Parliament, when I certainly will attend you at the Cockpit and help make the speech at the time, tho' I had little or no hand in the last. The weather is now so fine, the hounds in such order, and such plenty of foxes, that I really can spare no time from my sport but what necessity obliges me to.

The Duke went on to invite the Duke of Newcastle to stay at his hunting lodge at Charlton (now let to the Landmark Trust).[1]

In Singleton church is a memorial eulogising Thomas Johnson, the 18th-century huntsman of the Charlton Hunt who was said to have no equal. It was erected by a handful of aristocrats 'in memory of a good and faithful servant, as a reward to the deceased, and as incitement to the living. Go, and do thou likewise.' (St Luke, 10:37)

Here Johnson lies. What human can deny
Old honest Tom the tribute of a sigh?
Deaf's the ear which caught the opening sound:
Dumb the tongue which sheer'd the hills around;
Unpleasing truth; Death hunts us from our birth
In view, and men, like foxes, take to earth.

One of the great huntsmen and horse trainers a hundred years ago was J.P. Hornung of West Grinstead Park. Despite his great girth he rode to hounds 'like a thrusting cavalry officer and every moment of a fast hunt to him was bliss'. His daughters exercised the heavyweight hunters and were severely drilled by him in matters of turn-out and behaviour.[2]

One of the first questions asked of a locality by *nouveaux riches* inspecting the site of a country house was 'What about the hunting?' Sales Catalogues from the 1870s to 1939 invariably mention the numerous meets in the district, including Lord Leconfield of Petworth, the Crawley and Horsham, the Burstow, the Eridge, the Southdowns, the Warnham Stag Hounds, the Brighton Harriers and several others. Good hunting facilities attracted new country house owners and, as farming became less profitable, woods, hedgerows, coverts and shaws were managed principally for sporting purposes and allowed to extend outwards at the expense of fields, so that the Sussex Weald acquired an even more park-like character than formerly.

108   *Former kennels of the Goodwood Hunt, Goodwood House, recently demolished to upgrade golf facilities.*

109 *Fox Hall, Charlton, now a Landmark Trust property, was formerly the base of the Charlton Hunt. Drawing by Michael Fleetwood.*

SHOOTING

The invention of the breach-loader from the 1860s led to social shooting, as we know it today. Earlier the partridge had been king, then the hand-reared pheasant by the thousand, cossetted and guarded day and night, became the main quarry of luxurious country house parties. Before the breach-loader a spaniel would have pushed up a solitary bird for a simple 'poking' shot. Now pheasants were flushed up high over grouped batteries, twenty or more at a time, and a Labrador dog raced to collect the fallen.

One of the shooting celebrities was Wilfrid Scawen Blunt of Newbuildings, Shipley and Crabbet Park, near Crawley. Desmond McCarthy has described how in old age he would swing slowly into the saddle of a white Arab mare, looking like Count Tolstoy only more handsome and worldly. McCarthy walked at one stirrup with his gun, while a man-servant carrying a light bamboo chair over his arm, the keeper and a few beaters follow behind. At the cover the chair would be placed at one spot and McCarthy was stationed at another. 'With a startled hiccup, a snapping of twigs, and whirring of wings, a pheasant would presently fly out followed by another and another … it was ten to one my host from his armchair brought them down.'[3]

165

A.E. Knox was a great sportsman in the 1840s and tells of the relentless attack on predators of game:

> 23 June 1842. Denyer has just come up the house, to tell me that during the last two days he has missed several of the young pheasants. He went at daybreak this morning to the coops, in the neighbourhood of which he lay concealed. Soon afterwards a loud screaming and cackling among the hens announced the arrival of an enemy, and by the time D. has emerged from his hut of oak boughs, gun in hand, he had the mortification of seeing a hawk, out of shot, carrying off one of the young pheasants in its claws. I have no doubt that the thief is a sparrow-hawk, and that unless we can extirpate the family we shall lose several of our tame birds.
>
> 26 June. Returned home yesterday evening; and the first object that met my eyes on driving up to the hall door was a row of dead sparrow-hawks, seven in number, which D. had impaled, each upon its own peculiar stick, with its wings spread and tail expanded, as if to make the most of it. It was not long before Denyer made his appearance with a game-bag in his hand. [After killing the parent birds and five young nestlings] he then proceeded to empty the nest, and could hardly trust his eyes at the sight – here he shook out upon the grass for my inspection the contents of the bag – there were fifteen young pheasants, four large partridges, five chickens, a bullfinch, two meadow pipits and two larks, all in a fresh state.[4]

From the 1870s 'sporting estates' multiplied in the Sussex Weald and woodland became more valuable as a game preserve for deer and pheasants than for traditional timber or

110   *Drawing by Michael Fleetwood of an interior at Fox Hall, Charlton.*

coppice wood. Most estates stocked coverts for rural sports for London businessmen. Game habitats were well managed and new woods were planted, along with hedgerows for foxes and game birds, and much of this is still evident on the face of the landscape. In the past hundred years or so the county has been shaped by sporting pursuits as much as by axe and plough. Trout fisheries were also expanded, in the Ouse catchment for example.

Shooting increased as small properties were turned from commercially run properties into 'pleasure farms'. Until the declaration of war in 1939 innumerable properties in the Sussex High Weald were advertised as excellent shooting boxes where pheasants were reared, examples including Nettlesworth Farm in Heathfield, Wivelsfield Hall near Haywards Heath, Buxhalls in Ardingly, the Buchan Hill Estate near Horsham, the Whyly Estate in Framfield and East Hoathly and at Herstmonceux and Warbleton.[5]

CRICKET

Sussex, with Surrey and Kent, can claim to be the cradle of cricket. The game was being played on village greens and at country houses in the early 17th century, mainly in the triangle between Arundel, Midhurst and Chichester, which had the space and the ideal surface of springy turf. Here, too, were aristocratic patrons of the game such as the 2nd Duke of Richmond, whose Slindon team was notable enough to play London teams on the Artillery Grounds in the mid-18th century. It was this game, eventually adopted all over England, that led historian G.M. Trevelyan to argue that if only French milords had done the same the Revolution would never have happened.

A true cricketer, perhaps, is one who loves village cricket but whose form is worthy of 'good' cricket on the county ground. Edmund Blunden was one such person. His best memories were of the informal village game, the village blacksmith striding out from his shop to the wicket in braces, working clothes and leathern apron to bat with the squire's younger son in whites. The sturdy smith moistened his hands with spit and got his bat ready for huge blows at any ball in reach, but Blunden could not remember whether his hammering was as successful here as in the glow of his fire.[6]

Cricket-loving parson Charles Townsend, who held livings at Preston (Brighton) and Kingston Buci (Shoreham), preferred village cricket to the 'too scientific' game at the Marylebone ground, as far back as the 1830s. An account of one such game comes from H.B. Morton ('Beachcomber'), who played in a match at Rodmell in 1922 against Sir John Squire's team, which came down from London annually:

> So many people came and went during the day that it was difficult to know who was playing in the match and who was not. It was light-hearted cricket of the best kind. The match was played in a field with a magnificent view over the Brooks, with Caburn dominating the Vale of Glynde … The village inn did a roaring trade on these occasions, and you could never be sure that there were eleven people fielding, or that the next man in would not have to be hastily summoned from the inn. The central point of the match was the lunch which Allison [in the newspaper world] gave in one of his great barns, and one did not need to be fond of cricket to try to get into one team or the other, and if that failed, to slip in as a hanger-on … After the match the merriment used to go on far into the night, and on one occasion there was a complaint made by a very respectable spinster that she had found dozens of empty bottles on her doorstep.[7]

(Morton said that one of these Rodmell matches was used by MacDonell in his classic account in *England Their England*.)

S.P.B. Mais, broadcaster, writer and rambler, also relished village cricket. In his account of a match in a cricket week he organised on Southwick Green, an event still held on the same ground, he says:

> When the Civil Service began, they began well. They put on 150 for no wicket before lunch, a cold collation taken at the *Cricketers' Arms*; where I performed the double function of saying grace and supplying the first round of drinks … The village was in the end soundly beaten, the Civil Service declaring at 293 for 7 and getting us out for 6.
>
> The cricket was lively, and the crowd of motorists, old men on the benches, young men on the rails, girls in deck-chairs, errand boys on bikes, and children sprawling all over the grass showed, partly by their numbers and partly by the two guineas they put into the collecting box, their appreciation of the play.[8]

Information on village cricket can reveal much about the villages themselves. Describing cricket at Storrington, Hugh de Selincourt's *Tillingfold* (1924) noted the atmosphere of peacefulness 'in which unkindness and discontent would appear impossible … no wonder bungalows are springing up on all sides'. The village was prosperous, with two general stores, a London emporium, three butchers, four bakers, three cobblers, a barber, three builders, a bank, a dissenting chapel, two cycle shops, three tea-shops, a garage and seven public houses.

The 3rd Lord Sheffield (1832-1909) made a great contribution to Sussex cricket. His ground, acclaimed as one of the finest, hosted matches from 1846, including first-class games between 1881 and 1906 which included Australian teams. In 1891-2 he took an English team captained by Dr W.G. Grace at his own expense to Australia and his donation in appreciation of the host's hospitality inaugurated the Sheffield Shield, still played for by Australian State teams. The cricket pitch at Sheffield Park which once hosted the Australian side, now owned by the National Trust, was restored and England internationals and Australians played a match in 2009 to celebrate Lord Sheffield's contribution to cricket and to commemorate his death 100 years earlier. It was partly due to the patronage of the game by Sussex estate owners that the County Cricket Club is the oldest in England, having been founded in 1839.[9]

Chapter 18

WALKING FOR PLEASURE

> Give me the clear blue sky over my head, and the green turf beneath my feet, a winding road before me, and a three hours' march to dinner – and then to thinking!
>
> William Hazlitt, 'On Going a Journey', 1822.

For centuries walking was looked upon as demeaning. Being astride a noble, well-groomed horse was the sign of a gentleman, and as late as the 1950s an army officer in Kenya asked to be excused from foot patrol because his family had never walked. When walking for pleasure came in with the Romantic movement, William Cobbett scorned it as one of the absurdities of the age, and since then Bernard Shaw and Max Beerbohm have memorably dissociated themselves from it, though with tongues in cheek.

The first walkers in the South Downs appear to have been those too frightened to ride their chaises up or down the steep hills. Walking on the Downs in the late 18th century was done not for the sake of walking, but to improve digestion after gourmandising in Brighton. The first genuine country walker in Sussex was naturalist the Rev. James Hurdis, curate of Burwash and subsequently vicar of Bishopstone, whose poems *The Village Curate* (1788) and *The Favourite Village* (1800) show how familiar country walks made him with places in all seasons and weathers, and not just on roads but on footpaths across fields. Very few followed his example. Mrs Merrifield in her *Sketch of the Natural History of Brighton* (1860) noted that:

> Travelled by few is the grass-covered road
> Where the hunter of deer and the warrior strode,

and added that when she was gathering downland plants 'here and there a wandering pedestrian might be met', although groups of equestrian ladies under a riding master more frequently passed by.[1]

A landmark in country walking in the Downs was the publication of Louis J. Jennings' *Field Paths and Green Lanes* (1877). This was the first book written for ramblers on the South Downs and thus, as E.V. Lucas remarked, can be regarded as that which brought the first tidings of the Promised Land of Sussex. Walkers at that time were mainly road men, not pathfinders, maps not showing most bridlepaths and footpaths, and Jennings gave detailed directions to them in the belief that for jaded persons

> there are few things better worth living for than the pleasure of starting out on foot, in fair health, and with no particular anxiety pressing upon the mind, for a long day amid all the beauties which Nature spreads before her true lovers by every hedgerow, brook and hill-side in England.

Jennings was a native of Norfolk and a New York editor, but wrote the preface of his next book, *Rambles in Southern Hills*, from Kingston manor near Lewes, where he then lived, anecdotally telling of downland villages with no accommodation, squalid inns with only frugal food if any, natives as suspicious of strangers as Shakespeare's rustics, and snobbery and suspicion among well-to-do people towards walkers, whom they mistook for vagrants.

Clearly Jennings was a pioneer in country walking for, despite the 'irresistible call of the open road' described by writers such as Stevenson, Borrow and Walt Whitman, he could walk for miles without seeing a single human being (except, perhaps, artists), and the only other walkers he mentions are tramps and travellers. Walking for pleasure began in the era of stage coaches but until the dense pattern of railroads was built it was impractical for any but the wealthiest to travel to Arundel, Brighton, Lewes or Eastbourne to walk on the Downs and return home on the same day. The Brighton railway brought wayfarers in less than an hour to Balcombe Forest, and only a little further on the green Downs rolled down to the sea where Londoners already came for sea air. Within three years of the opening of the railway Thorne had published a guide to walks starting at Balcombe railway station.[2] By travelling down with one railway company and returning with another it was possible to undertake a round journey of some ten or twenty miles on the same day, and for this only a well-perused Bradshaw was required.

'Muscular agnostics' among the Victorian and Edwardian intelligentsia were simultaneously taking up long-distance walking but their passion did not filter downwards socially until after the First World War. E.V. Lucas, in *Highways and Byways in Sussex* (1904), wrote that few South Saxons were aware of the Downs. As late as 1909 Arthur

SOUTHERN
RAMBLES
FOR LONDONERS
by
S.P.B. MAIS

Published by the Southern Railway
PRICE SIXPENCE

Stanley Cooke, in *Songs of the Sussex Downs*, remarked that to the majority of visitors the Downs were unknown, and his *Off the Beaten Track in Sussex* (1910) laments this fact. Among the few who did walk were Richard Jefferies, before he became ill, and the inspirational Hilaire Belloc, who should be nominated the Prince of Sussex Walkers, not only for his pioneering walk in four to five days along the South Downs Way in 1897 and his other great walks in Sussex, but for his introduction to *The Footpath Way* anthology (1911) and, above all, *The Four Men* (1912), which although unclassifiable might be validly indexed under walking literature. Sidgwick in *Walking Essays* wrote that Belloc 'not only records walks, but writes in the true walking mood, with plenty of irrelevancy, plenty of dogmatism, and thorough conviction on the matter of eating and drinking'. His books must surely have increased the vogue for walking, for few men of his persuasion could have resisted his inspired call to see Sussex in the open air.[3]

111 *Book for ramblers by S.P.B. Mais, 1930s.*

112 Punch *cartoon of ramblers on Beachy Head, 1930s.*

THE AGE OF WALKING

Country walking reached its peak as a national pastime during the inter-war years, boosted by the advent of broadcasting and such newspapers as the *Daily Herald*, which advertised walking in the countryside as never before. It was mainly the preserve of the new lower middle classes, though Oxbridge students also took to long-distance walking for exercise and meditation. The passion was helped by the establishment of youth hostels from the mid-1930s and by the advent of hikers, a new breed in English life which had been inspired by the organised walking of the *Wandervögeln* in Germany. They were mostly shopmen, clerks and secretaries seeking respite from industrialisation in the peace and beauty of the country. These young people liked the comradeship and adventure inherent in hiking and believed in the Simple Life; to them the health of the mind was connected with the health of the body and a close connection with Nature. They pledged to respect the property and privacy of country people, not to disturb game or stock, not to leave gates open, not to light fires where damage may be done, and never to leave litter about or disturb the quiet and peace of rural life with noisy vulgarity. They tended to have an international outlook, as lovers of peace, although some university undergraduates, as David Fowler has noted, displayed Nazi sympathies in their quest for the regeneration of rural civilisation. In 1926 Virginia Woolf cringed at the sight of assertive women, clerks or secretaries, in jerseys and short skirts with rucksacks on their backs.[4]

That doyen of Sussex walkers, Southwick writer and broadcaster S.P.B. Mais, wrote of walking as 'the healthiest and cheapest exercise and one of the purest of human pleasures', the best remedy for the cares and ills arising from life in towns. His organised walks into the countryside for people in London were intended to offer them a complete change from ordinary life and help regain the senses of sight and smell dulled by traffic. He was strongly influenced by keen walkers such as Sir George Trevelyan, a foremost historian of his day and devotee of George Meredith, a poet and novelist who was also passionate about walking. The former wrote, 'Whether we like it or not, we are children of the earth, and removed from her our spirits wither and run in various forms of insanity.' Mais crusaded on behalf of the healing powers of nature and thought his organised walks were the nearest to

113   *Police assisting ramblers, 1930s.*

heaven the participants would get; without them they would be reduced to walking down the Camberwell or Wandsworth Road.[5]

Solitary walking in the afternoon for its own sake, whether in London streets or on the Downs, had an indispensable role in Virginia Woolf's writing. Walking, together with the exhilaration inspired by the freedom and beauty of the Downs, quickened her thinking. She would compose sentences, collect thoughts and toss ideas about for her present and future writings, catching them 'hot and sudden' as they rose in her mind walking up Asheham Hill, or over to Telscombe, for instance. (It had also been her father's favourite exercise and mental stimulation.) The delicious sense of freedom 'whirled her like a top miles upon miles over the downs', and she would recite sentences and phrases to herself as she walked so as to reinforce them in her memory before putting them in her Diary on return. Dirk Bogarde heard about this habit when he met her in boyhood while fishing on the banks of the River Cuckmere. On enquiring of a local friend he was told, 'She is of the London sort and a bit doo-lally.' Rebecca Solnit has remarked that thoughts gathered while walking tend to be associative and digressive, and this is evident in *Mrs Dalloway*, where the jumble of thoughts and recollections of the protagonist unfold best during her walks.[6]

The experience of country walking also quickened the thinking of Ernest Raymond, the novelist. He fell in love so much with Newtimber Lane, one of the lanes he rambled along at the foot of the Downs near Poynings, that its name was adopted as the title of one of his works. Repeated walks across country in mid-Sussex was Halsham's way of detaching himself from society and drawing on nature, and both Habberton Lulham and Richard Jefferies, solitary walkers to the core, worked themselves into a mood of exultation through this activity.

114   *Ramblers and motorists, 1930s.*

Railways continued to convey large numbers of ramblers into the country, and Mais wrote publicity matter for them as well as booklets with weekend rambles, but the motor omnibus became a keen rival and by the 1930s was the most popular way of starting and finishing a walk. Gerard Young's parents took their children by bus from Worthing into the Downs, and Arthur Beckett's close colleague, R. Thurston Hopkins, a manager of the Southdown Bus Company and an entertaining and knowledgeable writer on the Downs, appears to have travelled all over the Downs by bus using his bus pass. He assumed his readers would do the same. Hopkins, described as 'one of Sussex's most faithful, dutiful and grateful adopted sons', repaid his debt to the county by founding the Society of Sussex Downsmen (now the South Downs Society) to protect the South Downs in 1923 and, with his son Thurston junior and friend Cecil Palmer, walked all over Sussex preparing his *Lure of Sussex* (1928), a pocket-book of walks designed to get people onto field paths which he feared would otherwise be closed to the public or built over. In several other books he promoted the cause of rambling in the county.[7]

Mais's notable account of an excursion to Hassocks illustrates the deprivation some Londoners suffered as a result of loss of countryside nearer their homes. On a cold grey morning a special train drew out of Victoria station carrying hundreds of ramblers with haversacks containing mackintoshes, maps, sandwiches, a change of socks, and perhaps a book of poems or a pack of cards. At 10.59 the train pulled into Hassocks station and eight groups, each with a leader, set off in different directions onto the Downs. As they climb:

> Everybody stops to breathe in the pure air coming up from the sea, to gaze over the scores of miles of open country, to stretch their arms as symbol of the scene of perfect freedom in a scene of pure loveliness.
> It is difficult not to give vent in some way to the ecstasy that suffuses us.
> Hazlitt used to leap and sing. Some of our number lie down and hug the sun-warmed mossy earth for sheer joy ... We wonder, as we wander along in this warm, bracing air, over these pleasant ridges, how we can ever bring ourselves to go back to the cramped greyness of the towns. This is so obviously the right life to live, unhurried, slow, deliberate, with time to absorb beauty, and beauty at every turn waiting to be absorbed.[8]

Also notable was his abortive night-time walk to Chanctonbury Ring to see the sunrise. A pink railway leaflet advertised the walk and Mais met four special trains from London at Steyning station near midnight carrying more walkers than he had expected. The moon had sunk below the horizon before their arrival and it began to rain. At 4 a.m. Mais was asked to explain the absence of the sun.[9] Gosse takes up the tale:

> I am told it was extremely cold up there. I was in bed at the time. To cut a long and sad story short, the sun never rose at all, or if it did it rose so modestly and coyly behind heavy clouds as to be undiscerned, so that the promise made by Mr Mais and the Southern Railway that the ramblers would 'experience the novel thrill of watching a Summer Dawn from the first streaks to the full sunrise' was not fulfilled.
> Few, if any, took advantage of a kindly offer of a further lounge or ramble, and there was a hurried rush to catch the 7.30 a.m. breakfast train home. But many of the ramblers lost their way and missed the train, and the approaches to Steyning station were blocked with shivering sun-worshippers sheltering from the rain.[10]

Yet walking for pleasure, as we have seen, has never been universally popular. Graham Greene illustrates the resistance to country walking in his 'masterpiece of horror', *Brighton Rock*. Pinkie Brown of slummy Nelson Place just off the Steine is a precocious juvenile delinquent who murdered two people and married Rosie to prevent her testifying against him:

'Where'll we go, Pinkie?'

'Somewhere,' Pinkie said, 'out in the country. That's where you go on a day like this.' He tried to think for a moment of where the country was; the racecourse was country; and then a bus came marked 'Peacehaven' and he waved his hand to it. 'There you are,' he said, 'that's the country. We can talk there. There's things we got to get straight.'

'I thought we were going to walk.'

'This is walking,' he said, roughly pushing her up the steps. 'You're green. You don't know a thing. You don't think people really *walk*. Why – its miles. When people say "Come for a walk," they mean a bus or car.'[11]

Brisk exercise in fresh, salty air had been one of the elements in the health cure of Regency Brighton. Among the forerunners of modern ramblers is Arthur Beckett, whose opening chapter in *The Spirit of the Downs* (1909) talks of striding along the crest of the Downs near Eastbourne in seven league boots, 'lungs labouring like small bellows, eyes smarting with brine in a south-westerly gale, blissful to be alive'.[12] He (and naturalist W.H. Hudson) yearned for wings 'that they might skim along the lean sides of the grey-green downs and float over their backs'.[13]

At the end of the 19th century R. Thurston Hopkins conveyed the sense of release from urban life that the Downs brought: 'I feel that for months I had been in a dungeon and that I have suddenly been given my liberty … My dominant feeling … is a new companionship, a glow in the heart, as though the Downs and hanging woods of the hills had suddenly embraced and succoured me.'[14]

One of the Downs' most appealing qualities was the close greensward of old chalk grassland. Before 1939 this covered between a third and a half of the Downs, but is now one of the rarest habitats in Europe, accounting for only about three to four per cent in scattered parcels, almost worthless for wildlife purposes. This turf, singled out for praise as early as 1691 by the botanist John Ray, is a multitude of miniature clovers,

115 *Edward Thomas, whose walking inspired his* South Country *(1909).*

116 *Horseshoe Vetch on the Mill Hill Nature Reserve, Shoreham, 1995.*

flowers and creeping herbs, like aromatic thyme, marjoram and horseshoe vetch, and is a consequence of age-long nibbling by sheep and rabbits.

The spring of the step on the turf made it feel like a soft carpet, like standing on India rubber. Everyone, every living creature, was fleeter of foot. Ramblers strode or leapt for joy; cyclists had the sensation of flying through the air; horses seemed to grow wings, and hounds, foxes and hares ran faster here than anywhere else. The turf was superb to play cricket on. In 1900 this physical feature of the Downs was recognised as quintessentially English by Lord Avebury, in his *The Scenery of England* (1902): It is said that when the older generation of walkers stepped on a thick Persian carpet the remembrance of the soft springy turf with its miniature flora suddenly flashed upon them.

Another of the joys of walking on the Downs was the relentless wind. Arthur Beckett, that early enthusiast for downland walking who ran a mile on the springy turf in sheer delight, knew nothing more stimulating than a walk on the Downs when a brisk breeze was blowing. 'Go there on an autumn day, when the clouds are racing across the sky, and run with them. Throw off your starched dignity, put your cap in your pocket and bound across the brow of the hill and down the declivity to the next.'[15] Wind on the Downs was ecstatically received by poet John Davidson, who was recuperating at Shoreham:

> It sings its own triumph; and laughs like a conqueror … The wind was east by north-west, exceedingly fresh and virile, round, bold and splendid. Everything bowed to it, made way before it … The stark hedges ruffled it bravely, as the wind went by; the grass-green budding crops, soft like down, rippled at its feet. Over the shires from the Atlantic, it trampled with the rush of a charging host across Erringham Valley, took Thundersbarrow Hill at a leap, and reached the North Sea through Sussex and Kent.[16]

Maurice Hewlett sang in his exultation while walking against the wind on the Downs:

> My heart leapt to meet the wind, and I ran, and I ran. I felt my legs under me, I felt the wind buffet me, hit me on the cheek; the sun shone, the bees swept past me singing; and I too sang, shouted, World, World, I am coming![17]

Richard Jefferies was acutely conscious of wind; in his ill-health it freshened and invigorated him. On climbing towards Ditchling Beacon he noted how every step exposed him to the force of the unchecked wind:

> The harebells wing before it, the bonnets whistle, but the sward springs to the foot, and the heart grows lighter as the height increases. The ancient hill is alone with the wind … Standing presently at the edge of the steep descent looking into the Weald, it seems as if the mighty blast rising from that vast plain and glancing up the slope like an arrow from a tree could lift me up and bear me as it bears a hawk with outspread wings.[18]

Another who walked the Downs with the wind bellowing in each ear and swirling him round in a mighty sea of air which he called a 'cleansing countryside' was Barbellion (Bruce Cummings), who in his state of bad health felt blown clean and resonant as a sea-shell, and he was so healed and refreshed as to be free and transparent as a disembodied spirit.[19] George Gissing was also filled with gladness when the breeze on Beachy Head freshened his forehead. On the short, soft turf he felt capable of walking with an unwearying lightness and rejoiced in his love of England.[20]

The windy season of the year was the most inspiring for Hilaire Belloc. It was in October, when glorious days of wind, rain and sun brought great clouds over the Downs, loud noises were in the high woods with the beeches moaning and clouds of leaves being stirred up by the foot, and waves were leaping on the surf, that he could feel intoxicated by Sussex. He had the same joy of life as did dancing wild ponies, and one feels the wind blowing from the hills in all his writing about Sussex, testimony to the curative properties of the superb landscape.[21]

Chapter 19

THE DITCHLING
ARTS AND CRAFTS COMMUNITY

Ditchling's journey from rather obscure agricultural village dominated by Ditchling Beacon, highest point in East Sussex, to rival to St Ives in Cornwall as leading centre of the Arts and Crafts movement in England is one of the most remarkable Sussex developments. The experimental land reforms carried out at the Ditchling colony give it further significance. The background to these events was the growing disillusion towards the end of the 19th century with mass-production and urbanisation. Some abandoned the city for the country, rejecting the factory system and taking cottage life, rural handicrafts and the ordered regularity of the country workshop as ideals, together with all the charms of the countryside.

The two craftsmen colonies established at Ditchling and on Ditchling Common were the first and the most significant of those established in Sussex. The founders were four men who had been drawn to William Morris at Hammersmith, where he had lived at Kelmscott House on the Mall until his death in 1896. Eric Gill, letter-cutter, sculptor, wood-engraver and typographer, arrived in 1907, temporarily ending his restless search for an ideal environment in which to live and work, and took on assistant Joseph Cribb a year later. In Gill's *Autobiography* he wrote nostalgically of the Downs when he first knew them, in boyhood:

> If you have been a little child and brought up in those hills and in those days you will understand their moral loveliness … but not otherwise. No one who was not there as a child can know that heaven, no grown-up can capture it.[1]

Following in Gill's wake in 1912 was Edward Johnston, the calligrapher and foremost letter-designer of his day. He regarded the rural way of life as the embodiment of Morris's ideals, and his presence at Ditchling was the reason for the arrival of Douglas (Hilary) Pepler, the third to arrive from Hammersmith in 1918. Pepler took up hand-printing and was influential, although later controversial, in the community until his death in 1951. Mural artist Frank Brangwyn, who had worked for William Morris at Hammersmith as a young man and was thought of as the grand master of the Arts and Crafts movement, also came in 1918 and, although reclusive, was to contribute to the reputation of the village as an artist-craftsman's colony. Printer Gerard Meynell of the Westminster Press and his wife Esther, a prominent writer on Sussex, also came to live in Ditchling from Hammersmith, and Habberton Lulham, the most distinguished downland poet, arrived about the same time as Gill, drawn by his beloved boyhood home at nearby Abbotsford, Burgess Hill.

117 *Eric Gill.*

Other arrivals included Lawrie Cribb, Joseph Cribb's brother, and the painter Louis Ginnett.

The Guild of St Joseph and St Dominic was a group of Catholic craftsmen set up by Gill and Pepler in 1921 with the assistance of Father McNabb, whom many members regarded as a saint. The community began to grow in earnest during the early 1920s, its ethos set by Eric Gill's absolute insistence on the Catholic faith not only in personal lives but also in workmanship and on individual responsibility for all aspects of a craftsman's work, which involved the principle of ownership.

In 1913 Gill with Douglas Pepler adopted an extreme version of the Distributist ideals of Belloc and Chesterton. He wrote:

> A Catholic family bought a house and two acres of land at the south end of Ditchling Common. Their object was to own home and land to produce for their own consumption such food as could be produced at home, e.g. milk, butter, pigs, poultry and eggs, and to make such things as could be made at home, e.g. bread, clothes, etc.[2]

118 *Ditchling village, 1920s.*

119 *Joseph Cribb, Eric Gill's first disciple at Ditchling.*

120 *'On Ditchling Beacon', drawing by the potter Bernard Leach in 1936 on the occasion of his visit to the Guild of St Joseph and St Dominic.*

After Gill had settled on Ditchling Common his Catholic protégés began to arrive, including Desmond Chute, painter-poet David Jones, artist Philip Hagreen, loom-builder George Maxwell, weaver Valentine Kilbride, Ethel Mairet's assistant, who made fine vestments, and silversmith Dunstan Pruden (from Hammersmith), who achieved international fame for his croziers and chalices. The last to join the Guild, in 1949, was etcher and graphic designer Edgar Holloway, who had married Gill's model Daisy Hawkins. C.R. Ashbee, a key figure in the Arts and Crafts movement, visited Ditchling in 1923, and Bernard Leach, the celebrated potter, visited on several occasions and founded a link between Ditchling craftsmen and organisations in Japan inspired by the Ditchling model. In the 1930s the watercolorist Charles Knight came, drawing inspiration from Cotman and Arthur Hammond. Gill left the village for the Common in 1913 and left that in 1924, when he trailed his family, cats, ducks, geese and goats to Capel-y-ffin in the Black Mountains.

The Guild was a unique religious experiment in British artistic life, an attempt to create a Catholic fraternity in the countryside sustained by handicrafts, as Morris's federated community in utopian romance *News from Nowhere* (1890) had been. The chief architect of the community was Father Vincent McNabb, who propounded the teaching of St Thomas Aquinas with galvanic energy. These doctrines, together with Belloc and Chesterton's idealistic land-sharing proposals (Distributism), were the basis of the Guild's philosophy between 1917 and the late 1920s. A simple chapel and incomplete quadrangle of workshops on the Common was its focus and a Calvary was erected. In 1989 the Guild was finally wound up and all the buildings have recently been demolished.

The life of the community has been substantially recorded:

> Hilary Pepler ran the St Dominic's Press from one of the Guild workshops on the Common. This was in an old army hut one side of the Guild's courtyard, dismantled at Southwick Green and resited after the First World War. On the opposite side of the courtyard was a brick building housing Valentine Kilbride's weaving shed and Dunstan Pruden's silver-smithy. On the east side was Joseph Cribb's stone-mason's premises, higher to allow for lifting tackle, a little affair at the end. Stone lay in a heap at the rear. In a nearby shed lay several old weaving looms and part of a potter's wheel, plus skeins of wool. Joseph Cribb was carrying on the Eric Gill tradition in stone carving, and Valentine Kilbride and Bernard Brocklehurst were weaving cloth by hand on their looms. Among other things, they made cloth for suitings, and for Fr. McNabb's habits, and as a sideline hair-shirts for the Carthusian monks at Parkminster, near Horsham. But they began to specialise in the weaving of silk for vestment making, which was later to be their chief activity. In the carpenters' shop George Maxwell and his assistants made domestic and church furniture. He had built his own house and the Press workshop, and two or three houses that were owned by the Guild. His buildings were remarkably good for a man who had not been trained as a builder. His houses were well designed, but they had one defect; the windows

121 *Edward Johnston, portrait by Arthur Henry Knight-Hammond, painted at Cleves, Ditchling, 1937.*

were seldom completely waterproof against the heavy rains which the winter winds drove across Ditchling Common. He was a simple soul, albeit a highly intelligent one, the philosopher of the group. He was a real student and thinker, and knew a good deal about the thought of St Thomas Aquinas and other philosophers both ancient and modern. He held rigidly to the stricter school of Distribution, and thought that even Belloc and Chesterton were not quite orthodox on certain points.

Eric Gill, a controversial figure owing to the circumstances of his departure from Ditchling, had fallen out of favour with the group to some extent. When it became known that Gill had a motor car at Piggots and had become an Associate of the Royal Academy there were some severe comments during the morning coffee break.

At the St Dominic's Press the pace of work was leisurely. Electric power and the activities of the monotype machine had not yet intruded, and were disapproved of. The type (Caslon Old Face) was set by hand; and almost everything, from books to beer-bottle labels, was printed on hand-made paper. The printing was done on ancient but serviceable iron hand presses. Hilary Bourne's own work was usually in the 'comping' rooms. There are few pleasanter tasks than to set up type by hand. The keeping of the word-spacing as even as possible and the 'justifying' of the line in the composing stick requires considerable skill, but the work is compatible with a certain amount of conversation, singing, or even prayer and meditation. The standing is tiring, certainly; but if the compositor sits down at his work he is restricted in the movement of his arms and body. The typeface before him is as wide and broad as the top of a small desk, and a long reach is needed to pick up the letters from the compartments on the upper left and right hand sides of the case.

The work was enjoyable. The actual business of printing was a rhythmic and exhilarating affair; one man inking, another running the bed of the press in below the plates, and a third pulling the lever and taking the impression, while one would open the frisket and remove the printed sheet. Dumping the paper (for handmade paper had to be printed dry), was a very skilled business and Hilary usually took the guillotine and stacked up, every seventh sheet being put quickly through a sink full of water. It was left all night and weighed down by a caseful of type. During the night the water from the camped sheets worked through the whole pile, and the art was to judge next day the moment when the paper was neither wet or dry, but just deep enough to make a good impression on the type. [Pepler thought his Stanhope iron press the oldest in the country and used hand-set Caslon Old Face type devised by William Caslon in the 1730s. It is now in Ditchling Museum.]

A pleasant daily gathering took place in Dunstan Pruden's workshop at the coffee break at eleven o'clock. Often the session would last for a full hour or more, with good talk on every conceivable subject. Each craftsman was his own master and could begin and stop work whenever he liked. The assistants and apprentices usually stopped work at five o'clock, but the master craftsmen were often still hard at it at ten o'clock at night. These men, unlike the modern factory worker, felt themselves really free.

To a great extent the strength of the Ditchling community lay in its family life. The place was always full of children, and they always seemed to be of exceptional grace and beauty. The families were all poor, but certainly were looked after by the Providence they believed in. So for these families life was hard, with periods of anxiety as to the future. This was particularly hard on the wives and mothers, and it was due in great part to their patience and fortitude that the Guild survived.[3]

Conrad Pepler recalled the exacting religious routine of daily life on the Common in 1982. The Office of Prime and the reading of the martyrdom was at about 7 a.m. For breakfast he returned home to nearby Hallets and then began work in his father's printing shop until nine o'clock, when the Guildsmen met in the chapel for Terce. The Angelus was rung and said at noon, and at 6 p.m. Vespers was held.[4]

The manifesto issued by Father Vincent McNabb on behalf of Eric Gill's Guild at Ditchling advocated the abandonment of the modern city and a return to the land. It cited St Thomas Aquinas's chapter 3 of *De Regimine Principum*, which concluded that it was best to be self-sufficient and to avoid trading as much as possible. The Guild members had a copy of William Cobbett's *Cottage Economy*, originally written at Worth in Sussex and republished by St Dominic's Press in 1916. It was one of the two predominant influences on the Guild, the other being a translation entitled 'A Philosophy of Art' by Father O'Connor. Booklets on various social and religious subjects, including town planning, were printed in batches and scattered at public meetings by members of the Guild. On the occasion of a lecture by Marie Stopes on birth control, the Guild dropped around their own hostile leaflet on the subject before she could speak.[5]

The increasing polarisation between craftsmen in Ditchling village and the members of the Guild on the Common arose not only from the increasingly devout Dominican orthodoxy but also from the growing spiritual involvement in small-scale rural subsistence. Pepler and the Guildsmen were inspired by the agrarian tradition at Ditchling: its Tenantry Down, still legally common, the open sheepwalk on the Beacon, and the fact there were still, in and near the village, shepherds, weavers, tanners, brick-makers, lime-burners, millers, blacksmiths and wheelwrights, supporting farming and living near their work while the rest of the village lived on holdings around.[6]

Agricultural experiments were made which were linked with Ashbee's School of Handicraft at Chipping Camden and with American Waldo Emerson's Brook Farm in the USA. Pepler and Desmond Chute purchased in 1916 Fragbarrow Farm, 160 acres adjoining the Common, and proceeded to farm it broadly on the basis of the Catholic Distributist principles of Chesterton and Belloc. These prescribed 'three acres and a cow' for the post-industrial society and economy. Home-made bread, bacon and beer was produced with the aid of Johnston, Gill, Philip Mairet and others. Mairet recounted that:

> We mowed the hay with a scythe, cut our corn with the swophook … thrashed the barley with a flail, winnowed it with a fan, and malted the grain on a slow fire [for beer] … Some of the old men still wore the smock (so beloved by Gill) and so did the shepherds on the Downs, with their crooks, dogs and brollies. It was meat and drink to us to have such an 'unspoiled' rural economy, and we were sure that nothing could be more pleasing to God than to keep it so.[7]

After 1918, when Father McNabb received novices into the Tertiary Order of Dominicans (for lay artisans), he brought the land experiment within the Catholic social policy of Pope Leo XIII's Encyclical Letters between 1878-91. The support of Johnston, who had engaged in the Distributist land experiment but could not accept Catholic dogma, was thereby lost. He returned from the Common to the village but his work suffered as a result. Catholic remedies enshrined in the Pope's 'manifesto' for the social evils of industrial and urban life included the reinforcement of the family as the basic unit of society and the cultivation of land by small property owners. Dunstan Pruden always felt McNabb would have liked to see a community of jolly Catholic peasants drilling the soil in boots as big as his own, and only thrown back on art when weather interrupted their struggle with the Ditchling Common clay.[8] McNabb's vision was to extend eventually the ethics of the Ditchling Catholic village across the whole of England, but the hasty departure of Gill to Wales in 1924 and dissension between Pepler and other Guildsmen ultimately rendered the scheme a failure.

In 1917 Ethel Mairet, with her husband, actor and writer Philip Mairet, bought land on the southern edge of Ditchling after leaving Ashbee's colony of craftsmen at Chipping Camden in the Cotswolds. The land became a successful hand-loom weaving and dye works called Gospels, specially designed with high-ceilinged rooms, ample light for weaving, and spring water for dyeing. A special feature was well-crafted doors of oak and other traditional timbers. Here Ethel wrote the seminal handbook *A Book of Vegetable Dyes* (1917) and took in apprentices, including Hilary Bourne, a founder of Ditchling Museum, and Valentine Kilbride, who later moved into Guild premises on the Common. Before the Second World War Mairet sold her goods in local shops and in the West End of London. The village artists had given up the city to practise a rural primitivism, but were no more than a short horse-drawn bus ride from Hassocks station on the main railway line to London, and went to the capital at any time for their commissions.[9]

Despite the rigour of the regime, the daily mood of the Community was light-hearted. One of their cheerful songs was written and sung to the tune of 'Sally Brown', from *Sea Chanties* edited by Cecil Sharp.[10]

122 *Ethel Mairet's contribution to weaving.*

And when the Spring comes and it's nice and
Warm
Way-ho, a-carting we will go
We'll cart the Press and ourselves up to Hallett's
Farm,
As the old carters carted carting long ago,
And now to God, Father, Son and Holy Ghost,
Way-ho, a-printing we will go.

Chapter 20

'ANYTHING GOES': 1918-39

THE BRAVE NEW WORLD

In the 1920s and '30s the coastal belt underwent a frenzy of development at a time when public taste was low and local controlling agencies operated landscape protection and civic design with restricted powers. The mood of the age following the First World War was to provide 'homes for heroes', with gardens back and front, and either semi-detached two-storeyed houses or bungalows, a new craze among the retired. Farmland was sold to builders and speculators, advertisers, industrialists, caterers and retailers indulged in indiscriminate development with impunity, obliterating villages and turning downland hedges and flint walls into lamp-posts and kerb-stones in a manner that destroyed the character of the countryside. Arthur Schofield despaired at the indiscriminate growth, which was confining Nature to 'beauty spots' into which people 'pried with pocket cameras'. A craving for the lost order manifested itself in enthusiasm for the antique. This resulted in mock-Tudor houses, 'ye olde tea shoppe', and absurd 'rustic' buildings. Schofield thought people seemed fated to fly from their own towns to others in search of novelty: 'They speed along the roads and are confronted with the country they have themselves destroyed – ribbon-bungalow development, and advertisements of the fare to be had at the next inn.'[1]

Hundreds of despairing letters were addressed to national and local newspapers and journals on the 'desecration' of the countryside. Campaigning organisations established against spoliation included the CPRE. In 1931 Thomas Sharp, a town-planning expert, considered the catastrophes greater than the battlefields of the First World War and summed up the crisis: 'We curse the callousness of the men who create those towns and we creep out of them into the country – which we, in our turn, destroy with an equal blindness.'[2] Historian Sir George Trevelyan attributed this to man's power over nature outstripping his moral and mental development.[3] Vera Brittain thought it due to the death of so many of the best of her generation in the First World War.[4]

It was a common experience for a person to visit some familiar spot and find it devastated by one of the many spoliators of the countryside. This was most notable on the edges of Brighton, where housing estates, light industry and golf courses sprawled and a motor-racing track and aerodrome were proposed. Gigantic pylons carried electricity lines across the landscape, telegraph wires were strung up through villages, advertising hoardings proliferated along roads and railway lines, and the electrification of railways to the coast extended the suburbs. Antagonistic observers likened the effect to a shrapnel bomb hurled from London. Sharp termed it a 'negative semi-suburbia' and Ian Nairn invented the word 'subtopia' for the sprawling downland suburbs of Brighton.[5] Hadrian Allcroft described the back of Brighton in 1924 as:

surely one of the most heart-breaking bits of all the Sussex coast – four miles of gravel-pits and drying-grounds, of allotments, of those decrepit black shacks which are the peculiar fungus of such allotments, makeshift hen-houses and glass-houses and out-houses of every uninviting kind, all the rusted *débris* of the Iron Age, all the dead odds and ends of things that gather on the shore of a port [Shoreham] that has not made good punctuated at wide intervals with chemical works, with the wreck of a great military camp, with a cemetery or two. It is, as it were, all the backyards of a great town gathered into one ... The massed ugliness of it all is intolerable. In the good old days there were neat little villages dotted at every mile.[6]

This jerry-built ribbon development had occurred within ten years.

The revolution in motor transport increased the radius of Sunday afternoon excursions and created 'beauty spots', litter-strewn sites which congregating tourists were subtly suburbanising. Arterial roads began to appear, and cars raced along them doing serious damage to whole communities. Old Shoreham, Findon, and Sompting villages near Worthing were sliced in half to deal with the demands of horsepower, and others were smothered by gimcrack ribbon development, along the widened A22 from Eastbourne or the A26 from Hastings. Car-led suburbs sprouted on the Downs around Brighton, which Ian Nairn in the 1950s called an 'outrage'. For centuries the mean area of towns had been confined to an area which could be covered in about one hour's walk. Urban places in the Weald, like Horsham, Uckfield, East Grinstead and Hailsham, remained tiny until recent times, as did Steyning, Midhurst and Petworth below the Downs, but now the better-off tended to move further out and, joined by newcomers, return daily to work, a process which transformed the local character. As cars became cheaper the weekending population increased.

In *Don John's Mountain Home* (1936) Ernest Raymond vividly describes the mechanical making of a new road for a housing estate, then a widespread Sussex phenomenon, at 'Avonsmead', a place within the composite of Haywards Heath, Burgess Hill and Hassocks. He expresses the dismay felt all over the county at the overthrowing of hedges, the destruction of little lanes and the levelling of banks, all done by monstrous machines 'rolling and pitching, grunting and spitting', on caterpillar feet like some huge dockyard crane.[8]

The petrol station was singled out for special censure. Most were erected without regard to sound construction or appearance.

THE DESTRUCTION OF RURAL BEAUTY.

As they are now.

As they might be.

123 *New scenery along main roads depicted in* Punch.

A number were designed as sham antiques, equipped with rustic features such as thatched roofs and pumps disguised as trees. After the passing of the Town and Country Planning Act in 1925, planners looked forward to the day when the utilitarian petrol station would be made beautiful by correct placing and the use of modern materials and design, a dream that has still not been fulfilled.[9]

124 *A residence in Summerhill Grange,
Haywards Heath, by Harold Turner.*

The London to Brighton railway created new types of town at Haywards Heath and Burgess Hill. Late Victorians were divided about Haywards Heath, 'the town of the London sort', which rapidly grew in the central Sussex Weald. Mark Antony Lower wrote approvingly in 1870 of the 'many villas and pleasure residences having sprung up almost by magic', and it was highly approved of by many Victorians and Edwardians.[10] But John Halsham, with neighbouring Lindfield in mind, likened it in 1898 to a 'congeries of stucco villas and builders' lots, nursery grounds and brick yards fenced with corrugated iron and barbed wire … round about a dreary wooden pile of buildings perched high on a red clay embankment'.[11]

The character of much of Haywards Heath between the wars is due to Harold George Turner, who started his architectural practice in 1920 and designed Franklands Village, the Summer Hill Estate, Mill Hill Close, Birchen Lane and numerous other individual houses. A Turner house was distinguished by quality of design and materials and by good craftsmanship with attractive detailing. His inspiration came from the traditional Wealden vernacular and was greatly influenced by the Arts and Crafts movement with its focus on natural materials and honest craftsmanship. Each Turner house is unique, its special features including ornamented oak staircases, individually designed fireplaces, window surrounds of steel made by the Crittal company and containing leaded panes and stained glass (now difficult to obtain and in danger of being replaced wholesale by UPVC units), decorative chimney stacks, dormer windows, and imposing porches and doors. The grounds of each house were landscaped and the roads given wide verges, lending a rural flavour to the neighbourhoods. The overall effect is an attractive built environment which is not easily matched in the county. Haywards Heath, Burgess Hill and, later, Hassocks burgeoned into the largest urban development in inland Sussex.

Over a thousand acres of undulating park-like farmland of southern aspect offered for sale at neighbouring Lindfield in 1875 was thought to offer 'eligible sites for the erection of Mansions, and is worthy of the attention of capitalists'. Into the 1920s and '30s Lindfield expanded continuously, mainly by destroying small estates created earlier such as Summer Hill, where 'good class' houses were built within ten minutes of Haywards Heath railway station in 1926, and at the early Georgian Sunte Estate on a beautiful gentle hill near Lindfield church in 1928. Apart from its lime avenue, stately trees and hedges, this was replaced with 'quality' residences. 'Magnificent' building sites on rising ground were sold at neighbouring Scaynes Hill in 1929.

125   *Downland edge,
Portslade, Foredown.*

On the whole, the estates of the aristocracy held out against the trend, partly through sentimental attachment to land owned for centuries and partly through reluctance to being bordered by residential housing. The Duke of Norfolk's great estate based on Arundel survived almost intact (although the Duke sold Amberley Castle), as did the Firle Estate of Lord Gage and that of Lord Hampden of Glynde, but Lord Abergavenny parted with extensive downland at Lewes, for council housing at the Neville and Landport Estates, and with 1,300 acres at Patcham. His sale in 1919 of land at Rodmell and its vicinity was

126   *Unsightly development
on the Downs at Southwick.*

127 *The* Peacehaven Post, *a magazine of developer Charles Neville.*

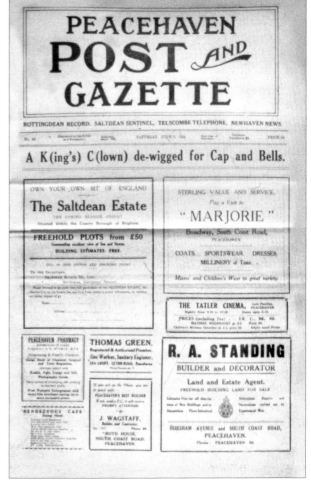

to allow entry by the Woolfs and a colony of literary contemporaries on new freeholds.

One of the saddest days for the Earl of Chichester and for the Downs was the sale of the Chyngton estate in Seaford as a result of death duties on two earls who had died within a short time of each other. The Sales Catalogue was endorsed 'At Low Reserves to Ensure Sale' and stated that the estate 'occupies probably the finest position on this part of the coast, stretching as it does to Cuckmere Haven and the sea'. The supremely beautiful location adjoining the Seven Sisters, already protected by Eastbourne Corporation, and extending westward along the cliffs almost to Seaford Head aroused national concern. The Chichester family and trustees of the estate acknowledged their regret in having to dispose of it and hoped that it would be acquired in its entirety for national purposes. The auctioneer, announcing its withdrawal from sale, stated, 'We have only one Sussex in England and only one Sussex coast, and thank God we have a family in Sussex who wish to preserve the amenities of the South Coast.' In the event, most of the estate disappeared beneath housing, but land adjacent to the Cuckmere river and its Haven and along the cliffs to Hope Gap was saved from building.[12]

Lord Abergavenny's Lewes sales are particularly interesting because they were intended to provide working-class housing in the beautiful downland valley of the River Ouse, and aroused much opposition. A photograph of the lovely setting in appeared in *The Times* of 3 December 1936. To a casual observer, Lewes was a prosperous, 'smiling' town, one of its chief residents, authoress Mrs Dudeney, describing it as 'the most divine spot in the world', but a considerable proportion of the population lived in slum housing in a part of the town called the Cliffe which had failed to meet the minimum requirements of the Housing Act of 1935. Lewes Council built neat small houses around a 'village green' and the old farm track to Offham survived, and the result was a much loved habitation amid natural beauty which was a credit to the local authority. Despite fears that the erection of so many houses would spoil the view of Lewes from the north, the much needed residential Landport estate has been carefully screened from that direction.[13]

128 *'It's all a Matter of Road-Sense, Old Boy',* Punch *cartoon, Summer 1936.*

What was significant about the subsequent development on the estate at Seaford was the lack of ribbon development, and stipulations imposed on each of the 195 plots regarding minimum cost of various types of housing resulted in an orderly zoning of working-class dwellings, 'artistic villas' and shops on the lower slopes, and provision for 'superior' detached houses on the upper. Only one private detached or semi-detached house was to be erected on plots of 50ft frontage. No hotels, public houses, beer-shops, asylums, letting houses, caravans or temporary buildings, or any traders or businesses (including 'blacksmith, bell-hanger, gasfitter, locksmith, tinman or slaughterman') were permitted, with the exception of certain shops in the working-class areas. The building programme began soon after the end of the war and was largely completed by 1939. Some parts were built later, but they always conformed to the original proposals of 1914.[14]

129 *Osbert Lancaster's* Drayneflete, *1940 (an imaginary Littlehampton), from his* Littlehampton Saga, *1984 edn.*

THE CRISIS IN AGRICULTURE

In the Sussex countryside life went on despite the severe crisis in agriculture. The halcyon days of local farming were over by the 1880s; imports of grain, meat and wool in the name of Free Trade as championed by industrialists had seen to that. The First World War saw a return to prosperity but in peace the poorer land slipped out of production, and the county was now looked upon as something pretty to be preserved for landscape gardening, hunting and fishing, or hiking and tourism. A tremendous agitation would take place whenever somebody threatened to spoil a beautiful view by building houses or erecting an eyesore, but stories of rural distress among the farming community went almost unnoticed by the urban population.

One of the few to write about the crisis was Julian Bell, son of Clive and Vanessa Bell of Charleston, whose decision to write about the Sussex countryside in rhyme shows that Charleston was no weekend cottage or funk-hole from the town. His was a clear-cut delineation of the farmscape, neither jingoistic or sentimental, and with a real feeling for the land itself:

> As, one by one, the farmers break and fail
> And barns are emptied and the bankrupt's sale.
> Mark from some hill, across the fertile Weald,
> The arable retreating field by field,
> The waste advancing as the corn recedes
> Where the team bullocks chew the fallow weeds.
> See rotting gates hang by the rusted catch,
> The untopped hedges and the mouldering thatch,
> The milweed hay beneath the August rain
> The fly rott'd trumps and the shredded grain,
> Thistles and brambles cloak the stinging tracks
> And deep corruption rots the rumbling stacks.
> Here, in a language all can understand,
> See plainly told the history of our land.[15]

One solution to the crisis was to switch from sheep, which had competition from Australia and New Zealand, to milk production for the seaside resorts. This was first achieved on the Glynde Estate and the example was emulated widely along the coast and Downs from the 1920s. At Glynde the dairy still exists, though it is now put to other uses.

Leonard Woolf thought the traditional life of a Sussex village had completely disappeared, but did not regret it, believing that in many ways it had been a hard life and the society, both physically and spiritually, an uncivilised one:

> It was full of Mrs Hawkesfords [the wife of the vicar of Rodmell in the 1930s], village women worn out by child-bearing and domestic slavery, men of considerable brutality. It took ten to fifteen years before the villagers regarded one as other than a stranger – and all strangers were regarded with distrust and hostility. But when they got to know you and allowed you to get to know them, you found that beneath the surface, side by side with the grimness and brutality, life was complex, with deep down sometimes happiness and sensitiveness to beauty.[16]

130 *Motor vehicle disguised as a hay wain in a pathetic attempt to recover 'Olde Sussex',* Punch *cartoon, 1934.*

Progressive farmers were mechanizing in Sussex on the eve of the Second World War, the farrier having to turn himself into a mechanic and the carter into a lorry driver; saddler's premises had become tea shops and other tradesmen had disappeared, yet villages were still recognisably agrarian communities. Few of the old farmhouses had yet been sold off and the hop-oasts had not been turned into residences. Water-courses, now filled with reed, were running clear.

You could still hear talk of the old countryman and his way of life. One old rascal who went to the nearest market town to buy some ferrets was induced to buy a pig. After spending the evening with convivial companions he was confronted with the problem of conveying pig and ferrets several miles to his village home. He nailed up the pig in a sugar box, put it on a borrowed wheelbarrow and set out to walk, arriving in the dead of night with one ferret round his

131 *The Old Dairy at Glynde, created by the Glynde Estate, lessened dependence on Southdown sheep and brought prosperity from milk production for the seaside resorts.*

neck and others burrowing in his pockets. The pig was left to pass the night in the sugar box with the help of a packet of Quaker Oats.

Although company water pipes were being laid in the country districts there were still a large number of wells. The old men would tell you the depths of the surrounding wells, who dug them, what mishaps accompanied their building, and how the water in some wells would suddenly go bad for no discoverable reason. At Ditchling the poet Habberton Lulham knew it was time for tea when he heard villagers drawing up water for the kettle.

But the most characteristic feature of country villages was the young men in the old cottages bursting forth with a motor cycle, collection of books, and strong and well-informed opinions as to the state of society, or young women cutting their hair, discarding their skirts for shorts, and getting about the world with lightweight camping gear.[17]

SUSSEX COTTAGE TEAS

One of the most obvious signs of a changed Sussex in the decade or so before the Second World War was the rapid spread of premises selling 'Morning Coffee' or 'Tea with Hovis'; redundant forges, saddler's shops and water-mills, in fact any building which had enough beams, even if actually rather new, became tea-rooms, generally with a garden attached. Tea gardens were established at Bramber, Wannock and Litlington, and every seaside resort and country town had more sophisticated tea shops. This was a measure of the success of the tourist trade, but also indicated a change in social mores. It was considered unseemly for a lady to enter a public house before the Second World War. The growing number of

132 *Woodingdean, 1920s.*

THE BEAUTY SPOT

133 *Tea Gardens, a cartoon in* Punch *magazine, 1923.*

ladies travelling with the opposite sex while unchaperoned went instead to tea-rooms or places offering non-alcoholic refreshment.

The Bramber tea gardens were well-known to trippers from Brighton and Worthing. When the young Vaughan Williams stayed in 1898 at the village in a Temperance hotel – actually a refreshment room and tea garden with apartments attached – he found so quiet a place to work that he wrote four pages of full score in a day.[18] Virginia Woolf's *Diary* records a visit there in 1926 when it was full of overflowing charabanc parties of 'the lower middle class', quite unappreciative of the historic surroundings of the ruined castle of the medieval Braoses.[19]

The Litlington Pleasure Gardens and Tea-Rooms, about ten miles from Eastbourne, were the brainchild of Frederick Russell in 1863. A pavilion was built for large parties and a number of evergreen arbours and wooden chalets provided for refreshments. A double-gabled house was built next door as a hotel. By the late 1870s the Gardens had entered their heyday: factory employees from the London area and the Eastbourne Cycling Club met annually in summer from 1877 for 'high tea, bathing, a concert and a strawberry feast'. The present-day Gardens were modified by the naturalistic movement of William Robinson and Gertrude Jekyll, but they retain their quaint Victorian atmosphere.[20]

Chapter 21

WRITERS AND THE NEW SUSSEX

Sussex never had as many poets, novelists, dramatists, short-story and 'country' writers as it did between 1900 and 1939, and no English county was ever more promoted by them. As Amy Sawyer, the Ditchling artist and playwright, said of the popularity of Sussex in the early 1930s: 'Sussex at present is *the* thing. No novel is complete without a Sussex manor. Put 'em altogether and they'd circle the world twice.'[1] Belloc thought the view of the Downs near Arundel was perhaps the 'most verse producing mile in the world'.[2] There was such a host of prolific writers in the 1920s it was not unusual for the *Poetry Review* to receive two or more slim volumes of Sussex literature published in a single week.[3]

THE 'INVENTION' OF SUSSEX

Sussex writers had a cultural as well as a creative importance. It has been said that Hilaire Belloc and Rudyard Kipling 'invented' Sussex, the former by making the Downs one of the Englishman's minor religions and the latter by 're-inventing' the county as a rustic idyll locked in the past for some 'complex psychological, political or other reason'.[4] This over-simplifies and misrepresents what actually occurred, but it is true that the two writers of genius helped Sussex acquire a new, super-charged identity.

Belloc's *South Country*, of haunting wistfulness and charm, was a forerunner of his mystical and spiritual relationship with the land of his boyhood which had shaped his imagination to an extraordinary pitch. His intense patriotism for Sussex, to which he had felt indebted since childhood, which had entered his soul and enlarged with age, created in him a desire to serve the county and commanded his admiration. Kipling's immensely popular *Sussex*, which appeared almost simultaneously with Belloc's earliest works in 1900-2, reclaimed for literature the bare, open Downs from Shoreham in the Adur valley to their termination in Beachy Head, which Regency tourists and the following generations had judged treelessly dismal and forlorn. At Rottingdean he immortalised the unbroken downland turf and gleaming chalk cliffs in verse. He also introduced a wide readership to the Sussex Weald in his Burwash days, with *Rewards and Fairies*, *Puck of Pook's Hill*, his classic story *The Habitation Enforced* and the exquisite *They*. Until this time the Weald had been almost unknown territory.

Yet there are signs that Sussex was becoming popular with an urban audience a generation and more before Belloc and Kipling wrote. The former noted that one of the effects of modern communication was that men could tell others what their landscape was like and compare one part of England with another in a way they could not have done before. Copley Fielding was painting the South Downs as early as 1829-35, and he was followed by Henry George Hine and William Nicholson, who made studies at Rottingdean. A glance at *The Studio*, an illustrated magazine of Fine and Applied

134 *Hilaire Belloc,* Punch *magazine, 1909.*

Art, reveals that Sussex had become the object of a veritable cult even before the publication of Belloc's and Kipling's verses. An article in the popular journal *Once a Week* in 1865 asserted that 'There is not a more picturesque county in England than Sussex, or one that possesses a higher degree of interest to the historian, and holds forth more tempting sources of research to the antiquary.' In 1862 *The Quarterly Review* had mentioned the Downs admiringly (p.31). Richard Jefferies enthusiastically advertised Sussex to the following generation in his short essays, and he was followed by John Halsham, whose *Idlehurst* is a masterly picture of the central Sussex Weald in 1898, and W.H. Hudson, who wrote the brilliant *Nature in Downland* (1900).

Belloc and Kipling took the tenacious hold the Downs and Weald already had on the national psyche and greatly enhanced the legend, a literary example of how to exploit a good thing to the fullest possible extent. Both men chose to describe Sussex in its 'golden age' in the past, an approach psychologically congenial to those struggling with modernism and matching their political beliefs.

It was largely on account of the fame Belloc and Kipling brought to Sussex that the varied and influential host of immigrant authors subsequently settled in Sussex and reshaped its regional identity. They preferred country to town, following in the footsteps of writers who had held the same ideals a hundred years previously, and consequently the strongest theme running through Sussex literature is withdrawal from urban life and a conscious rejection of contemporary civilisation symbolised by London and the industrial towns – a theme so continuous and predominant that it might be called the 'Sussex tradition'. It rose to greatest prominence when poets and authors started to write for an urban readership. Despite being ignorant of its wants and needs, urban society governed the countryside; it painted and photographed it, and hungered to read about it. Sussex writers were engaged in what Raymond Williams has called the literary remaking of the countryside as a complement to the triumphant urban economy following the Industrial Revolution.[5] Theirs was a vision of Eden.

So one is not surprised by Sussex's exceptional place in England's imaginative geography. Hardly a natural feature or artefact, animate or inanimate, or aspect the Sussex landscape has gone unnoticed or unrecorded, possibly to a degree unparalleled in any other English region, the Lake District not excluded. Some towns, too, had an extraordinary amount of attention: Brighton is probably among the most publicised cities in the world, and more than two hundred visitors and residents at Hastings found their way into print over two centuries. Even a minor port like Shoreham inspired a dozen or more authors in little more than a generation.

At the outbreak of the Second World War, in a number of favourite Sussex villages, novelists, poets, dramatists, critics, artists and university teachers outnumbered those working the land. G.K. Chesterton claimed in 1904 (with pardonable exaggeration) that 'short story writers leapt from behind hedges. Minor poets dropped from the trees like ripe fruit. Philosophers, sociologists and artists ran like rabbits about the woods.'[6]

After Alfred Noyes had joined Kipling and Belloc, no county could boast three poets of similar stature. Henry James had taken up permanent residence at Rye and was entertaining leading literary figures, including neighbours H.G. Wells, Conrad, Kipling and Ford Madox Ford. Sussex became the holiday home of the most urbane of artistic coteries, the Bloomsbury Group. Virginia and Leonard Woolf's home was the refuge of E.M. Forster, William Plomer, Aldous Huxley, T.S. Eliot and many more, and Vanessa Bell's Charleston, only

a few miles away, had Lytton Strachey as a visitor and Maynard Keynes as neighbour at Tilton. To Rottingdean gravitated numerous literary and artistic celebrities, including Burne-Jones, Kipling, Enid Bagnold, Noyes, William Watson, Maurice Baring and Angela Thirkell, and Greatham, near Pulborough, was the home of poet Alice Meynell. D.H. Lawrence was a visitor, as were Francis Thompson, Eleanor Farjeon, John Drinkwater and others, all of whom left literary legacies. More writers gravitated to the Surrey border in the footsteps of Tennyson, including Bertrand Russell and Logan Pearsall Smith. On the border of Ashdown Forest in 1926 A.A. Milne wrote *Winnie the Pooh*. At Ditchling and other villages were colonies of handicraftsmen. The safety cycle and motor car and cycle made Sussex reachable and contributed to the avalanche of 'country writing', some of which secured a worldwide readership.

135 *Rudyard Kipling, John Collier, 1910.*

If writers had an aim it was to offer consolation, stir the spirit and entice people into the open air. The life of pleasure they evoked for the hard world beyond was close to Keats' idea of paradise: 'fine weather, and health, and books, and a fine country and contented mind and, please heaven, a little claret-wine cool out of a cellar a mile deep!',[7] or Charles Lamb's:

> Sun and sky and breeze, and solitary walks, and summer holidays, and the greenness of fields, and the delicious juices of meats and fishes, and society, and the cheerful glass, and candlelight: and fireside conversation and innocent vanities, and jests, and irony itself – do these things go out with life?[8]

Paradoxically, as Raymond Williams noted, there was an inverse relationship between the decline of the agricultural economy and the cultural rise of rural ideas. In Sussex this was even more evident because most writers had not spent their lives in the country and had no knowledge of practical farming or care for it.[9] Missing in their work is, for example, Edmund Blunden's felicitous evocation of the lives of country men and women based on his connections with Yalding in Kent (*Poems*).

Their cherished existence was the time and space of yesterday. While they could still see plough oxen on the Downs and hear sheep-bells, the shepherd calling commands to his dog and the flock moving away into silence, leaving them alone on the hillside, they had found their heart's content. By concentrating on such survivals they propagated the myth of an unchanging countryside. Their literature developed into a distinct genre. Out of this calm little world came calm little poems and essays, not usually the kind of writing which burns itself into the memory and deeper consciousness. No whiff of the great world, with its harsh, exigent realities, seemed to reach them, the international situation in the 1920s and 1930s seeming to pass them by.

This is because Sussex poets no longer engaged with the facts of modern life. They did not sing of work, or of strife, of noise in crowding streets, of 'the ratapans that beat the march of millions of hurrying feet', nor of the drum and fife on the battlefield. They did not write about life at all; but of ways of alleviating its weariness and doing nothing whatever. They were invariably in holiday mood, their appreciation of the countryside being that of a happy hiker enjoying green fields and 'birds twittering in the copses'.

From the pens of Belloc, Kipling, Habberton Lulham and Charles Dalmon came verse in the first third of the 20th century which is the last and most admirable version of the English tradition of the pastoral, which persisted from the classical Georgics and through Spenser, Milton and Blake. A love of nature in a rural landscape has been characteristic of English verse since a poet in Surrey dialect celebrated the nightingale singing in a woodland clearing in the late 12th or early 13th century.

The output of lesser lights has had a very mixed reception, being treated to mingled appreciation and derision and found both consoling and exasperating. As a quirky footnote in literary history, Sussex verse has been stereotyped as the tweedy effusions of lyrical pastoralists. It was scorned by the modernist set of T.S. Eliot, W.H. Auden and Aldous Huxley as undisguised propaganda for the tourist trade, little more than a succession of beautiful sounds and a conscious straining after effect.

Indeed, everyone was against it except townspeople, who bought the published volumes in thousands. People generally did not take to the unfamiliar views and opinions of 'modernists' and preferred to read poetry rather than analyse and squabble about it in literary journals. Culturally, therefore, the poetry should not be underestimated. 'Ordinary' Sussex literature lacked literary distinction but satisfied the emotional and spiritual needs of the urban public. Particularly gratified were veterans of the First World War trying to re-make their lives, and the vast majority with no knowledge of the beauties of the county outside what they could read. It could be argued from the perspective of the present that the 'Georgian literature' despised by a handful of intellectuals brought more enjoyment to members of the urban public than works aimed at fellow professionals which they found impenetrable.

THE LAND THAT HEALS: SUSSEX AS A RURAL SANCTUARY

The quest for the Land of Promise is a theme running right through the cultural history of Sussex over the past two hundred years. Louis Jennings, in one of the first books on the Sussex countryside, found it in the ancient park of Wiston, where he thought the 'healing hand of Mother Nature' would heal wounds made by the anxieties of life.[10] As Hilaire Belloc remarked in 1909 of his new home, the sparsely peopled Weald blocked in by hills and sea 'was a perfect refuge, exactly the place for a seclusion from men'.[11] An example of the restorative effect of its topography is William Benham of H.G. Wells' *Research Magnificent* (1915). He climbs to the crest of the North Downs and surveys the great expanse of the Weald to the South Downs in an attempt to find new purpose again after troubled times in London:

> It is after all not so great a country this Sussex, nor so hilly. From the deepest valley to highest crest is six hundred feet, yet what a greatness of effect it can achieve. There is something in those downland views which, like sea views, lifts a mind out to the skies.[12]

By the time Wells wrote this the Weald was seen as the sanctuary of England. Vera Arlett's griefs took wing in the Downs but the 'quiet Wealden country' was her most 'beautiful friend' and greatest comfort; it caressed and healed her, and she wrote to console the less fortunate.

The author who voiced most emphatically the need for a rural sanctuary in difficult circumstances was Ford Madox Ford, who recovered the strength of mind he needed to return to novel-writing in the deep Sussex countryside after shellshock in Flanders. He craved country, just country – 'not heaths, moors, forest or famous views' but just ordinary, commonplace fields, hedges and country lanes – the countryside one saw from the windows of a train. He was evidently like his character Gringoire, in *No Enemy*, whose sustaining vision in the depths of terror in the trenches was some future green nook. Ford found his 'green nook' at Red Ford and afterwards at Bedham near Pulborough. He described his cottage at Red Ford with the imagery of war still uppermost in his mind. With his new vision of life and society he made a devastating attack on London, which he associated with wars, follies, drabness and dullness.[13]

THE OPEN AIR

Sussex literature has a predilection for the joys of the outdoors. William Watson, who lived at Rottingdean for a time, voiced the thoughts of the movement when he wrote:

> May cloud and mountain, lake and vale,
> never to you be trite and stale.

The scanning of horizons was particularly loved by Alice Meynell, and revelling in cloud-worship was a constant inspiration to John Halsham; Richard Jefferies rejoiced in the sun. Unsurprisingly, Sussex has a large quantity of literature for the wayfarer. Charlotte Smith's botanical books for children were based on her forays into the Arun valley and the South Downs, and Gideon Mantell's *A Day's Ramble in and about Lewes* (1846) has become a classic. Memorable as a pioneering book on footpaths in the South Downs is Louis J. Jenning's *Field Paths and Green Lanes* (1877). Hilaire Belloc's evocation of the open road has no peer: people thought in the 1920s that no one could handle a book such as *The Four Men* and not be instantly infected with a desire to be out and doing in the open air. He was followed by Thurston Hopkins, who published walking guides and outdoors books on rural Sussex and by S.P.B. Mais, the Southwick author and broadcaster who brought London's countryside to the reach of thousands at weekends.

LOAFING

Despite the Victorian work ethic, life in towns created the need for periodic rest. From a literary point of view, Sussex was also an old man's and woman's country, attractive to the incoming retired, and most writers had settled there in later life. Accordingly, the literature reflects this.

One of the great gifts of the Downs, according to the poets, was the opportunity for loafing and doing nothing. Drinkwater's poem *At Rottingdean*, where he was a guest of poet Alfred Noyes, conveys no hint of anything happening at all:

> The days are sweet at Rottingdean,
> And very sweet at Rottingdean,
> Where leagues of downland travel north and southward leagues
> Of sea
> A sea that flashes blue and green
> With purple shadows thrown between,
> And downs that gather up the song of all the winds that be.

Ford Madox Ford's *Love in Watchfulness on the Sheep Downs* finds him resting drowsily on a hot day, watching moving clouds for hours at a time:

> Sail, oh sail away,
> Oh sail, you clouds, above my face.
> Here where I lie.
> Trail, oh trail away.

> *(Selected Poems)*

Maurice Baring, who retired to Rottingdean, also evoked the drowsy midsummer sense of peace:

> I have loved summer and the longest day;
> The leaves of June, the slumberous film of heat
> The bees, the swallow,
> And the waving wheat,
> The whistling of the mowers in the hay.

And Coulson Kernahan has said that not even Sussex-born and bred poets have painted a picture of summer's tranquillity more perfect than Drinkwater's *Of Greatham* (1917), a glad and grateful note addressed to his fellow poet and hostess Alice Meynell:[14]

> And peace upon your pasture lands I found,
> Where grazing flocks drift on continually,
> As little clouds that travel with no sound
> Across a windless sky.

G.D. Martineau, who had served with the Royal Sussex Regiment in Ireland on the Foyle and wanted to go back to the 'wholesome calm' of Sussex to ease the pain of his experiences, expresses the lifestyle of the retired elderly person perfectly:

> I like it when the day is warm,
> And I can laze at ease,
> Untroubled by the world's alarm,
> Beneath the kindly trees.
>
> ('On the Downs', in *Old Sussex*)

One imagines Martineau lying in the sunshine when the only sounds are those of sheep-bells and the drone of bees, and his poems give the feeling of deep repose and freedom. Habberton Lulham's *Kettle Songs* (1922), a collection of village gossip before a roaring fire in his retirement cottage, is a fine example of the genre.

Kenneth Grahame, author of *The Wind in the Willows*, brought loafing to high perfection not only on the Thames but also on the Downs, where he writes of the experience at first-hand in the manner of a Romantic poet:

> A holy calm possesses the village. All vestiges of a sordid humanity disappear. The loafer is alone with the breeze and the vista and the blue sky. Only a carolling of larks and a tinkling from distant flocks breaks the brooding noon-day stillness … Prone on his back on the springy turf gazing up into the blue sky, his fleshy integument seems to drop away, and the spirit ranges at will among the tranquil clouds. This way Nirvana nearest lies. Earth no longer obtrudes herself.[15]

THE WORLD OF FAERY

The generation of writers up to the 1930s often extolled the virtues of 'Old Sussex' by drawing on folklore and the fantastic to distract an urban readership from contemporary concerns. In their hands, Sussex became Hesperides, one of the places where people had long felt in contact with a supernatural presence, usually exceptionally beautiful, remote and mysterious. This was, to use the old word, the land of faery.

The new world of the imagination, of folklore and fairy tales, in the early years of the 20th century was a reaction against science and technology. But folk tales among country people went back many centuries. Before the 19th century the Sussex natives had remained unobserved, and had claimed the 'fairy-rings' on the Downs were the work of 'Pharisees', a corrupt plural form of 'fairy'. But the county is not peopled with literary Rosalinds and Orlandos and there are no tales of Oberon or Titania, such as frequented Arden in the 16th century.

CONSEQUENCES

In 1909 A.S. Cooke remarked that the Downs 'to the majority of visitors are simply unknown'. Rediscovering Sussex and making it familiar to thousands in London and the southern counties who knew little of its beauty was the role of great writers, such as Hudson, Kipling and Belloc, as well as the lesser authors and popular press of the inter-war years. Without doubt, the writers' admiration for the county has to be seen as a major reason for the haphazard development which brought to an end traditional rural life and landscape. This killing of Sussex by kindness and loving it to death was perceived as one of England's greatest environmental catastrophes. As the *Manchester Guardian* cynically observed in 1926: 'The beauties of the county [Sussex] seem to have been fairly safe until the "Sussex school" of writers descended on the land and proceeded to elaborate on Mr Kipling's well-known appreciation.'

Kipling himself came to deplore the motorists and charabanc visitors in, for example, his verses entitled *Very Many People* (1926); but he had himself invented the genre of motoring tales:

> They take our land to delight in,
> But their delight destroys
> They flay the turf from the sheepwalk
> They load the Denes with noise.

Chapter 22

THE ROLE OF THE ARTIST'S EYE

The Sussex landscape has long appealed to the painter. Turner learnt to draw on the Kent and Sussex border and represented in watercolour the wildness of surviving Wealden woodland for John Fuller of Brightling Park. He was also inspired by the coast at Rye and Brighton and made memorable paintings of Petworth Park and the House's interior. His sketchbooks contain numerous lively Sussex scenes and his *Views in Sussex* (1817) are engravings of watercolours taken on his many visits to the county. Constable visited Brighton in 1824 and, though he disliked the place, made sketches of seascapes, and consummate paintings of the Chain Pier and of windmills in the surrounding rural district.[1] Had he lived he would probably have depicted the hanging woods over the Arun near Arundel, which in 1834 he thought the most beautiful view he had ever seen.

A Journey through Trees

From the 1840s artists of Ruskin's generation were moved to paint *plein air* landscapes according to the fashionable criterion of truth-to-nature, eloquently insisted upon in Ruskin's *Modern Painters* (1843-60). Samuel Palmer, whose brilliant decade at Shoreham in Kent had ended in discontent in North Kensington, was haunted for years by a hill range with wide prospects in 'uncockneyfied' countryside. He plaintively thought 'the sight and smell of sunshine and new-mown hay are more congenial with our pursuits than those of smoke and sewers'. Artists had previously found surviving *rus in urbe* enclaves in London that provided an rich source of inspiration to the landscape watercolourist, but by the 1860s land in the city was being appropriated wholesale for railways, obliterated by palatial offices and warehouses or covered with colourless streets. Open spaces and vistas were lost and villages which had lain for centuries within half an hours walk of St Paul's were built over. The loss of confidence in London, with its accompanying canopy of smoke, as a subject of landscape painting led to an invasion of the countryside which writers subsequently emulated.

Certain rural districts entered into artistic consciousness for the first time, such as the middle Thames valley, but the gravitational centre to which most would-be landscapists drifted was the Weald, comprising the counties of Hampshire, Surrey, Sussex and Kent. It was to become the centre from which a new naturalistic movement radiated. Multiplying artists' colonies turned the Weald into a vast open-air studio, a modern *locus ameonus* of paradisal topography. The earliest artists were trained in the Vale of Mickleham in Surrey and painted in the Dorking district, which was both convenient and diverse in scenery.[2]

The almost instantaneous effect of railway travel on artistic lifestyles can be illustrated by the commuting between Bayswater and Balcombe, in the central Sussex Weald, of landscape

136 *'Straying Sheep', William Holman Hunt, 1850s.*

painter John Linnell. In 1847 he decided to paint landscapes instead of portraits, and his selection of Balcombe in 1848, a remote village about thirty-five miles from London that was virtually unknown until the siting of a convenient railway station in 1841, was possibly due to his reading of John Thorne's *Guide to Walkers in Sussex* (1844). This early example of a travel guide intended for railway travellers used Balcombe as the start of a prescribed walk and extolled the beauty of its trees and rocks, Linnell's principal interests as a newly fledged landscape painter.

His repeated visits to Balcombe, recorded in his Diaries from 1848, make him one of the first of the commuters who were ultimately to transform the county. The Diary throws light on arduous travel to and from the capital and show how Linnell set about learning to paint landscapes in a diverse country, deeply humanised and utterly 'wild' by turns, a 'disordered order' of woodland, heath, fields and streams. He spent days on end observing, note-taking and sketching the superabundance of detail there, first the trunks and branches of trees, then the rock formations which abounded in the district, and then the effects of sun and shade on water and woodland glades.

Like so many contemporary artists, who chose to reside in places commanding extensive panoramas, he bought Redstone at Redhill, convenient for the Brighton railway, on the sandstone ridge overlooking the Weald in 1851. Over thirty forceful years of landscape painting were ahead of him, during which he became England's most popular landscape artist, depicting the expressive Sussex and Surrey Wealds with their changing backdrops of cloud and light. In his delineation of extended space, paradise became synonymous with prospect, a largely untried experiment that contrasted with Constable's view of the Weald as an unpaintable immensity. Linnell and his followers made the Weald as seen from its ranging summits a Victorian dream of tranquil English beauty. Many of his Wealden paintings, which mined a deep vein of popular taste, were acquired for permanent public exhibition by art galleries in the northern industrial towns, including Preston, others being acquired for the private collections of businessmen in the Midlands and North. Linnell influenced, among others, George Vicat Cole. His artistic reputation declined as the repetitious pictures he produced from his Redhill 'art factory' for a insatiable market became mere commodities. Although he pandered to public taste, however, he had a moral message to convey. He shared the fears of Ruskin, Arnold and the writers discussed in the last chapter of a godless society and of a civilisation under threat. In paintings such as *On the Eve of the Deluge* (1848) and *The Last Load* (1852) he is responding to the loss of human values in the face of the spread of cities and the threat to nature their growth implied.[3]

For artists of Linnell's generation the landscape was a place where the spontaneous activity of nature, in the manner of Wordsworthian religion, was predominant. This vision was animated by the scientific curiosity which geologists and botanists, in newly constituted laboratories of field studies, had regarding the rocks and plants of the Weald. But it was also in keeping with Ruskin's advice that the landscape painter should 'keep away from clover fields and parks and so hold to the unpenetrated forest and unfurrowed

137   *Alfred Glendening, 'A View of Rye', 1897.*

hill', in opposition to Gower Street. Ruskin was particularly inspired by woodland such as the trees in the hanging woods above Arundel which Constable had earlier described as 'beyond everything beautiful'. This was a response to the contemporary England, whose commonland ('wastes') and natural pasture was disappearing, whose hedgerows and trees were being rooted out. Wildlife was extirpated and every available rood brought under cultivation by 'High Farming'. Sussex, though developed for agriculture for millennia, had retained an uncommon profusion and diversity of nature. Woodland extending past the horizon into infinity, echoing Turner, gave the overwhelming impression of an aboriginal England before its remodelling by man. The power of landscape art to refresh wearied minds was seen by artists as a social responsibility. In the words of G.F. Watts, a contemporary painter, the urban patron saw nothing beautiful around him 'excepting always sky and trees and sea; these, as he is mainly a dweller in cities, he cannot have enough of'.[4]

The Coles, George Vicat and his son, Rex Vicat, also painted extensive Wealden landscapes with consummate skill. The former dwelt for a time high up on the Surrey-Sussex border and his *Harvest Time*, which looks across a great wooded landscape to the South Downs, and his paintings of the hanging beech woods in the Arun valley in autumn helped make him the most popular painter in the Royal Academy. His son was so stirred by the view from high ground at Bedham, near Pulborough, that he and his family lived in a labourer's cottage there contentedly for 20 years until Elgar took a sub-let on it during the First World War. Cole's *The Weald of Sussex from Brinkwells* (1906) shows the extensive sweep of woodland from his cottage of that name. Rex Cole painted for years in this small area. His wife, writing in about 1910, described their dwelling 'as dropped bodily, garden and all, into an enchanted wood … It really makes you wonder where you are.' Rex revelled in Brinkwells, with its garden orchard and thatched outbuildings, decorating the interior with small wooden panels bearing sketches of flowers and leaves and furnishing the cottage with sturdy oak. The studio, partly built from a disused railway carriage, has since been moved to a site more than a mile away. This country home was central to his imaginative processes, and from 1906 to 1915 nearly all Rex's paintings were of woodland within walking distance of Brinkwells. His range of colours grew, his brush became broader and the green ways overhung with trees inspired him to experiment with sunshine through leaves. His greatest source of inspiration was trees, the principal subject of his pictures, and he wrote *British Trees* (1907), containing superbly drawn descriptions by himself of a particular tree or group of trees. He later wrote *The Artistic Anatomy of Trees* (1916) in which he taught, among other techniques, stylising them as a method of pictorial composition. The setting clearly influenced Elgar following his arrival at Brinkwells in 1917 and both his Violin Sonata and the Piano Quintet have a strong sense of the mystery of woodlands.[5]

From the 1880s artists descended on Sussex in crowds, especially in the Chichester district, at the foot of the Downs, in the High Weald, and at Brighton. The landscape was so alluring that artists spent a lifetime painting it. The comparative popularity of the Weald among painters can be gauged by the numbers of exhibitors at the Royal Academy before 1904, the Weald accounting for a third of them, by far the largest for any region; research suggests that the percentage increased still further in later years. In 1910, for example, the *Sussex Daily News* reported that no fewer than 36 residents of the county had exhibited at the Academy that year.[6] The desire for 'country' pictures among middle-class visitors

138 *Surrealist art commissioned by Edward James at Monkton, West Dean.*

led to 'pretty' watercolours turned out with little inspiration and limited technique, just as it had spawned run-of-the-mill poetry and prose. Artists were not true countrymen but metropolitan in their business relations. In order to achieve prominence they had to establish close connections with London picture dealers, and as soon as yellow leaves began to fall about their easels they returned to London for exhibitions, business contacts and the enjoyment of the city in the winter season.

Their fondness for cottages and their gardens, developed as a main motif by Frederick Walker about Horsham, by Helen Allingham, C.S. Elgood, P.L. Clifford, Alfred Parsons and many others, was their special vision of arcadianism. Typically an image of peace, pleasure and retreat, this was one of the clearest signals of a town-weary society. Cottages increasingly entered into the possession of artists, writers and weekenders, and ever since the Weald has been thought of as the garden of gardens, especially in the Wealden idiom of William Robinson and Gertrude Jeykyll. If some of the cottages suggested destitution, they were disguised with roses so as not to offend the sentiments of buyers in Kensington and Sydenham.

IMAGES OF THE DOWNS

The rolling Downs, which came to be regarded as beguilingly English, have been recorded in drawings, paintings and watercolours for nearly two hundred years now. There is little realism in the works of the more distinguished artists; the images are mainly romantic and dream-like, half-imagined and half-recollected. It was the mission of most artists to represent a fine summer's day with any signs of modern technology removed. Their work established the county's reputation as a place for relaxation and consolation.

For lovers of the Picturesque a bare chalk landscape was considered unpaintable in its whiteness. This attitude was overturned by Copley Fielding (1787-1855), the first artist to paint the Downs, between about 1829 and his death in Hove. He was a true innovator. With astonishing skill, expressed through flowing lines, washes of lovely colour, a sense of atmosphere and Turner's facility for handling immense space, he created an image of the Downs that became the model for most of his successors. *On the Downs* (1838) aimed to evoke a romantic mood rather than adhere to scientific or historical fact, and his downland topography, often seen through a mist or shimmering haze, is largely imaginary; but he successfully captures the region's essence. His fine series of paintings from Arundel Park was commissioned by the 13th Duke of Norfolk.

A notable successor to Fielding was Henry George Hine (1811-85). Before the onset of Victorian realism he, like Fielding, aimed to create a romantic mood, but his reputation has suffered from repetition. He was born in Brighton and made familiar to his generation the Downs between his birthplace and Beachy Head, more so than any other artist. As a boy he was befriended by the Rev. W. Townsend, vicar of Kingston Buci and friend of Copley Fielding, who showed him a collection of Fielding's drawings which appear to have made a lasting impression on him. It is, however, probably a sign that downland paintings had not yet become fashionable that he had reached middle life before they become his inspiration. He recalled how difficult and subtle it was to model the shapes of the Downs, which resembled a human body. From the 1860s he visited frequently favourite places such as chalk pits above Eastbourne, Bible Bottom near Lewes, Mount Harry, Wolstonbury Hill and Cissbury Ring. His watercolours are mainly views from these places, made various by weathers, seasons and times of the day. There are downland paintings by him in the Towner Art Galley, Eastbourne, and at Lewes Town Hall.[7] A masterly painter of the western Downs was La Thangue, who had a magical touch in depicting woods, orchards and pools, as at Graffham in 'The Farm Under the Hill'. His painted labourers working in the fields, such as 'The Weed Burner' and 'The Sower', have an almost sculptural form. Notable, too, is Edward Stott who experimented with the effects of light at Amberley under the strong influence of Millet.

Sir William Nicholson, who first came to Rottingdean to meet Rudyard Kipling, was a much more innovative painter. His superb evocation of 'Judd Farm' (1909), then perched on the cliffs near Rottingdean, captures the profound silence and simplicity of the Downs. It uses skills acquired in producing graphics for posters and pioneering coloured woodcuts. Nicholson often chose to paint on a late summer evening, when buildings stood out boldly against the smooth lines of the chalk and a huge sky. The bookplate depicting Rottingdean windmill, designed for his publisher William Heinemann (1897) and adopted by Heinemann for his firm's colophon, was a site from which he often painted.[8]

Thereafter the Downs became part of artists' England. Ruth Dollman (d. 1965) illustrated Richard Jefferies' *Nature near London* and painted the Downs around her home near Ditchling. She conveyed the serenity of empty downland in a flowing style which has been called 'weak' and 'pretty', though her works are still much sought after. Wilfrid de Glehn (1870-1951), John Singer Sargent's painting companion, depicted some evocative scenes in 1908-19 around his friend's home at Cooke's House, West Burton, near Arundel. This included the barn and the archway into the garden, done in a manner that recalled the luscious colour and varying shade he had adopted in Italy.

In the 1920s and '30s the Downs were the nation's favourite sketching and painting grounds for both professionals and amateurs. In the county's art galleries are collections which attest to thorough exploration of the local surroundings. In the Towner Gallery at Eastbourne are Edward Stott's 'Lambing Time' (1918), Charles Knight's tranquil 'Ditchling Beacon' (1935) and Frank Wootton's 'Windover Hill in Snow' (1945). In the Worthing Art

139 *Rottingdean Mill, by William Nicholson, designed as a bookplate for William Heinemann and later adopted as a colophon by the publishing company.*

Gallery are paintings by Mark Fisher and Shoreham's Marlipins Museum holds paintings by Brooking Harrison and James Aumonier.

The most successful attempts to express the sculptural folds of the eastern Downs were those of Eric Ravilious. His great achievement was to abandon the hackneyed vision of idyllic downland that was the playground of the urban and suburban patron. He experimented with light effects, such as the pallor of chalk in winter, which few artists had hitherto tackled. He had an eye for barbed wire, wind pumps and other modern machinery, but did not depict the darker side of country life – the drudgery, the insanitary cottages, the struggle with heavy clay or hungry sand. His earliest sketchbooks date from the period when he was at school in Eastbourne. After attending Eastbourne College of Art and the Royal College, he became a talented wood engraver, lithographer and ceramic designer, before turning to watercolours. His 'Firle Beacon' (1927), showing the influence of Paul Nash, his tutor, has an iconic intensity in the way the great sculptural folds on its escarpment are presented. His finest series of Sussex watercolours date from the mid-1930s when he stayed at Peggy Angus's rented cottage at Furlongs near Beddingham, two fever wagons from the war acting as additional accommodation for artists weekending from London. Here he tackled new themes, including the 'Dolly' engines in a nearby cement works, the winter arable, which he evoked by characteristic ribbing, ships in Newhaven harbour, and the interior of Angus's house (more curious and beautiful than Charleston) when the weather was too bad to paint outside. This was the period of 'Downs in Winter' (1934), a stark and dramatic scene, 'Tea at Furlongs' (1939), 'Farmhouse Bedroom' (1939), 'The Wilmington Giant' (1939), 'Cuckmere Haven' (1939) and 'Channel Steamer Leaving Newhaven Harbour' (1935). In one of his last Sussex paintings, 'Beachy Head' (1939), he appears to be experimenting in a design resembling a Chinese painting, with a few shapes drastically simplified. Ravilious's works are things to measure, observe, and react to, but rarely to be fully absorbed by. There is a selection at the Towner Art Gallery. He was lost on an air sea rescue mission in 1942.[9]

From 1916 Charleston farmhouse near West Firle was home to Vanessa Bell and her ménage, including Clive Bell, her husband, writer and art critic, artist Duncan Grant, art critic Roger Fry, her lover for a time and life-long admirer, and writer David Garnett. Charleston was also periodically visited by the Woolfs, Maynard Keynes, Lytton Strachey and E.M. Forster. It became famous, or notorious, for its assault on conventional social mores and as home to the Post-Impressionist movement in English art. Everything Victorian was scorned. From his Omega workshops Fry supplied household designs influenced by the force and colour of Cézanne. They matched the exciting Charleston interior, an idiosyncratic mix of subtle and exuberant colour streaked and splashed on every surface in sight. Charleston was not so much a house to live in as a canvas to be painted.

The art of Bloomsbury never attained the heights reached by Cézanne, Matisse and Picasso to whom it owed so much, but conveys a love of life in an avant-garde manner which was refreshingly different. Angelica Garnett termed the creativity 'a fountain of vitality springing from the earth of sleepy Sussex'. It was 'fun' art, spontaneous and do-it-yourself, what might be called 'holiday' art with a French feel. Grant and Vanessa Bell were painters to the core and their sole motivation was satisfying the eye. The same feeling was extended to the garden, where the influence of Cézanne prevailed again, many different flowers being planted for their colour. Grant painted with verve his massively rounded women, portraits, pottery and glass, and Vanessa Bell supplied bold and spontaneous Post-Impressonist still-lifes and portraits, including those of Lytton Strachey and Iris Tree, plus self-portraits. Berwick church near Charleston is remarkable for the modern wall paintings executed by Grant, Bell and other family members. The pictures were painted at Charleston on large sections of plaster-board and then fitted to the church walls with wooden battens. Angelica Bell was the model for the angel in Vanessa's 'Annunciation' and 'Nativity', and a friend was the adoring angel in Grant's 'Christ in Glory'. A local shepherd and others acted as models, and two Australian servicemen posed as disciples in Quentin Bell's altarpiece. For Professor Sir Charles Reilly, an originator of the project made possible by Bishop Bell's enthusiastic support, the heavenly feeling induced was like stepping out of foggy England into Italy.[10]

Frank Newbould's 'The South Downs', a Second World War poster depicting Birling Farm and the former lighthouse of Belle Tout on the chalk cliffs of the Seven Sisters near Beachy Head, encapsulated the English heritage the nation was fighting for at the time.

Chapter 23

AGAINST THE CURRENT: REPELLING THE CONTEMPORARY AGE

You cannot know
In your bald cities, where no cowslips blow,
How dear life is to us.

W.S. Blunt, 'Worth Forest'

Fade far away, dissolve and quite forget
What thou among the leaves hast never known,
The weariness, the fever, and the fret.

John Keats, 'Ode to the Nightingale'

Great things are done where men and mountains meet.
These are not done by scurrying in the street.

William Blake, 'Great Things Are Done'

One of the most worrying matters before the Second World War was the periodic arrival of disagreeable 'London smoke', first observed by Gilbert White of Selborne in the late 18th century. As the capital became bigger it became blacker, and all Sussex within forty to fifty miles of the capital experienced the occasional haze wafted down on a northerly wind from the 'stupendous volcano with a million fumaroles'. The climatic effects were quite dramatic. When a canopy of soot hung over 100 square miles of countryside, light became dull and hueless, the temperature fell, air became raw and damp, bird song ceased, and nostrils were filled with the tang of sulphur. Wilfrid Blunt imagined that Sussex was being held in the grip of London's dark arms. Ruskin called it a 'poisonous plague wind' in *Storm Cloud* (1884), one of the earliest reports of pollution and its adverse effects. John Halsham reckoned in 1898 that, partly on account of this canopy of soot defiling the Home Counties, summers had degenerated from the time when grapes had ripened on almost every house in Lindfield, near Haywards Heath, and landscape gardener William Robinson of Gravetye, near East Grinstead, wrote in 1917 of the surface of his ponds being covered by a 'mass of greasy wreaths' when the wind blew from the Wen for several days.[1]

The majority of contemporaries endorsed the views of Herbert Spencer and H.G. Wells, or later writers such as C.P. Snow and E.H. Carr, who held that the future meant accepting the technological advances that were lengthening human life spans and raising standards of living, but a substantial Sussex population kept as far as it could from modern realities. After all, it was the essence of the Sussex dream, for both incomers and the old society, to escape from growing cities. They conceived landscape as not only solace but as morally regenerative, indispensable to the soul's salvation. The anti-urban culture of the British middle classes that Martin Wiener derided was nowhere more prominent in the inter-war years than in Sussex, the county most transformed by urban migrants.[2] They were heeding the warnings in Aldous Huxley's *Brave New World* (1922) of the dangers of the frightening Utopia which could come with purely technological progress.

National and local newspapers tell this side of the story. The man round the corner bewailed changes which made his home district unrecognisable, and newspapers took up the issue, broadly supporting a curb on housing, identifying areas of natural beauty to be regarded as sacrosanct, and decrying 'Londonisation' generally. Strong opposition also came from the established landowning class, notably the Gages of Firle. Then, gravitating to the earthly paradise, were misfits, rebels, utopian dreamers, Simple Lifers, 'Back-to-the-Landers', and escapists generally at odds with the world, and these people regarded Sussex as a refuge, the relic of a purer, pre-industrial, world. An influential few, inspired by Ruskin's and William Morris's example, abandoned London to take up cottage life and practise rural handicrafts in a Back-to-the-Land movement. These, like Eric Gill and his followers at Ditchling, considered their actions a defiance of the system of mass production. Ford Madox Ford retreated from the capital after 1918 because it signified the society and way of life that had betrayed him and his fellows into world war. Hilaire Belloc's Distributist ideals on the wider ownership of land, worked out with G.K. Chesterton and published in *The Servile State* (1911), may well have been influenced by his long familiarity with the small family farmers of the Sussex Weald.

These dissenting elements inform the light lyrical poetry and other writing on the county. An accompanying strand of explicit anti-urbanism in Sussex literature was incensed at the inroads of London into the surrounding countryside and the insidious changes to traditional rural life caused by modern urbanisation. Writers varied in their approach: some had a bunker mentality, like Rudyard Kipling and John Halsham; others adopted a battlefield strategy, like W.S. Blunt, Hilaire Belloc, Ford Madox Ford and C.E.M. Joad. They wrote with the pugnacity and dedication of William Cobbett or took Habberton Lulham's quieter, more contemplative look at the world's ills. These authors supported the revival of rural civilisation, in line with Baldwin's assertion that 'England is the country, and the country is England'. The avalanche of run-of-the-mill Sussex literature has impeded recognition of this finer tradition.

Three separate but interlocking strands in their defence of Sussex can be identified. Firstly, at the core of their philosophy, the writers questioned the moral, political and spiritual standards of *laissez-faire* capitalism and proposed alternatives based on agrarian traditions, still regarded as more ethical and sustainable today. Their objective was the reform of urbanisation and industrialisation, and with single-mindedness they took on the role of social critics, looking for antidotes to what they considered the 'sickness' of man in modern society. They crusaded for the salvation of England.

Secondly, they vigorously denounced the insidious 'Londonisation' of the Sussex countryside, demanding landscape protection, possibly for the first time in England.

Far from regarding this as impossible appeal to the god of retrogression, they became active champions of the culture and sensibility of an older England, openly defying the prevailing national mood.

Thirdly, their love of the rural life, that was disappearing as developers eyed up tempting sites, induced them to record the remnants of ancient beauty for an urban readership. A new class of writer pioneered a rich genre based on the search for rural survivals. The habit of regarding them nostalgically through sepia-tinted glasses is traceable to Miss Mitford's *Our Village* and the other works mentioned on p.199.

THE ORIGINS OF URBAN DENUNCIATION

The roots of the withdrawal from urban life, the strongest theme in Sussex literature, is traceable back for more than two hundred years. It is clearly evident in William Blake's imaginative renunciation of the consequences of the Machine Age for mankind, which appears to have emerged initially during his stay at Felpham – the 'sweetest spot on earth'. He stated in his own words, on his return to London, that 'Jerusalem' grew 'out of the three-years slumber on the banks of the Ocean'.

A predilection for traditional rural life appears in the pastoral poetry of James Hurdis's 'The Village Curate', published in 1788 and set in Burwash. Hurdis (1763-1801), a friend of Cowper, was appointed to the curacy of Burwash and remained there until about 1791. He compared the beauty of the hop gardens with the people 'pent up in city stench, and smoke and filfth', and asked what were the charms of the formal gardens of Ranelagh or 'boasted Vaux' in London compared with his own ravishing natural scene.

> Tell me not,
> Ye who, in love with wealth, your days consume
> Pent up in city stench, and smoke, and filfth.
> O tell me not of aught magnificent
> Or fair as this, in all your public walks.
> What are the charms your Ranelagh affords
> Compar'd with ours? Search all your gardens round,
> Ye shall not find e'er at your boasted Vaux
> A haunt so neat, so elegant as this.
> Long let us stray, and frequently repeat
> Our ev'ning's homage to the blossoming hop.[3]

The antipathy to the city is also strong in the poetry written by Charlotte Smith between 1784 and 1797. The district around Bignor Park offered a complete and credible alternative to London, a world of roses and comforts. She preferred her native southern hills to 'polluted, smoky atmosphere and dark and stuffy streets'[4], and yearned for the western South Downs, 'unspoil'd by man', as a means of escape from sophistication which, to her as a woman, meant suppression, injustice and folly:

> How often do I half-abjure Society,
> And sigh for some lone Cottage, deep embower'd
> In the green woods, that these steep chalky Hills
> Guard from the strong South West.

140 *Hurdis's birthplace, Norton, Bishopstone.*

> For I have thought that I should then behold
> The beauteous works of God, unspoil'd by Man
> And less affected by human woes
> I witnessed not.[5]

Throughout her works she reveals an extraordinary knowledge of the botany of the chalk, heath and woodland flora, and her pen brings to life the banks of the Arun with yellow broom and silver birch, willowherb, and flags sheltering in the reed beds. She was an expert on the wildflowers of the chalk and, unusually for her time, saw beauty in heathland and studied the geology and archaeology of the Downs.

In later poems she widened her denunciation to the moral condition of England. In her long poem *The Emigrants* (1792-3), which opens on the cliffs east of Brighton, she takes up the cause of the French émigrés in the style of William Cowper's *The Task*. She reflects on the turmoil in France and adopts a political standpoint on the condition of England which she considered was as hapless and suffering as were the wretches of France. Her own story led her to argue that the much vaunted freedom, justice and liberty of England was a sham. Her powerful phrases must have surprised and angered many a Sussex mansion, manor house and rectory and, coming from a woman, were probably completely insufferable. Even in the delightful view from the cliffs she saw evidence of class warfare in the trees hiding the parish church, 'with care conceal'd/ by verdant foliage, lest the poor man's grave/ Should mar the smiling prospect of the lord'. She openly attacked 'the venal, worthless hirelings of the Court' and the parasites who giddily rise to scorn those who in reality were superior in worth. Such free thinking in a county housing the Prince Regent's Palace was strong stuff, which her friends and readers would have seen as revolutionary. She was alienating herself from the high society in which she was born and bred – though not completely: 'half-abjure' was her phrase, and she appeared to be taking on the mantle of middle-class morals and proprieties. This is probably part of the explanation for her patron Hayley's abandonment of her, and Lord Egremont's extraordinary statement (after a period of strong support) that her worthless husband was 'the best of the bunch'.

In the novel *The Old Manor House* (1794), set on a large landed estate in West Sussex, her aristocratic characters are mainly dissolute rakes, lawyers, despicable rogues and clerics riddled with nepotism. A key spirit that defined the age to her was the supercilious behaviour of the rich towards the poor, the oppressed and depressed, the atmosphere of public rudeness. On account of her general disillusionment she took the side of Americans in the War of Independence, and hinted that some of the reforms of the French Revolution could happily be applied to England. In what is clearly meant to be an unattractive picture of her social times, the hero receives justice, despite the wickedness of the age, when he and the heroine, an orphan dubbed a servant by 'society', ultimately share a large country estate.

LATER 19TH-CENTURY OPPOSITION

Wilfrid Scawen Blunt (1840-1922) lived an autocratic life at ease in beguiling estates at Crabbet Park near Crawley and at the stone-and-brick house of Newbuildings in Shipley, near Horsham. He was proud of his Sussex birth and, when not denouncing British imperialism in Egypt and Ireland or declaiming his respect for peoples uncorrupted by the false values of western society, was declaring his passionate love for his native Weald and tenaciously defending it against what he regarded as adverse change. One forms the impression that over a period of years every field, wood and copse and every fence and road on his estates was overhauled to make it beautiful. He took care to retain the historical character of his countryside of deep oakwoods, ancient forest wastes, sheltering hedgerows and deep brown fallows, including the sub-parallel old droveways, 30 to 40ft and more wide, that thread the Newbuildings estate in a north-south direction,

141 *The title page of the 17th edition of Cobbett's* Cottage Economy, *published in the forlorn hope of reviving the English peasantry. It was reprinted by Douglas Pepler and used as a manual by the Guild of St Joseph and St Dominic at Ditchling.*

"COTTAGE ECONOMY:

CONTAINING

Information relative to the brewing of BEER, making of BREAD, keeping of COWS, PIGS, BEES, EWES, GOATS, POULTRY, and RABBITS, and relative to other matters deemed useful in the conducting of the affairs of a Labourer's Family ; to which are added, Instructions relative to the selecting, the cutting and the bleaching of the Plants of English GRASS and GRAIN, for the purpose of making HATS and BONNETS ; and also Instructions for erecting and using Ice-Houses after the Virginian manner.

BY WILLIAM COBBETT

SEVENTEENTH EDITION.

PUBLISHED BY ANNE COBBETT, 137 STRAND, 1850

B

213

142 *Crookhorn Farm near Horsham, 1993, on the estate of Wifrid Scawen Blunt. It was shown to William Morris as a gem in the landscape.*

worn by men and animals travelling between the Downs and woodland pasture in the deep Weald. Blunt was so proud of his handiwork that he showed it to William Morris, himself haunted by the Middle Ages and a lover of country exquisitely fitted for life's gentler uses. It was a perfect setting for the pastoral poet, who fell under its spell and found in the Wealden countryside a physical beauty that suited his temperament. This appears to have shaped his own set of values which included championing the small Wealden farmer, his ways and traditions.

Blunt expressed his deep love of his homeland as a young man in *Chanclebury Ring*:

> Say what you will, there is not in the world
> A nobler sight than from this upper Down.
> No rugged landscape here, no beauty hurled
> From the Creator's hand as with a frown:
> But a green plain on which green hills look down
> Trim as a garden plot. No other hue
> Can hence be seen, save here and here the brown
> Of a square fallow, and the horizon's blue.
> Dear checker-work of woods, the Sussex Weald!
> If a name thrills me yet of things of earth
> That name is thine. How often I have fled
> To thy deep hedgerows and embrace each field
> Each lag, each pasture – fields which gave me birth
> And saw my youth, and which must hold me dead.[6]

The last six lines of this sonnet are carved on his tombstone in a yew grove at Newbuildings. He writes in this vein again in old age:

> A love of English country things, more especially of the actual clay soil of Sussex with its deep hedgerows and deeper oakwoods, is still with me the most permanent instinct in my mind that I can hardly imagine happiness in my old age with[out] some local anchorage, and I find it difficult to recognise beauty if it were not of the Weald.[7]

143 *Scawen Blunt's tomb in the grounds of Newbuildings, Shipley.*

On the outbreak of war in 1914 he drove to the top of Stammerham Hill to take his mind off the awful prospect ahead. He could imagine no more perfect picture of peace and confessed the Weald meant more to him 'than all the British colonies put together'.

Richard Jefferies' extraordinary autobiography, *The Story of My Heart* (1883), contains the most radical and imaginative alternative society dreamt up in Sussex, a community that would 'enjoy their days, the earth, and the beauty of this beautiful world; that they may rest by the sea and dream, that they may dance and sing, and eat and drink'. The book commences with his experiences in his Wiltshire chalkland home at Litlington Hill near Swindon, but concludes with his intense feelings at the Devil's Dyke in the South Downs above Brighton, where the book was written. Jefferies' mind soared into mystical exaltation on chalklands: the immensity of open space and its inexpressible beauty; the pure air; the mystery of the mighty forces that wore and shaped the groove-like hollows; the feeling of antiquity and continuity engendered by grassy tumuli, fosses and 'camps' over thousands of years old which one could see, touch and enter into at every hand. The opportunity to withdraw from the everyday world and be utterly alone left him rapt and carried away with a quickened aspiration to understand more of the universe and his place in it, and learn how mankind might lead a better life through the search.

His story has not hitherto been thought of as a 'Sussex' one because it is a record of his spiritual development over the previous 17 years with little that is specific to Sussex, but his inspiration was the ancient stones of Pevensey Castle, which he visited in 1880, and it was written during his stay in the county. Moreover, it is clear his innermost feelings were fed by the presence of the sea and of the Downs during this period. He took enjoyment in long walks over the South Downs, 'in the long-drawn breath, the spring of the foot, in the act of rapid movement', and experienced the exquisite joys of the senses. The depth of feeling aroused by the Devil's Dyke figures in his notebooks:

> After a long interval I came to the hills again, this time by the coast. I found a deep hollow on the side of a great hill, a green concave opening to the sea, where I could rest and think in perfect quiet. Behind me were furze bushes dried by the heat; immediately in front dropped the steep descent of the bowl-shaped hollow which received and brought up to me the faint sound of the summer waves. Yonder lay the immense plain of the sea, the palest green under the continued sunshine ... Silence and sunshine, sea and hill, gradually brought my mind into the condition of deep prayer. Day after day, for hours at a time, I came there, my soul-desire always the same.[8]

It was on the Dyke one evening in the dusk that he understood for the first time the mysticism exalting an individual's soul and perfected a way of making human life longer, less painful and more pleasurable. He described the feelings of rapture when he reached the Sussex coast and could experience physically and spiritually what he called the fullness of life – sea and sun, earth and air.

> I found the sea at last; I walked beside it in a trance away from the houses into the wheat. The ripe corn stood up to the beach, the waves on one side of the shingle, and the yellow wheat on the other ... The great earth bearing the richness of the harvest, and its hills golden with corn, was at my back ... The great sun shone above, the wide sea was before me, the wind came sweet and strong from the waves ... I lifted my face to the sun, I opened my lips to the wind. I prayed aloud in the roar of the waves.[9]

It was in Sussex that he meditated upon his bafflement at the 'madness' that 'after twelve thousand written years' the human race should still live from hand to mouth like animals, slaving for the barest of necessities in the midst of a cornucopia of riches, declaring, under the infatuation of money, that work is the main object of man's existence, although the power of the rise and fall of the tides alone would save most of the human labour. W.H. Hudson considered the book was powerfully influenced by Jefferies' stay in Sussex, where his literary and imaginative powers developed greatly, but A.H. Anderson concluded it was largely inspired by his origins in Wiltshire.[10] If Hudson is correct, the book is the most utopian vision of the future to emerge from all the Sussex reformers we have encountered. In the middle of the second cataclysmic collapse of the capitalist system, it should not be dismissed as the hopeless delusion of an early 'hippie'.

AGAINST THE TWENTIETH CENTURY

By the 1890s London was over-running parts of rural Sussex and altering traditional habits faster even than bricks and mortar. This aroused strong feelings for rural Sussex, which was given a 'supercharged national identity' by Hilaire Belloc and Rudyard Kipling, who arrived almost simultaneously in the county to do it justice.

For all Belloc's vitality and restless travel writing around Europe, his exploration of the history of France and his engagement in national politics and religious issues, the inspirational centre of his universe was Sussex, where he had been brought up by his mother and lived almost all his life. To him Sussex was 'that part of England what is very properly called her Eden', the Arun valley the 'ante-chamber to heaven for beauty', and Gumber Corner, his favourite summit on the Downs near Slindon, the 'high watch-tower of England'. This glorious arrogance, as his admirers termed it, signified his vision of Sussex as a civilisation entire in itself, permanent, stable and salutary, the centre of the good things of life, and somewhere he himself could be healed. Sussex was the source of his best work because it filled his soul and gave wings to his imagination. Sussex was England at its most quintessential. It was a 'Not-London', a civilising heart of England, the very sentiment of his neighbour Blunt at Shipley.

His exceptional patriotism for Sussex was possibly due to the fact that, born in France and settled in England, he felt like a man without a country. As a man who did not belong, he needed its support, which was also Kipling's position. Belloc established a quasi-mystical relationship with Sussex and conceived the notion that as the county had 'nourished him and given him his being', he should in return try to lend it glory and serve it faithfully; it would be his friend forever and he would, in a sense, outflank death.[11] 'The Sea compels me, and my County calls me', he wrote in one of his poems. He developed the idea most fully in a superb lyric, 'The Boy that Sings on Duncton Hill', which concludes *The Four Men* and is, in effect, his epitaph:

> He does not die that can bequeath
> Some influence to the land he knows,
> Or dares, persistent, interwreath
> Love permanent with the wild hedgerows;
> He does not die, but still remains,
> Substantiate with his darling plains.

The affection for Sussex never became stale or trite, but increased with age. H.B. Morton says that Belloc's eyes never rested on the Downs above the *Crabtree Inn* at Lower Beeding, or admired the view from Bury Hill or the Arundel Gap under Rackham Hill, without an exclamation of pleasure. Belloc himself remarked on the thrill 'which comes upon a man as he travels south from Victoria Station and hears, almost at the same time that he first smells earth, the South Country tongue'.[12] He had a special relationship with rivers, the Arun and the Western Rother, which he worshipped not as inanimate things, but as living beings.[13]

He compared rural life in 'this Eden which is Sussex still' with the 'slavery being undergone by people in the industrial districts', and as late as 1937 considered the characteristic Englishman to be a countryman. His own generation still remembered an England where most old people belonged by birth to villages and country towns. In *The Servile State* (1912) he denounced the corruption of state capitalism; his Catholicism and his familiarity with the Sussex Weald and its society of small farmers, with whom he lived for over forty years, underlay his own political dream of a property-owning democracy based on 'peasant' farms and smallholdings. This, it was hoped, would bring classes more closely together and encourage people to work harder on land they owned.

His criticism of modern living led to his hating towns of 'the London sort' such as Haywards Heath, and he roundly condemned ignorant urban newcomers who pronounced 'Hor-sham' for Saxon 'Hors-ham'. He was haunted by a fear of the disappearance of the Sussex he knew following the advent of the motorcar. Melancholic distress runs through all his writing, such as his remarkable *The Four Men* (1912) and *Halnaker Mill* (1913), which ends:

> Spirits that call and no one answers;
> Ha'nacker's down and England's done.
> Wind and thistle for pipes and dancers
> And never a ploughman under the Sun.
> Never a ploughman. Never a one.

Little attention was paid at the time to Belloc's alarm at the desecration of the county, voiced in *The Four Men* (written in 1902), the most passionate and original book on Sussex ever written. In it he predicted that Sussex was doomed, his purpose in writing being to set down what he then saw before it was forgotten and became a different thing, 'its people never more being what they were'. In *Sussex* (1936) he took on the role of 'Deplore-Laureate' of Sussex; it is a sustained elegy for the loss of the Sussex he knew, brought about by the railway and the internal combustion engine. He concludes with the question:

> Which of us could have thought, when we wandered years ago, in the full peace of the summer Weald, or through the sublime void of the high Downs, that the things upon which we had been nourished since first we could take joy in the world would be thus rapidly destroyed in our own time, dying even before we ourselves should die? Yet apparently it has come. London broke out like a bursting reservoir, flooding all the ways to the sea, swamping our history, and our past, so that already we are hardly ourselves.[14]

Kipling's search for a haven from trippers at Rottingdean, whom he found unbearable after his daughter Josephine's death, ended in 1902 when he found Bateman's on the banks of the little river Dudwell at Burwash. He wrote to a friend, 'I have moved from Rottingdean to an old stone house about 300 years old, in the middle of the most English country that ever you dreamt of.' He loved modern technology and science, but over the next decade Kipling became absorbed in the Sussex past, and no other author has interpreted it with such realism and historical imagination. This period of creativity is marked by his rediscovery of the history, traditions and folklore of the Sussex Weald, centred on fictional persons such as the Roman Parnesius and Old Hobden, the archetypal hedger and poacher whose family had been rooted in the soil for centuries.

Where Kipling succeeds is in his reconstruction of the Wealden landscape, enthralling adults as well as children of his generation, the history being largely a fantasy of his own imagination. As Seymour-Smith has remarked, 'The evocation of the district around him rings but true and clear. To do this he writes himself into the landscape with a touch of genius.' *Puck* is interspersed with realistic little details of Wealden life, generally centred around Old Hobden, the hedger. There are also touches of folklore, such as the singing of 'Old Mother Laidinwool', a song sung in the hop gardens around Burwash in the 19th century. He writes an imaginative history of the Weald, with which he had fallen in love as 'the most English England', but is also acutely conscious of what should be preserved (unlike Hardy, who dwelt on decay). Moreover, his short stories with a Sussex theme and his poem *The Land* appear to mark a deliberate eschewal of the values of industrial society. He remarks on the waste of rural skills and craftsmanship when young people leave the countryside to take up menial work in towns, and displays, perhaps unfairly, an animus against 'second-rate' intellectuals from the city. He has insight into the harmony which Wealdsmen in the past had with the soil and, regarding it as a corrective to the modern materialistic attitude to life and society, wanted to see it eventually re-established. This is most evident in the verses 'Recall' and 'An Habitation Enforced', when he speaks for the

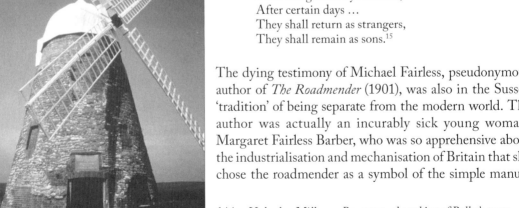

Weald and makes plain that he yearned for the day when those migrating to the towns would return again to the thousand-year-old district:

> I [The Weald] am the land of their fathers,
> In me the virtue stays,
> I will bring back my children,
> After certain days …
> They shall return as strangers,
> They shall remain as sons.[15]

The dying testimony of Michael Fairless, pseudonymous author of *The Roadmender* (1901), was also in the Sussex 'tradition' of being separate from the modern world. The author was actually an incurably sick young woman, Margaret Fairless Barber, who was so apprehensive about the industrialisation and mechanisation of Britain that she chose the roadmender as a symbol of the simple manual

144 *Halnaker Mill near Boxgrove, the subject of Belloc's poem.*

145 *Kipling's watermill at Bateman's.*

worker who laboured for the benefit of others. She asked only to serve, live and commune with her fellow countrymen without avarice or anxiety. Her book had such pathos, vision and charm that, published posthumously, it became a bestseller in Britain and the United States. It also revealed a Franciscan love of nature in all things, great and small. It was written at Mock Bridge House, Shermanbury, on the River Adur, where she spent her last two summers. The sycamore tree under which she lay in warm weather still thrives and the white gate through which she imaginatively passed into Heaven is identifiable.

Ford Madox Ford kept up the most consistent attack on modern civilisation. Written in a mood of bitter disillusionment, *The Inheritors* (1901) attacked the modern age, with its frauds and cold-blooded exploitation of humanity, and *Mr Apollo* (1907) satirises contemporary London, boasted of as 'the largest city that the world has ever seen'. After his war service at the Front in the First World War, Ford, like so many others, was even more convinced that the values which had held good before the war must now be wrong if not responsible for causing the war. He recuperated in his little 'green nooks' at Red Ford and Bedham near Pulborough, where he tried a little farming. He was tremendously disheartened at what he felt was a betrayal by the British ruling classes of the chance for peaceful and humane government. In his novels he offers a sound and penetrating analysis of what he considered the moral and material collapse of the western world, and particularly of England and the United States. The fortunes of Christopher Tietjens in *Parade's End* (1921-8) illustrated the situation in England and, in the *New Statesman* for 1919, Ford made vitriolic comments about London:

> One had had [in the London of 1919] little sense of the values of life, if indeed one had the sense that life had any values at all. Now it was as if some of the darkness of nights of air raids still hung in the shadows of the enormous city. Standing on the Hill that is high above that world of streets one had the sense that vast disorder stretched into those caverns of blackness. A social system had collapsed. Recklessness had taken the place of insouciance … Now we are drifting towards a weir.[16]

One of the most representative Sussex poets was Habberton Lulham. He was from a Brighton family and hungered to return from Sydenham and Croydon after he qualified as a medical practitioner. The need to escape into the country, a conventional theme of the Sussex poet, is particularly predominant in his work. In 'Escape' (1908) he pleads for his lover to leave with him the 'reeking streets' for the 'wave and star and heather', and in 1913 he returns to this idea:

> We were not made for cities, you and I,
> And in the reek lies poison for our souls.
> Their riches but impoverish our hearts,
> Make but a wedge to rive us from our best.
> Escape, pure heart, escape! Break free to me,
> And with me bare your tired brow to the breeze
>
> ('Come')

And although he and his lover are always on breezy sea cliffs or in unspoilt countryside he feels his wooing is at a disadvantage:

> How dare I dream to wind our woodland grace
> With this poor city soul, and form and face?

His love of the countryside leads him to speak directly to the hills themselves:

> What do we ask of you and, asking, find?
> That which the glittering cities may not give,
> What in the fields of flowers can never live,
> Nor all the hurrying seasons leave behind,
> Unchanging shelter from the blast unkind,
> Refuge and solace for the unquiet mind.
>
> ('To the Hills')

Simple Life colonies tended to be transient and ultimately unsuccessful, but a remarkable example called the Sanctuary was founded by Vera Pragnell, daughter of a prominent textile manufacturer. Her aim was to create a Christian community which carried out the teachings of St Francis of Assisi and was devoted to rural life and handicrafts. She trekked over the Downs with her donkey in 1923, searching for suitable land, and discovered 19 acres of sandy common, eight acres of arable, a heather-covered hill and two derelict cottages on part of Heath Common between Washington and Storrington. On the hill she built a Calvary, divided the area into allotments and allocated land for huts, built by the colonists themselves, and camping pitches. Her vision and achievements are set out in her booklet *The Story of the Sanctuary* (1928). This explained her goals for a better life but, sadly, the colony fell short of her ideals.

Her guest house, free to anyone, had a statue of the infant Jesus standing with outstretched arms in the porch. When Gerard Young visited the colony in 1928 the artists living there were holding an exhibition of their work, and an old wheel-less omnibus provided the schoolroom; there was a tiny community shop and a little hall where plays were enacted and folk dancing and discussions took place. People tramping over the Downs would drop down from the hills to join in the dancing and alfresco concerts round the great camp fire, and watch the sunset from Calvary Hill. In the early 1930s the guiding philosophy began to wane. Pragnell provided title deeds for the colonists' parcels of land and these were swiftly sold. She was married and the future of the colony passed into other hands.[17]

Chapter 24

SAVING THE COUNTY

'I dunno what my old Daddy would say, boy. Look at it. Houses, Houses, Houses – that
makes me prostrate with dismal.'
(Jim Copper talking to his son in the 1930s in *Bob Copper's Sussex*, 1997).

On account of its fast-changing character, Sussex acquired a reputation for being rather
built-up and overdone. Critics scornfully dismissed the 'cosy palaces' of wealthy
newcomers, the mock-Tudor and other period houses everywhere under construction,
the actors' weekend cottages full of fake oak beams and furniture, banal pictures in the
Summer Exhibition of the Royal Academy and the hackneyed tags of Belloc and Kipling
as a chocolate box stuffed with trippers, or an extension of Oxford Street. But this gives a
misleading impression of Sussex as a whole. There were still in 1939 little roads under the
Downs or through the woods of the Weald where on fine Sundays one could drive without
meeting another car, and one could walk up to Chanctonbury Ring on midsummer nights
when the glow worms were about and hear the fox and nightingale. The terns diving in
the sea near Chichester, wild daffodils in secluded places like West Dean, lonely groups of
flint farm buildings, and dew ponds on the Downs, all remained until after 1940. As one
contemporary writer put it, 'Even though a few more houses should be built in Sussex, and
even if a few more verses be written about it, I don't think I should leave.'[1]

Philip Gosse, who lived below Chanctonbury Ring, was not so charitable to the county
in which he had come to live. One senses his boiling rage when he declares he cannot
forgive a Sussex that has become plastered with hoardings, petrol stations, bungalows,
tea shops and shanties. He thought foreigners would assume the two principal industries
of the English were the supplying of cakes and petrol. His greatest venom was reserved
for teas – 'dainty and otherwise' – for he was convinced that wherever there was a tea
shop there came a petrol station next, and to reactionaries like him the Sussex tea shop
was a symptom of the landscape degeneration he detested. Gosse recommended that
the traveller in search of Sussex get a third-class train ticket from Victoria Station to
Steyning, via Horsham, because it avoided the recent degeneration along the roads.[2]

Some liberal thinkers objected to the new notion of preserving countryside which was
then gripping the middle classes. Evelyn Waugh, for example, regarded as menaces to the
integrity of the countryside the preservation of ancient monuments, transplantation of
Tudor cottages, collections of pewter and old furniture and debased arts and crafts, indeed
anything connected with the mania for 'ye oldness' and 'picturesque bits', including Eric
Gill's Ditchling and Belloc.[3] Waugh would have been disgusted by Lord and Lady Moyne's

146 *Edward Shanks' cottage, Rodmell.*

collection of ancient houses from Wiltshire and Somerset dismantled and re-erected at Bailiff's Court near Littlehampton between 1927 and 1933.

Cyril Connolly, one of the leading literary figures of the day, was educated at Eastbourne and lived for a while at the foot of the South Downs near Firle before finally ending up at Eastbourne again. He loved the unpraised Downs and is buried in Berwick churchyard. With idiosyncratic melancholy, he thought of the Downs in 1929 in terms of the 'awfulness' of the people who wrote about them – Kipling's thyme and dew ponds, Belloc's beer and Chesterton's chalk; he despised the lyricism of the Georgian poets, the 'Drinkwaters', the 'Squires' and the 'Shanks', all of whom were connected with Rodmell (and also despised by the Woolfs). He was also driven to distraction by the people of the 'country habit has me by the heart variety' and the 'England, my England' sort whom he found spreading all over the Downs: ardent cyclists, beer-swilling ramblers, brass rubbers, charabanc trippers and motorists picnicking 'over a space for building lots'. In the next decade he dismally wrote that English civilisation was dying, and saw no reason to preserve the South Downs in their final moments of distress. He thought saving the countryside would merely convert it into an open-air museum, under siege from the 'crows' of the semi-detacheds heading down the new arterial roads from the suburbs. His pessimistic vision was of an Americanised England, with slagheap cities in rubble fields, but without American vitality or variety of race.[4] In *Enemies of Promise* (1938, revised 1948) he thought a bomb-proof ivory tower might even be necessary from which to continue the celebration of beauty which the rest of mankind would be 'too guilty, hungry, angry or arid to remember'.[5]

147 *Saltdean Lido, designed by Charles Neville.*

So much Sussex countryside has been erased by sprawling residential estates that it is difficult to visualise what it was like as farmland. On the urban fringe there may be glimpses of surviving 'green belt', as at Haywards Heath, where a fragment of the undulating park-like scenery beloved by John Halsham is a locally cherished open space. Useful documents in this regard are Sales Catalogues. These exist in substantial numbers for large estates sold since *c.*1880, and their illustrations and descriptive detail are invaluable sources of information as to the former appearance and usage of the land, even if the 'brochure-speak' of the auctioneer sometimes falsifies reality.

With Sales Catalogues, we can discern at Haywards Heath the Lucastes and Harland Farms before they were 'ripe for development' at throwaway prices, and discover at Sunte the outlying fields of a country house lined with detached houses; at Summer Hill the elegant pleasure grounds before the mansion became a Preparatory School and a 'high-class' residential estate are once more laid out. The Sales Catalogues of the 1920s help depict the three landed estates which make up modern Seaford – East Blatchington, Sutton and Chyngton. Surviving catalogues reveal much about the transformation of the Weald from a landscape of small family farms to the parks and pleasure grounds of the country houses of urban newcomers.

On the eve of the First World War the sale of land on the Downs for housing began almost overnight; it went into overdrive from the mid-1920s and lasted until the declaration of the Second World War. Over and over again, the various schemes were judged a catastrophe by middle-class opinion and architectural critics alike, with Peacehaven held up as a national disgrace. It was not the fact of housing itself that provoked outrage as much as the jerry-building and total lack of design, done on open landscapes that were widely visible and among some of the noblest natural beauty in England. Weak planning controls and an indifference to landscape design characterised the generation that survived the First World War.

There was a widespread middle-class bitterness that more was not done to protect the Sussex countryside from despoliation. The matter was brought to a head by concerns about Peacehaven (initially called Anzac Cove), built haphazardly on the cliffs along the coast road between Newhaven and Brighton by developer Charles Neville, 'with superb views of the sea'. Critics claimed it was cheap, greedy and meretricious; Virginia Woolf thought Wembley beautiful and the Mile End Road respectable compared with Peacehaven's gimcrack houses and raw roads. Her Diary entry for 5 September 1927 expressed the hope 'that a really comprehensive statesmanlike mind would take stock of all this human activity and direct and weld it together', something that was to be tackled spasmodically and feebly until 1947 when the Town and Country Planning Act began to bring some order and principles to development.[6]

In the 1920s and '30s people anxiously scanned local newspapers for announcements of the sale of extensive downland estates that would almost certainly presage an assault by speculators. There were widespread doubts that Sussex would survive the unchecked development. O.G.S. Crawford, the Archaeological Officer of the Ordnance Survey, who called downland turf a 'priceless manuscript', which would be irretrievably destroyed by development, was in pessimistic mood. He predicted in the journal *Antiquity* in 1929 that it was unlikely, with *laissez-faire* capitalism, that any open country or downland would remain in southern England in a hundred years time.[7]

Crawford's unpublished manuscript account of contemporary England, written in 1938 and entitled *Bloody Old England*, envisaged the English countryside not in the light-hearted manner of H.V. Morton's books, bought in their thousands by tourists, but as a place vandalised and degraded by a car-bound civilisation which valued the countryside as a resource to be plundered. This was Hilaire Belloc's view in 1936.[8] Crawford's pessimism was justified by inadequate government control over the situation, but he had underestimated the growing effect of middle-class opposition to the building on the Downs which had almost ruined them. A new appreciation for the English countryside was partly a consequence of patriotic feeling after the First World War, and it led to the creation of voluntary environmental and amenity organisations such as the Society of Sussex Downsmen (founded in 1923 and now the South Downs Society). It was also a principal reason for the formation of the Council for the Preservation of Rural England in 1926 (now the Campaign to Protect Rural England). These bodies concerned themselves with the protection of natural beauty, the preservation of historic buildings, poor building standards, flagrant commercial advertising, and the problem of litter left behind by holiday-makers. In 1927 Douglas Freshfield of Forest Row wrote in his local newspaper of the recent changes for the better.

> Our County Council [the East Sussex Council] is enforcing control of roadside advertisements, Brighton is stirring itself to secure the neighbouring Downs, Eastbourne is eager to add the Seven Sisters to Beachy Head and to preserve them from being converted into a dumping ground for bungalows, Hastings is striving to preserve some of the charm of the promontory of Fairlight.[9]

It is at this juncture, and it is on the Sussex Downs, that we first meet in England the emotional overdrive of radical environmentalists which was to peak in the 1960s.

The spectacular success of these projects showed that the tide was turning against the speculative builder, although much damage continued to be done and there were many lost battles and setbacks ahead. Despite the national concern over the South Downs there was so much desecration up to the beginning of the Second World War that it seems, in retrospect, the face of Sussex was only saved by the onset of hostilities and the years of austerity which followed. From the later 1950s onwards, wiser counsels prevailed and stronger government protection was provided for cherished landscapes.

Public concern was matched by the achievements of East and West Sussex County Councils in the years just before the Second World War. The former purchased the development rights from speculators and others on the open Downs, spending many millions in present-day terms, and prevented a rash of bungalows on high ground. It also secured voluntary agreements with landowners to restrict building development on open downland purchased for plotland at Cradle Hill, above Alfriston, and demolished shanties (still evident as brick foundations in scrubland). West Sussex County Council also entered upon a downland protection scheme of its own, securing voluntary agreements with more than 100 landowners to save some 125 square miles of downland over 200ft above sea level from being built upon.

Another landmark in saving the county was a letter published in the press in May 1929, signed by the principal landowners and supporting the measures being taken by the authorities (such as the Brighton Joint Regional Town-Planning Scheme of 1932). It expressed the hope that with the exercise of foresight and expert knowledge it should be possible to accommodate a larger population without destroying the Downs, but it regarded the lack of compensation for landowners who forewent development as an injustice.[10]

Eastbourne Corporation purchased downland at Beachy Head and the Seven Sisters; another part of the famous chalk cliffs was successfully acquired by public subscription led by the Society of Sussex Downsmen; the National Trust received the Newtimber estate from

148 *Rottingdean Tudor, designed by Charles Neville.*

Lord Buxton; and Brighton, inspired by (Sir) Herbert Carden, acquired a green belt which included Standean, the Devil's Dyke and Saddlescombe Farm. The Standean Estate in 1905 included 4,400ft of frontage to the old turnpike road from Brighton to London, which at 600ft above sea level commanded 'views of the most charming description overlooking Stanmer Park' and the sea. The Sales Catalogue added, 'The property possesses great possibilities for development, the frontage affording some fine building sites, unsurpassed for beauty on the South Coast.' Today, these views remain open and unspoilt for all who travel along the road over the Downs to Ditchling Beacon. Downland divisions between suburb and country are exceptionally sudden and sharp, the result of haphazard development. Examples are the setting of Rottingdean windmill and the island-like greenness protecting the historic Bishopstone church and village. Wherever open space survives among bungalows and semi-detached houses there is a person or authority, usually unremembered and thus unsung, who deserves the praises of posterity.

Virginia and Leonard Woolf's feelings about unplanned development in the South Downs can be read in the latter's autobiography and in the former's diaries and letters. Leonard explained that on the day war broke out in 1914 the Woolfs walked from their summer home at Asheham (near Lewes) down to the sea at what is now Peacehaven and Telscombe Cliffs. Leonard thought the walk, when he looked back on it, marked the end of the civilised country life he and Virginia had known. The haphazard creation of Anzac-on-Sea, which eventually became Peacehaven, epitomised to him and countless others the destruction of the way of life which existed in Sussex and vast stretches of England before 1914. He noted that there were tremendous evils in the former ways and much that needed to change, but he could see no point in destroying it unless something better were put in its place. Writing in 1965, he thought no sane man would then walk from Asheham to Peacehaven. 'If one had to choose between the sheep and the sheepdog, not to speak of the shepherd, of 1914 and the respectable devotees of T.V., football pools and bingo who flock into the hideous houses which in 1963 are flung together higgledy piggledy in Peacehaven, then I am not sure that one should not prefer the civilisation of the sheep.'[11]

149 *Steyning from the Bostal Road.*

Every solitary walk from her home at Rodmell brought Virginia Woolf fresh eyesores or threats of development. Whenever she came across anything new spoiling the cherished sweep of the Downs, whether houses, bungalows, shanties, race- and motor-cycle tracks, or chalk quarries and cement works, they provoked rage, despair or ungovernable nostalgia. She expressed her dread of being worried out of her walks and views repeatedly, and thought the Downs were being murdered and Sussex was doomed. She preferred to live in Tavistock Square, Whitechapel or any suburban slum, but occasionally, when in jubilant or more relaxed mood, shrugged off the losses of the Downs and imagined bungalows as haystacks, the new 'elephant sheds' at Asheham cement works as 'Greek temples' (in March 1932) and relished the sublime beauty of the works lit at night.

On 26 December 1929 she noted that Rodmell was always being risked and saved, and so perhaps would be again. Cutting down trees and spoiling the Downs she regarded as the two greatest iniquities. Their gardener told the Woolfs that Captain Byng-Stamper was to sell a 40-acre field on Rodmell Hill for building. Leonard made various moves to avert this, including writing to the Prime Minister, but failed to prevent the erection of several houses and bungalows in subsequent years which have one of the finest views in the Downs.

On 16 September 1931 she wrote to Vita Sackville-West of her rage at the prospective local Labour candidate who had bought land above the village and was putting up a bungalow with an immense view. 'What are we to do?' she cried, 'I don't see any point of living in a suburb of Brighton … My God, I wish one hadn't picked this age to live in. I hate my kind.'

At Ham Spray in Wiltshire on 18 January 1932, she was reminded by its beauty of how her own Downs were being ruined. Her diary entry on 2 February 1932 records Ethel Smyth saying, 'Really I think that building of the kind you describe at Rodmell is worse than death. After all, one may say of death it's natural, but this is wanton desecration.' Virginia was encouraged by the policy of Rupert Gwynne, landowner at Wootton manor, who thought beauty was something to retain and refused to sell his land for development, although it meant sacrificing money.

Returning from Greece on 2 May 1932, she noted that they had not seen a villa, tea shop, or kennel anywhere. In September 1934 a road was to be made along the Downs path up Rodmell Hill and she asked herself whether it was worth buying the land and saving one crumb when all was threatened. Her entry for 4 October 1934 is one of the most poignant: there were too many buildings already, alas, but the gossip was that a building company was buying Botten's Farm in Rodmell to build on it. The fate of her former home at Asheham, which had become a limeworks, was the most terrible of all. In the words of Quentin Bell, the hillside was 'blotted out of sight by vast corrugated iron sheds, the valley was coated with toxic white dust, the air with nauseating fumes, and the hill itself was hollowed out as though it had been a diseased tooth'.[12]

Cyril Connolly, staying at Hove, thought Sussex 'inconceivably ugly', the change from yellow brick and slate to red brick and slate being all that told of the move from town to country.[13] Philip Gosse described the whole south coast of England, from the South Foreland to Poole, as practically one long suburb of London, and thought the few unspoiled spots, such as Cuckmere Haven, would eventually go the way of the rest of the coast as there were no powers to prevent it. Only a few years earlier it had been a pleasant walk or drive along the upper coast road below the Downs, between Hove and Worthing, but he now warned people not to go there anymore, 'with its mile of silly little crowded bungalows and villas, built anyhow, and without a thought for dignity, arrangement or planning'. He thought that in the new 'Sussex by the Sea' it was becoming difficult to find a right of way between the houses, and lamented that no simple law had been passed forbidding any house being built within half a mile of the seashore. When playing cricket at Woodingdean

150 *Virginia Woolf.*

he was aroused to such fury by the scene that he missed an easy catch. He wished he had the wealth of a multi-millionaire so that he could buy up the whole village, with its villas, bungalows, shanties, henhouses, tea shops and all, and restore the hodge-podge to its original state as an enchanting downland valley.[14]

Gerard Young recalled his own anxieties about the future of the Downs when a young man in the 1920s. Worried that they might not always remain in a state of perfection, he was alarmed to discover that most people were not interested in preserving the beauty of the hills. He never forgot the shock he felt as a boy when he cycled to Eastbourne from Brighton and suddenly encountered Peacehaven. Such hideous sprawling on the smooth downland grass made him worried for the fate of other hillsides he knew more intimately. It was with sickening heart in later years that he watched the gradual despoilation of green slopes with harsh red brick and tile. He saw the housing estates of Worthing creep like a lava stream into the lovely Findon valley behind the town. High Salvington already had a rash of bungalows among its blackberry thickets, and now the ugly new houses were mounting higher up the hillsides further eastwards at Lancing, and making a mark across the wild thyme slopes like dirty water in a bath. It was disquieting to him to be confronted with an opinion opposite to his own, especially one that felt that if, by settling and living on new land, mankind could benefit itself then to hell with the scenery.[15]

Although the Downs engaged most attention, there was also a widespread spirit of resistance against the residential sprawl that was occurring on the coastal plain of West Sussex and turning it from an agricultural place into the home of a health and 'pleasure industry'. From the late 1920s the coastal plain was the fastest developing area in Sussex. This led to a common belief that housing, unless checked, would completely cover a region which mostly comprised first-class arable land, so removing the very amenities which made the region so popular. In fact, development was brought under some control by the planning committees set up under the Town and Country Planning Act of 1925, which collaborated with voluntary organisations and endeavoured to identify by means of a zoning system sites for urban use. As an alternative to the continuous promenade of ragged buildings lining the coast, the intention was to provide a series of self-contained communities, each separated from its neighbours by a girdle of open land containing planned recreational areas. The seaside township of Angmering-on-Sea was singled out as an excellent example to be followed. The smaller towns of West Sussex could not follow the example of Brighton and Eastbourne, which were buying outright large tracts of downland to save them from development, but a crucially important proposal in 1929 limited development on the Downs to below the 150ft contour (eventually revised to 200ft). This reflected the Society of Sussex Downsmen's opinion that the Downs should be preserved in their present state and have only agricultural buildings erected on them. The keynote of planning in West Sussex after the 1925 Act was the preservation of the greater part of the area in its existing condition. By 1929 both Bognor and Littlehampton had proposed schemes which provided for a ring road, an aerodrome, the protection of Bersted village's open land, and zoning of the built-up interior to prepare for more orderly development. Largely lost sight of was the proposal that some stretches of beach should be left in their natural state.[16]

The most sustained broadside on despoliation was by Ian Nairn, subsequently co-author of the Sussex volume in the *Buildings of England* series, who turned the searchlight on Brighton's downland, five miles deep and seven miles wide. Although

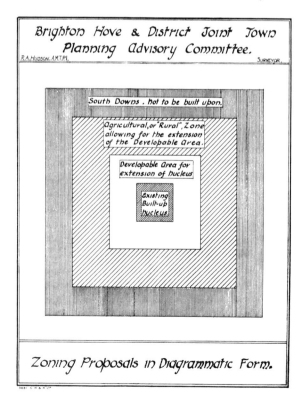

151 *Zoning Proposals for Development, Brighton District, 1932.*

152   *The Downs from Poynings village, 1932.*

post-war planning had rounded up and in-filled earlier damage to the Downs, he condemned the spatter of houses spreading like treacle over open downland, 'tied by their trolley-bus umbilical cords which lay between green gaps, tatty and narrow, between this careless romp of dispersal'. Prophetically he remarked that if development were allowed to proceed at the current rate, by the end of this century there would be no distinction between town and country, i.e. 'subtopia'. Nairn thought that the terror of subtopia would keep people sweating at night; instead they yawned and remained unmoved. His vision of an 'annihilating tragedy of Valhalla' still hangs over Sussex, but people's reaction today is as apathetic as was their grandparents'.[17]

The purchase of open spaces for the benefit of local communities, a feature of the Brighton, Eastbourne, Surrey and Middlesex county councils, led to the idea from the late 1920s that such large tracts as the Lake District and the South Downs should be set apart as National Parks on the example of the USA and Italy. The suggestion that parts of Sussex should have some special legislative protection on account of their exceptional natural beauty and vulnerability to development had come from John Halsham in his *Idlehurst* (1898). He advocated what he termed a 'Natural Museum' for the central Weald and adjoining Downs, an idea inspired by the growth of the Haywards Heath district and by one of his favourite views, from the Rectory Garden at Lindfield across the wooded folds of the Weald to the blue haze of the Downs in the distance.[18] Halsham's proposal was not addressed until the greater urban growth which followed the First World War, the government's Addison Report advocating the designation of National Parks (1929).

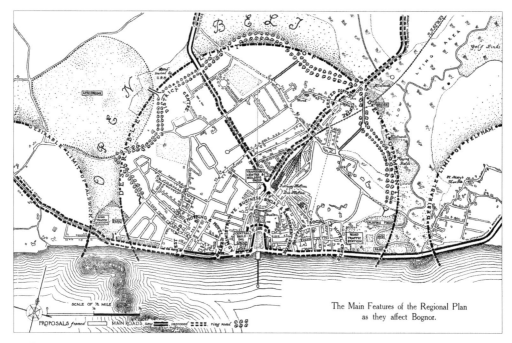

153   *The Bognor Regional Plan, 1929, from Arthur Schofield's West Sussex Coast and Downs (1929).*

But the aspiration did not find favour among the great landowners of the Downs, who for centuries had exercised a system of estate control which had created and preserved many of the finest features of the Sussex countryside. When Vaughan Cornish set out his vision of a National Park for the South Downs in 1930 he had in mind a central South Downs park between the Arun and Adur rivers.[19] He considered that the Downs eastward should be left in the care of the municipalities of Brighton and Eastbourne, and dismissed the western Downs towards Chichester as largely wooded and, though beautiful, less representative of downland. He remained uncertain whether the necessary powers of protection should be given to a National Park authority or whether that could be arranged by some other means, an ambiguity which has only been resolved in 2009 by designating the whole of the South Downs and the adjacent Western Weald as a National Park.[20]

One of the oddest paradoxes of the inter-war years was the public's intense love of the coastline and accompanying failure to preserve more than a tiny fraction of it for posterity, another example of the Englishman's predilection for destroying what he professes to love. Vaughan Cornish made the proposal, which is only now actively being pursued, of retaining a strip of public land along the top of cliffs or foreshore to preserve the view and provide public access. This he envisaged as complementary to the ongoing clearance of slums by the London County Council, the latter aiming to make towns fit for people to live in, the former guaranteeing a countryside fit for people to look at.[21] His aim to create a coastal path round England is now being taken up in Bills going through Parliament.

Cornish failed to influence events in one major respect, arguing in 1935 that the natural beauty and archaeological interest of the widespread turf cover of the Downs should be protected and maintained under powers provided by the Town and Country Planning Act, 1932. All but about three per cent of the turf went under the plough in the name of modern agri-business.[22]

The conservation movement also failed to protect British agriculture. As Malcolm Muggeridge observed in 1941, the Preservation of Rural England attracted adherents and money but the Productivity of Rural England aroused little concern, and fields were abandoned to rabbits while tall thistles grew among the corn. Farmhouses and labourers' cottages were coming into the hands of new occupants who were champions of countryside amenities, but not protective of its utilities.[23]

Cyril Joad's letter to the *The Times* is an example of how an individual's protest at desecration, widely publicised, often succeeds in stopping disaster. When Amberley was about to receive electricity, he wrote of the village's superb setting on the margin of the Wild Brooks and the Downs, describing 'a plum of the countryside', a reposeful land intimately praised by poets and artists, and the haunt of wild birds.

> The village of Amberley is composed of many thatched cottages … It is to the highest degree picturesque. It has a narrow winding street, an old village church, a half-ruined castle, and a perfectly placed cricket ground. Practically unspoilt by modern building, it is as good a specimen of the traditional village as one could wish to see. One cannot avoid the conclusion that if there is one [place where?] the visible approach of electricity supply is more unwise than any other, it is Amberley. It could be completely damaged by the introduction of the new ugliness or beauty – call it what you will – of the modern age. Are we, in a word, to preserve no place to record what it was once and will never be again. To run the wires underground will cost an estimated £370, far beyond what the village can pay.

The Times blazed away at a time when Dirk Bogarde's father was the photographic editor. It published three photographs of the village, including artist Edward Stott's cottage, a

154   *Lewes, view to Beddingham.*

155   *The new living conditions of the ultra-modern 1930s.*

156 *End of an era: tractors harvesting the first wheat crop on the former chalk turf at Falmer, 1941.*

map, and seven letters from correspondents, all but one supportive of Joad's opposition. R.A. Drury, ARA, wrote, 'There are few parts of our countryside which condense as eloquently as does Amberley the beauty of pastoral England.' As a result of the outcry the wires *were* put underground.[24]

For saving so much of the county from reckless destruction in the inter-war years we have to thank first the landowners, especially owners of downland, who supported the actions of those local authorities which were attempting to establish some control, and all those who strove to preserve the character and natural beauty of the county. Despite impoverishment since the First World War, partly from heavy death duties, most of the

157 *Looking forward to old times: a government war poster of 1941 showing a fair on Alfriston Tye.*

bigger landowners strove to protect as much of their agricultural land as possible. They were aware that haphazard 'development', although providing some immediate increase in wealth, could lead to the ruin of the Downs and the decrease in value of their remaining estates because of unsightly change on the boundaries. In 1929 Lord Gage of Firle, Lord Buxton of Newtimber, Ruth Chichester, the representative of the Chichester Estates, Humphrey Brand of Glynde, John Christie of Glyndebourne and other landowners united to prevent further ribbon development along main roads and stop all road building in the Downs.[25] The landowners' actions were not confined to the Downs. If one stands on the terrace of Balcombe Place at Balcombe, one of the loveliest parts of the High Weald, and looks across the Low Weald to the unspoilt Downs in the far distance, the sweep of unspoilt wooded country ranging for miles still resembles the unbroken Saxon Andredesweald. For this inspiring survival much is owed to the owners of large landed estates such as the Cowdrays and Burrells, and numerous owners of smaller properties who resisted the easy temptation of 'development'. The subsequent dissolution of most of these estates poses a threat of unchecked development in the future.

Then, to our roll-call of heroes, we should add the pioneer town and country planners and councillors of local authorities, such as Sir Herbert Carden of Brighton, originator of Brighton's green belt, officers such as R.H. Hudson, who was primarily responsible for the first regional planning scheme for the Downs in 1932, and the young Stanley Baker, who did much professional and voluntary work for the community in the 1930s and later. Among the host of volunteers of the period, the man who was foremost in the battle to save the Sussex countryside was Arthur Beckett of Eastbourne, who fought with the spirit of the famous Sussex marching song of the First World War: 'You may tell them all that we stand or fall for Sussex by the Sea'. As an inspiring propagandist in the *Sussex County Magazine*, which he founded and edited from 1926 until his death in 1943, he was influential in the cause of conservation. His books on Sussex were popular and inspired affection for the county, and as President of the Society of Sussex Downsmen he was persuasive in helping secure valuable amenities. As an expert on the Downs he contributed to the first Brighton scheme of 1932.

CONCLUSION

On the eve of the Second World War barbed wire was hooped on the cliffs, defences were dug along the foreshore, air-raid shelters were built in the towns and evacuees arrived by rail from London. Sussex had already undergone steady change over several generations. Much of the small and intimate life of farm and homestead, lane and footpath, gate, hedgerow and pond, not to mention incomparable trees, had fallen in the face of the developer; inexorable social change pervaded the traditional life of the county following its 'discovery' by an urban population. We have seen that Sussex people were not grudgingly reclusive or falsely modest about the exquisite graces of their county, but they were less than caring for the surroundings they admired so much. The county today stands on the brink of further change as mankind squares up to the new challenges that face him. This examination of earlier responses to change, and of the distinctive types of creative endeavour which have successively shaped and reshaped the county, is not merely a nostalgical look backwards. On the contrary, it is a means of learning from former mistakes in the hope of securing a better future.

NOTES

1 INTIMATIONS OF EDEN

1. Jefferies, 1929, pp.541-2.
2. Belloc, 1954, pp.35-8
3. *Sussex Express*, 1927
4. Noyes, 1950, 'The Tramp'
5. Lucas (ed.), 1904, p.4
6. Farjeon, 1921, p.231
7. Wells, 1924, p.25
8. Beckett (ed.), 1952, pp.183-4
9. Webb, British Library Ms. Webb, 271
10. Watkin, 1968, pp.158-9
11. Brandon, 2003, p.241
12. Belloc, 1906, p.176
13. Jennings, 1880, p.162
14. 'English Country; Four Landscapes', *New Statesman*, 23 August 1919
15. Lucas, 1918
16. Hudson, 1900, p.37, and *passim*
17. Lawrence, 1921, p.14
18. Copper, 1971 edn, pp.97-8
19. Robinson, 1938, p.2
20. Hudson, 1900, p.29
21. Hopkins, *c*.1930, p.17
22. Wilkinson, 1933, pp.60-70
23. Brandon, 2006, pp.374-5
24. Stockwood, 1984, pp.99, 196, 206, 214
25. Belloc, 1912, p.2
26. *Country Gentleman Magazine*, 1905
27. Charques, 1936, pp.51-2
28. Shanks, 1924, p.18
29. *Time and Tide*, 3 June 1939, p.724
30. Montague, 1928, p.147
31. Olson (ed.), 1980, p.55
32. Waugh, 1930, p.48

2 BEYOND THE SMOKE

1. Ellis (ed.), 1987, vol. 2, p.88
2. Carlyle, 1970-2001, vol. 12, p.292 (17 October 1840)
3. Rutherford, 1881, p.38
4. Stephen, 1878, pp.76-7
5. *The Times*, 4 December 1886, 11e
6. Hunter, 1880
7. Lamb, 1903 edn, pp.8, 246
8. James, 1987, pp.175-6
9. Cecil, 1975, p.154; Bell, vol. iii, 186; Spotts, 1990, p.249
10. Keegan (ed.), 'In a London Drawing Room', *Penguin Book of English Verse*, 2001, p.757
11. Gissing, 1903, pp.18-26
12. *The Times*, 2 December 1890, 3d
13. Trevelyan, 1931, pp.104-5
14. Mais, 1948, p.13
15. Thomas, 1912, pp.67-8
16. Holliday, 2007, p.127
17. Farjeon, 1986, p.191
18. Arlett, 1940, p.170
19. Barbellion, 1991 edn, p.39
20. Blatchford, 1931, p.217

3 CHANGING WAYS OF SEEING AND EXPERIENCING LANDSCAPE

1. Keats, 1947, p.176
2. Macky, 1732 edn, vol. 1, p.971
3. Allingham and Radford (eds), 1907, p.301
4. *The Guide to Goodwood House*, 1834, pp.1-2
5. Hare, 1896, vol. 2, p.143
6. Hare, 1900, vol. 6, p.487
7. *Poetry Review*, vol. 16 (1925), pp.363-7
8. Piozzi, 1884, p.91
9. Keats, 1947
10. Gilpin, 1804, 1792
11. Granville, 1841, pp.580-1
12. Merrifield, 1864, p.21
13. Brooke, 1865, pp.89-90
14. Massingham, 1946, p.202. For one the earliest pleasurable appreciations of bare chalk scenery see H. Ainsworth, *Ovingdean Grange* (1860), pp.1-6
15. *The Speaker*, 1898, p.765
16. Brandon and Short, 1990, p.217
17. Mrs Humphry Ward, 1888, pp.295-6
18. Cobbett, 1835, p.359
19. Massingham, 1946, p.248
20. Lang, vol. 5, 1883-90, pp.218-29
21. Bell, 1972-84, vol. v, p.346
22. Woolf, 1968, p.221
23. Beckett, 1909, p.8
24. Jennings, 1880, p.211
25. Thomas, 1990 edn, p.50; Bell, 1972-84, vol. iv, p.74
26. Mais, n.d. (*c*.1930), p.164.
27. Brandon, 1984, p.88
28. Belloc, 1958, p.48
29. Mantell, 1833
30. Wooldridge and Linton, 1939
31. British Library Webb Mss. 876
32. Reclus, 1881, p.141
33. Halsham, 1913, 214
34. Pater, 1917, pp.197-247
35. Halsham, 1898, pp.159-60
36. Cunningham (ed.), 1906, vol. ii, pp.178-9

4 WILLIAM COBBETT

1. This paragraph is based on Dr John Stevenson's Annual Memorial lecture to the William Cobbett Society, Cobbett's New Register, vol. 10, No. 10, 2009, pp.3-10
2. Cobbett, 1930, vol. 1, pp.152-60
3. *Op. cit.*, vol. 2, pp.542-7
4. *Op. cit.*, vol. 1, p.53
5. *Op. cit.*, vol. 1, pp.206-9
6. *Op. cit.*, vol. 3, pp.702-3
7. *Op. cit.*, vol. 1, p.149
8. *Op. cit.*, vol. 2, pp.246-7
9. *Op. cit.*, vol. 2, pp.532-41
10. Parliamentary Papers: The Poor Law, 466-7, 493-4. For further details of the Petworth emigration see Wendy Cameron, Shelia Haines and Mary McDougal Maude (eds), *English Immigrant Voices: Labourers' Letters From Upper Canada In The 1830s*, 2000. See also Sheila Haines and Leigh Lawson, *Poor Cottages and*

Proud Palaces, The life and works of the Rev. Thomas Sockett of Petworth, 1797-1859, 2007, pp.155-67

5 THE SOUTH SAXONS

1. Cobbett, 1930, vol. 1, pp.225-6
2. Cobbett, 1930, vol. 1, p.207
3. Halsham, 1913, e.g. pp.55-63, 97-105, 188-97
4. *Op. cit.*, pp.29-31
5. Halsham, 1898, pp.45-7, 120
6. Hudson, 1900, pp.83-4, 113-14
7. Parliamentary Papers, the Poor Law, 1834, pp.467, 486, 496
8. Powys, 1967, pp.211
9. Sturt, 1912
10. Ford, 1971, pp.141-3
11. This was the opinion of John Burton, the 18th-century visitor. British Library, Add. Mss. 11571
12. Andrew Hedger, in George Meredith's *Diana of the Crossways* (1908 edn), pp.82-3
13. Parliamentary Papers, the Poor Law, 1834, pp.728-8
14. Cobbett, 1802-35, vol. 27, 1830, p.453
15. Parliamentary Papers, the Poor Law, 1843, pp.487-93
16. *Op. cit.*, p.392
17. *Op. cit.*, p.412
18. Curwen (ed.), 1940, pp.87-90
19. Parliamentary Papers, the Poor Law, 1834, p.812
20. Cobden Unwin (ed.), 1904
21. Minutes of Evidence, the Royal Commission, 27 July 1881

6 EARLY ACCESSIBILITY TO ARCADIA

1. A record in the parish church of Horsted Keynes
2. Cunningham (ed.), 1906, vol. 2, pp.299-300
3. Cunningham, 1906, vol 2
4. Radcliffe, 1892 edn, vol. 1, p.44
5. Radcliffe, *op. cit.*, vol. 1, pp. 45-6
6. Cobbett, 1930, vol. 1, p.198
7. Egerton, 1892 edn, pp.57-9
8. Parry, 1833, p.99
9. Brandon, 1979, p.174
10. King, 1900, p.27
11. Cobbett, 1930, vol. 1, p.288
12. de la Garde, 1834, p.391-3
13. Andrews, 1934, vol. 1, pp.374-5
14. Cobbett, 1930, vol. 1, p.283
15. Fairless, 1901, pp.72-102, 131-5
16. Thirkell, 1951, p.27
17. Wood, 1938, pp.200-1
18. Hopkins, n.d. (*c*.1930), pp.20-1
19. Holliday, 2007, p.62
20. Blaker, 1919 edn, pp.90-1
21. Kaye-Smith, 1953, pp.14, 18-19
22. Holliday, 2007, p.190
23. Gosse, 1935, pp.66-9
24. Lower, 1870, vol. 1, p.225
25. Lucas, 1904, p.111
26. Verrall, 1988
27. Andrews, 1934, pp.1, 352-3, 357, 367, 372-3
28. Wood, *op. cit.*, p.76
29. *Ibid.*
30. Jennings, 1880, pp.189-90
31. Belloc, 1912, pp.115-16

7 DIALECT, FOLKLORE AND FOLK SONGS

1. Belloc, 1936, p.37
2. Lower, 1861, pp.219-31
3. Parish, 1957 edn
4. Halsham, 1898, p.186; Beckett, 1933, p.30
5. Wood, 1938, pp.112-13

6. Blaker, 1919 edn, p.98
7. Kipling, 1914
8. Beckett (ed.), 1952, p.viii
9. Hopkins, 1928, p.71
10. Dalmon, 1922, p.14
11. Hudson, 1900, pp.115-17
12. Cobbe, 2008, pp.43, 78
13. Morton, 1955, pp.23-4
14. Cook, 1928, pp.8-12
15. Holliday, 2007, pp.128, 167
16. Belloc, 1954, p.53
17. The words and music were by Ward Higgins, *The Folk Songs of Michael Blann*, ed. by Colin Andrew, which lists songs from the Barclay Wills collection at Worthing Museum.

8 CHURCHES AND CLERGY

1. Lethaby, 1919, p.225
2. *Spectator*, 2 September 1994, p.72
3. Marsh, 1990, *passim*
4. Ellman, 2006
5. *Ibid.*, pp.44, 131-2, 141-3
6. *Sussex Archaeological Collections*, Vol. xv
7. Jennings, 1880, pp.223-5
8. Ellman, 2006, pp.241-2
9. Philip Webb, British Library Mss. 476
10. Clive Bell, *Country Life*, 4 June 1943, pp.1016-17
11. Anon., 1924. See also Thomas Cocke, *Brighton Churches: the Need for Action now*, 2009
12. Raymond, 1924, pp.165, 168
13. Jerome, 1998, p.31

9 THE CALL OF THE SEA

1. 'Reminiscences of Old Hastings', *Cornhill Magazine*, 1910, p.71
2. P.F. Brandon, the Shoreham Census of 1881, 1985
3. *Ibid.*
4. Lang, 1962, vol. 5 (1883-90), pp.214-18
5. Moore, 1894, pp.8-16
6. Hopkins, n.d. (*c*.1930), pp.130-1
7. Brandon, 1985
8. The *Speaker*, 1898, p.474
9. Walker, 1982, p.4
10. Belloc, 1958, p.126, letter dated 4 Sept. 1922
11. Belloc, 1925, p.118
12. Powys, 1967, pp.211-12
13. *Op. cit.*, p.215
14. 'Reminiscences of Old Hastings', *Cornhill Magazine*, 1910, p.73
15. Wyndham, 1940, pp.82-3
16. Jennings, 1880, pp.271-2
17. Parliamentary Papers: the Old Poor Law, 1834, 487, 489-91
18. 'Reminiscences of Old Hastings' *op. cit.*, p.78
19. King, 1900, pp.13-18

10 SUSSEX BY THE SEA

1. Cook, 1928, p.114 (Hood, *c*.1800)
2. Johnson, G., 'Bathing in the Channel', *Cornhill Magazine*, 1845, pp.63-4
3. Jefferies, 1908, p.118
4. Lamb, 1914, vol. 2, pp.60-2
5. Schofield, 1929, pp.47-8
6. Granville, 1841, pp.594-6
7. Whitford, 1984, p.80
8. *Shoreham and Southwick Gazette*, 22 August 1903
9. Worlters, 1985, p.5
10. *Ibid.*, p.17
11. Walker, 1982, pp.57, 165-6

11 BRIGHTON

1. Antony Dale, 1957, pp.9-11
2. Taylor, 1851, pp.31-3
3. Berry, 2007, pp.4-5
4. Dale, *op. cit.*, pp.57-61
5. Beckett, 1952, pp.182-3
6. Cobbett, 1930, vol. 2, pp.600-1
7. Thackeray, *Papers of the Fat Contributor*, 1845, p.4
8. *Ibid.*, p.84
9. Jefferies, 1908 edn, p.48
10. *Ibid.*, pp.58-9
11. Williams, 1845, pp.23-5
12. Gill, 1940, pp.76-7
13. Asquith, Cynthia, *Diaries, 1915-18*, 1968
14. Shone, Richard, *The Observer*, 1 August 1993
15. Arlotts, 'Landmarks', 1943, pp.47-8
16. *The Spectator*, 7 December 1956

12 SOUTHDOWN SHEEP AND SHEPHERDS

1. Blauw, 1850, pp.35-70
2. White, 1836 edn
3. Baxter, 1846, p.lxi
4. Copper, 1997, pp.75-6
5. Blaker, 1919, pp.9-11
6. Wills, 1938
7. Edwardes, 1909, pp.291-4
8. Jennings, 1880, pp.200-1
9. Price, 1933 edn, pp.151-7
10. Shrubshall and Coustillas, 1985, p.46
11. Hubbard and Hubbard, 1922 edn
12. Edwardes, 1909, p.290
13. *Ibid.*; Hopkins, 1928, pp.18-19, 78, 81

13 COUNTRY HOUSES: HISTORIC AND NEW

1. Collin, 1970, pp.88, 93
2. Andrews, 1934, vol. 1, p.348
3. *Ibid.*, p.374
4. *Ibid.*, pp.366-7
5. *Ibid.*, p.351
6. *Ibid.*, p.363
7. *Ibid.*, pp.364-6
8. *Ibid.*
9. Gilbert, 1927, p.82
10. Andrews, p.375
11. Hare, 1873, p.68
12. Cunningham, 1906, vol. 2, pp.299-301; Andrews, *op. cit.*, pp.362-4, 367, 375; Venables, 1859, pp.125-202; Hare, 1873, vol. 1, pp.66-9, 71-3, 84
13. Wellesley, 2008, p.288
14. Wellesley, 1940, p.42; Wellesley, 1952, pp.157-64
15. *The Times*, 2 January 1936, 11d
16. Harris, 1998, vol. 2, pp.19, 22, 63-8
17. 'Wykehurst', *Country Life*, 1974, p.153. I am indebted to Arthur Shopland for information in this paragraph.
18. Hare, 1873, vol. 2, pp.74-6

14 LANDSCAPED PARKS AND GARDENS

1. Brandon, 1979, pp.182-3
2. *Ibid.*, p.186, n.76
3. Homewood, 1947, pp.68, 100
4. Hussey, 1927, p.129
5. Brandon, 1979, p.177
6. Andrews (ed.), 1934, vol. 1, pp.375-6
7. Halsham, 1898, pp.187-8
8. Meredith, 1972, p.220
9. Pichot, 1825, pp.20-1; see also p.16.

10. de la Garde, 1834, description in translation
11. Hussey, 1927 edn, p.14
12. Kipling, 'A Habitation Enforced' in *Actions and Reactions*, 1909, pp.27-8
13. Brandon, 2006, p.381
14. Robinson, 1870, p.6
15. Robinson, 1911, p.v
16. *Op. cit.*, p.12
17. *Op. cit.*, p.v.
18. Clarke, 1932, p.1
19. Patmore, 1886, pp.1-20
20. Robinson, 1909
21. Messell, 1916, p.iv
22. Noel, 'Leonardslee', *Country Life*, 15 January 1995, p.271
23. Godfrey, 1914, p.87
24. Hare, 1900, vol. 6, pp.487 and *passim*.

15 NEW FORMS OF TRANSPORT

1. Kipling, 1996, vol.3, pp.149-51,
2. Kipling, 1937, pp.101, 175-9
3. Woolf, 1942, p.67
4. *The Essays of Virginia Woolf*, ed. Andrew McNellie, 1988, vol. iii, p.440
5. Woolf, 1942, pp.7-11
6. Blunt, 1932, pp.622-4 (5 August 1908)
7. *The Times*, 26 August 1927, 7d
8. Wilkinson, 1933, pp.48, 63-5, 134, 188
9. Lucas, 1904, p.194
10. Abercrombie, 1926
11. Belloc, 1912, pp.vii-ix; Belloc, 1935 pp.202-3
12. de la Garde, 1834
13. Muggeridge, 1972, p.58
14. Roberts, 2008; Bel Bailey, 'Little Airport, Great Memories', *Country Life*, 1985, p.922
15. *The Times*, 14 June 1930, 6d

16 DOUBLE LIVES

1. The use of farms as weekend refuges for commuters is recorded as early as the 1770s. See Brandon, 1979, p.184n.
2. Plomer, 1958, pp.140-4
3. Young, 1950
4. Blatchford, 1931, pp.250-1
5. Bowen, 1928, pp.65-6
6. Dalmon, 1927, p.18
7. Lewes, 1997, p.468
8. Joad, 1937, pp.174-5
9. Brandon, 2005, pp.173-7
10. John Linnell Archives
11. Lewes, 1997, p.540; Connolly, 1945, p.33

17 SPORT

1. McCann (ed.), Sussex Record Society, 1984, vol. 73, p.117
2. Collin, 1970, passim
3. McCarthy, 1931, pp.29-33
4. Knox, 1845, pp.18-19
5. Sales Catalogues
6. Blunden, 1944, p.66
7. Morton, 1955, pp.34-5
8. Mais, n.d. (*c.*1935), pp.127-37
9. Clifton, 2008
For other sports the reader is referred to Peter Brandon, Sussex (2006), pp.236-54

18 WALKING FOR PLEASURE

1. Merrifield, 1864, p.21
2. Thorne, 1844, p.3
3. Sidgwick, 1912, p.21
4. Bell, vol. iii, p.104

5. Mais, 1948
6. Solnit, 2001, p.21; Trevelyan, 1931, pp.1-18
7. Hopkins, 1933; Mais, 1927
8. Mais, n.d. (*c.*1935), pp.220-5
9. *Op. cit.*, pp.182-3
10. Gosse, 1935, pp.113-15
11. Greene, 1938, p.193
12. Beckett, 1909, p.7
13. Hudson, 1900, p.22
14. Hopkins, 1928, p.12
15. Beckett, 1909, p.7
16. *The Speaker*, April 1898
17. Hewlett, 1908, p.26
18. Jefferies, 1908 edn, pp.190-2
19. Barbellion, 1919, p.39
20. Gissing, 1903, pp.481-4
21. Belloc, ed. W.N. Roughhead, 1954, pp.35-6

19 The Ditchling Arts and Crafts Community

1. Gill, 1940, pp.75-6
2. MacCarthy, 1989, p.116
3. Pruden, 1994
4. Holliday, 2007, p.232
5. Personal communication from Hilary Bourne
6. Holliday, 2007, p.177
7. *Op. cit.*, p.176
8. Pruden, 1994
9. Coatts, 1983
10. West Sussex Record Office, Eric Gill Ms., 34

20 Anything Goes, 1918-39

1. Schofield, 1929, pp.42, 48
2. Sharp, 1932, p.3
3. Trevelyan, 1949, p.95
4. Brittain, 1933, p.17
5. Nairn, 1955
6. Allcroft, 1924, p.148
7. Raymond, 1936, pp.261-5
8. Schofield, 1929, frontispiece
9. Lower, 1870, p.38
10. Halsham, 1898, pp.4-5, 187-8, 220.
11. Sales Catalogues
12. *The Times*, 3 December 1936
13. Sales Catalogues
14. Bell, 1937, p.88
15. Woolf, 1968, pp.60, 67-8
16. Wilkinson, 1933, pp.154-6, 198-9
17. Cobbe, 2008, p.33
18. Bell, 1980, vol. iii, p.105
19. Clarke, 1999, p.11

21 Writers and the New Sussex

1. Sawyer, Ditchling Museum Ms.
2. Belloc, 1906, p.165
3. *Poetry Review*, 1925, vol. 16, pp.363-7
4. Angus Ross, broadcast talk
5. Williams, 1973, p.18
6. Smart and Brandon, 2007, p.21
7. Forman (ed.), 3rd edn, 1947, p.259
8. Macdonald, 1907, pp.11, 35
9. Williams, 1973, p.27
10. Jennings, 1880, p.162
11. Belloc, 1906, p.178
12. Wells, 1915, p.141
13. Ford, 1929, p.13; 1933, pp.92-3

14. Kernahan, 1922, p.236
15. Grahame, 1893, pp.43-52

22 The Role of the Artist's Eye

1. British Library, Prints and Drawings, S5, 32, 33, 37, 38, 48
2. Brandon, 1984, p.219
3. *Op. cit.*, p.301
4. John Linnell Ms.
5. Brandon, 2005, p.231
6. Barringer, 1988, p.136
7. Brandon, 1984, *op. cit.*
8. Campbell, 1992
9. Constable and Simon, 1981
10. Shone, 1999

23 Against the Current: Repelling the Contemporary Age

1. Halsham, 1898, pp.15-19; Robinson, 1917, p.11
2. Wiener, 1981
3. Hurdis, 1800, lines 49-81
4. Smith, Book One, 1792-3, lines 291-3
5. *Ibid.*, lines 35-58
6. Blunt, 1914, p.87
7. Finch, 1938, p.304
8. Jefferies, 1908, pp.37-8
9. *Op. cit.*, pp.103-4
10. Hudson, 1900, p.14; Anderson, A.H., *Sussex County Magazine*, 1937, pp.524-30
11. Belloc, 1912, p.309
12. Belloc, 1906, pp.24, 190
13. *Ibid.*, p.212
14. Belloc, 1936, p.141
15. Rudyard Kipling, 'An Habitation Enforced' in *Actions and Reactions* (1914)
16. Ford, Ford Madox, *The New Statesman*, 1919
17. Young, 1939, pp.79-81

24 Saving the County

1. *Time and Tide*, 3 June 1939, p.72
2. Gosse, 1935, p.203
3. Waugh, 1930, pp.55-6
4. Connolly, 1945, pp.201-2, 207
5. Lewes, 1997, p.199; Crawford, *Antiquity*, 1929, 432
6. Woolf, 1986-1994, vol. iv (1994), p.290
7. Crawford, *Antiquity*, 1929, p.432
8. Belloc, 1936, pp.159-62
9. Letter in a local newspaper, 1927
10. Brighton Hove and District Regional Planning Scheme, 1932, pp.13, 307
11. Woolf, 1968, pp.146-8
12. Bell (ed.), 1972-84, vols 3, 4
13. Lewes, *op. cit.*, p.249
14. Gosse, 1935, pp.65-6, 166-8
15. Young, 1950, p.20
16. Schofield, 1929, pp.80 and *passim*
17. *Architectural Review*, vol. 117 (1955), pp.118, 261-2, 361-458
18. Halsham, 1898, pp.159-60
19. Cornish, 1930, pp.56-8
20. *Op. cit.*, pp.56-8
21. *Op. cit.*, pp.81-2
22. *Op. cit.*, pp.59-60
23. Muggeridge, 1941, pp.352-4
24. *The Times*, 8 December 1932, 14d; 10 December, 4e.
25. Brighton Hove and District Regional Planning Scheme, 1932, p.13
26. Hussey, 1927, p.1299

BIBLIOGRAPHY

Manuscript souces are quoted in full. Articles and books are cited by author and date, for ease of identification from the Notes. Unless otherwise stated the place of publication is London.

Abercrombie, P., *Bulletin of the Council for the Protection of Rural England*, 1926
Allcroft, A. Hadrian, *Downland Pathways*, 1924
Allen, Andrew, *A Dictionary of Sussex Folk Medicine*, 1995
Allingham, H. and Radford, E. (eds), *The Diary of William Allingham*, 1907
Andrews, C. Bruyn, *The Torrington Diaries*, 1934
Andrews, Colin, *The Life and Songs of Michael Blann of Upper Beeding*, Worthing, 1979
Anon., *Excursions in the County of Sussex*, 1822
Anon., *St Bartholomew's Church, Brighton*, 1924
Arlett, Vera, *Sussex Poems*, Sussex, 1940
Baldwin, Stanley, *On England*, 1925
Barbellion, W.N.P. (pseudo. for Bruce Cummings), *The Journal of a Disappointed Man*, 1919
Barringer, T.J., *The Cole Family*, Portsmouth City Museum, 1988
Barton, Margaret and Sitwell, Osbert, *Brighton*, 1935
Bates, H.E., *The Country of White Clover*, 1952
Baxter, John, *Library of Practical Agriculture*, Lewes, 1846
Beckett, Arthur, *The Spirit of the Downs*, 1909
    The Wonderful Weald, 1911
    Adventures of a Quiet Man, 1933
Beckett, R.B. (ed.), *Constable and the Fishers*, 1952
Bell, Anne Olivier, *The Diary of Virginia Woolf*, 5 vols, 1972-84
Bell, Julian, *In New Signatures*, 1937
Bell, Quentin and Nicholson, Virginia, *Charleston: A Bloomsbury House and Garden*, 1997
Belloc, Hilaire, *Hills and the Sea*, 1906
    The Four Men, 1912
    The Cruise of the 'Nona', 1925
    The County of Sussex, 1936
    Letters, ed. Speaight, Robert, 1958
    The Complete Verse, ed. W.N. Roughhead, 1954
Berry, Sue, *Georgian Brighton*, Chichester, 2007
Binyon, Helen, *Eric Ravilious: Memoir of the Artist*, 1983
Bisgrove, Richard, *William Robinson: The Wild Gardener*, 2008
Blaker, N.P., *Sussex in Bygone Days*, 2nd edn, Brighton, 1919
Blatchford, C., *My Life*, 1931
Blauw, W.H., 'Letters to Ralph de Nevill, Bishop of Chichester, 1222-1244', *Sussex Archaeological Collections*, vol. 3 (1850), p.54
Blencowe, R.W., 'On Shepherds and their Songs', *Sussex Archaeological Collections*, vol. 2, 1849, pp.247-56
Blunden, Edmund, *Cricket Country*, 1944
Blunt, W.S., 'Possibilities of Peasant Ownership in Sussex', *Nineteenth Century*, vol. 59, 1906, pp.955-67
    Poetical Works, 1914
    My Diaries, 1932
Bourne, George (pseud. for George Sturt), *Change in the Village*, 1912
Bowen, Stella, *Drawn From Life*, 1941
Brandon, Peter, *The Sussex Landscape*, 1974
    'The Diffusion of Designed Landscapes in South-east England', *Change in the Countryside*, Institute of British Geographers Special Publication No. 10, 1979
    'Philip Webb, the Morris Circle and Sussex', *Sussex History* 2, 1981, pp.8-14
    'Wealden Nature and the Role of London in the Nineteenth-century artistic imagination', *Journal of Historical Geography*, 10, 1984, pp.75-104
    The South Downs, Chichester, 1998
    The Kent and Sussex Weald, Chichester, 2003
    Sussex, 2006
Brandon, Peter and Short, Brian, *South East England from 1000 A.D.*, 1990
Brittain, Vera, *Testament of Youth*, 1933
Brooke, Stopford, *Life and Letters of R.W. Robertson*, 1865, pp.89-90
Campbell, Colin, *William Nicholson: The Graphic Work*, 1992
Carlyle, Thomas, *Collected Letters of Thomas and Jane Carlyle*, ed. Sanders, C., North Carolina, 1970-2001
Cecil, David, *Through A Library Looking Glass*, 1975
Charques, R.D., *This Other Eden*, 1936
Chesteron, G.K., *William Cobbett*, 1925
Clarke, Juliet, *Mr Russell's Little Floral Kingdom*, Alfriston, 1999
Clarke, R.S., *Catalogue of the Trees and Shrubs at Borde Hill*, Sussex, 1932
Clifton, E., *Cricket Match at Sheffield Park, 1900*, Hove, 2008
Coatts, Margo, *A Weaver's Life: Ethel Mairet*, Bath, 1983
Cobbe, Hugh, *Letters of Ralph Vaughan Williams*, 2008
Cobbett, William, *A Life*, 1835
    A Legacy for Labourers, 1834

    Political Register, 1802-35

    Rural Rides, ed. by G.D. and Margaret Cole, 1930, vol. 1

Cobden Unwin, Mrs, *The Hungry Forties*, 1904

Collin, C., *The Hornungs of West Grinstead Park*, 1970

Connolly, C., *The Condemned Playground*, 1945

Constable, Frieda with Simon, Sue, *The England of Eric Ravilious*, 1982

Cook, C.F., *Another Book of Sussex Verse*, Hove, 1928

Copper, Bob, *A Song for Every Season*, 1971

    Bob Copper's Sussex, Seaford Sussex, 1997

Cornish, Vaughan, *National Parks and the Heritage of Scenery*, 1930

    The Preservation of our Scenery, Cambridge, 1937

Cunningham, Peter, *Letters of Horace Walpole*, vol. ii, 1906

Curran, Stuart, *The Poems of Charlotte Smith*, 1993

Curwen, Cecil, *The Journal of Gideon Mantell*, 1940

Dale, Antony, *Fashionable Brighton: 1820-1860*, 1957

Dalmon, Charles, *Singing as I Go*, 1927

    A Poor Man's Riches, 1922,

Dennis, John, *Original Letters*, 1721

Ditchling Museum, *Edward Johnston: Lettering and Life*, 2007

Edwardes, Tickner, *Lift Luck on Southern Roads*, 1909

Egerton, the Rev. J. Coker, *Sussex Folk and Sussex Ways*, 1892 edn

Eliot, George, *Letters*, ed. Haight, Gordon S., 1954-6

Ellis, P. (ed.), *The Writings of Leigh Hunt*, vol. 2, 1987

Ellman, the Rev. Boys, *Recollections of a Sussex Parson, 1815-1906*, Sussex, 2006 edn

Fairless, Michael (pseudo. for Margaret Fairless Barber), *The Roadmender*, 1901

Farjeon, Annabel, *Morning has Broken: A Biography of Eleanor Farjeon*, 1986

Farjeon, Eleanor, *Martin Pippin the Apple Orchard*, 1921

Farrant, S., 'John Ellman of Glynde in Sussex', *Agricultural History Review* 26, 1978, pp.77-8

Finch, Edith, *Wilfred Scawen Blunt*, 1938

Ford, Ford Madox, *It Was the Nightingale*, ed. Killigrew, V., 1971, pp.141-3

Forster, E.M., *Room with a View*, 1980 edn

Foster, Paul (ed.), *Bell of Chichester*, Otter Memorial Paper, Chichester, 2003

de la Garde, Comte, *Brighton; Scènes detachés d'un voyage en Angleterre*, 2nd edn, Paris, 1834

Gibbons, Stella, *Cold Comfort Farm*, 1932

Gilbert, J., *Everyman's Sussex*, Sussex, 1927

Gill, Eric, *Autobiography*, 1940

Gilpin, William, *The Picturesque*, 1792

    Observations on the Coasts of Hampshire, Sussex and Kent, 1774, 1804

Gissing, George, *The Private Papers of Henry Ryecroft*, 1903

    Collected Letters, ed. D.P. Matthiesen, A. Young and P. Coustillas (1990-3), vol. 2, p.478

Godfrey, Walter, *Gardens in the Making*, 1914

Gosse, Philip, *Go to the Country*, 1935

Grahame, Kenneth, *Essays*, 1893

Granville, A.B., *The Spas of England*, vol. 2, 1841

Greene, Graham, *Brighton Rock*, 1938

Halsham, John (pseud. for George Forrester Scott), *Idlehurst: A Journey into the Country*, 1898

    Lonewood Corner, 1907

    Old Standards, 1913

Hamilton, Hamish (ed.), *Commemorative Anthology*, 1941

Hare, Augustus, *Memorials of a Quiet Life*, 2 vols, 1873; vol. 3, 1876

    Guide to Sussex, 1896

    The Story of my Life, six vols, 1900

Harris, John, *Lost Country Houses*, 1982

Hauser, Kitty, *Bloody Old Britain: O.G.S. Crawford and the Archaeology of Modern Life*, 2008

Hewlett, Maurice, *Pan and the Shepherds*, 1908

Holliday, Peter (ed.), *Eric Gill in Ditchling*, Delaware, USA, 2002

    Edward Johnston: Master Calligrapher, 2007

Homewood, R.A., *Three Farms*, 1947

Hood, Thomas, *Hastings*, c.1800

Hopkins, G. Thurston and R. Thurston, *Literary Originals of Sussex*, Gravesend, 1936

Hopkins, R. Thurston, *The Lure of Sussex*, 1928

    Sussex Rendezvous, n.d. (c.1930)

Hove Museum and Art Galley, *Eric Gill and the Guild of St Joseph and St Dominic*, 1990

Hubbard, Arthur and Hubbard, George, *Neolithic Dew Ponds and Cattle Ways*, 1922 edn

Hudson, W.H., *Nature in Downland*, 1900

Hunter, R., *Lectures to the Kyrtle Society*, 1880

Hurdis, James, *The Favourite Village*, Bishopstone, Sussex, 1800

Hussey, Christopher, *The Picturesque*, 1927

James, Henry, *The Complete Notebooks*, ed. by Edel, Leon and Powers, Lyall, Oxford, 1987

Jefferies, Richard, *Nature near London*, 1908 edn with illustrations by Ruth Dollman

    The Story of My Heart, 1908 edn

    'Wild Flowers', in Birkenhead, Lord, *The One Hundred Best Essays*, 1929, pp.540-8

Jennings, Louis J., *Field Paths and Green Lanes*, third edn, 1878

    Rambles in the Southern Hills, 1880

Jerome, Peter, *John Sirgood's Way*, Petworth, 1998

Joad, C.E.M., *The Testament of Joad*, 1937
    'The Face of England', *Horizon*, no. 29, May 1942, pp.335-47
    The Untutored Townsman's Invasion of the Countryside, 1947
Jones, D.K.C., *The Shaping of Southern England*, 1980
Jones, D.K.C., Rose, Francis, and Hebbert, M., 'The Downs that are England', *Geographical Magazine* 52, 1979-80, pp.618-31
Kaye-Smith, Sheila, *Sussex Gorse*, 1916
    Weald of Kent and Sussex, 1953
Keats, John, *Letters*, ed. H.B. Forman, third edn, 1947
Kernahan, Coulson, *Six Famous Living Poets*, 1922
King, Maude Egerton, *Round about a Brighton Coach Office*, 1900
Kipling, Rudyard, *Rewards and Fairies*, 1910
    A Diversity of Creatures, 1914
    Something of Myself, 1937
    Rudyard Kipling to Rider Haggard: A Record of a Friendship, ed. Cohen, M.N, 1965
    Letters, ed. Pinney, C., vol. 3, 1996
Knox, E., *Ornithological Rambles in Sussex*, 1845
Lamb, C., *Essays and Sketches*, ed. Macdonald, William, vol. 4, 1903
Lang, Cecil, M., *The Letters of Algernon Swinburne*, vol. 5 (1883-90), pp.214-15
Lawrence, D.H., *England, my England*, 1921
Leach, Bernard, *Drawings, Verse and Belief*, 1973
Leslie, P. (ed.), *Letters of John Constable to C.R. Leslie*, 1931
Lethaby, W.R., *Philip Webb and his Work*, 1919
Lewes, Jeremy, *Cyril Connolly: A Life*, 1997
Linnell, John, archive in possession of the Linnell family
Longford, Elizabeth, A *Pilgrimage of Passion: A Life of W.S. Blunt*, 1979
Lower, M.A., *Contributions to Literature*, 1854
    'Old Manners and Speech in Sussex', *Sussex Archaeological Collections*, vol. 13, 1861, pp.219-31
    A Compendious History of Sussex, 2 vols, 1870
Lower, Richard, *Stray Leaves*, Lewes, 1862
Lowerson, J.L., *A Short History of Sussex*, Sussex, 1980
Lucas, E.V., *Highways and Byways in Sussex*, 1904
    A Sussex Poesie, 1918
McCarthy, Desmond, *Portraits*, 1931
MacCarthy, Fiona, *Eric Gill*, 1989
MacDonell, A.G., *England, Their England*, 1932
Macky, John, *A Journey through England*, vol. 1, 1732 edn
Mahood, Molly, 'Kipling's Wheeltracks', in Paul Foster (ed.), *Seams Two*, Chichester, 2000
Mais, S.P.B., *Listen to the Country*, n.d.
    See England First, 1927
    Rambles in London's Countryside, 1948
Mantell, Gideon, *The Fossils of the South Downs*, 1822
    'Note of the Iguanodon, a newly discovered fossil of an herbaceous reptile from the sandstone of Tilgate Forest', *Philosophical Transactions*, 1825, p.1179
    The Geology of South-East England, 1833
Marsh, John, *The John Marsh Journals*, (ed.) Brian Robbins, New York, 1990
Massingham, H.J., *Where Man Belongs*, 1946, p.248
Mendell, Vera and Meynell, Francis, *The Week-End Book*, 1924
Meredith George, *The Letters*, Cline, C.L. (ed.), vol. 3, 1972
Merrifield, Mrs, *A Sketch of the Natural History of Brighton*, Brighton, 1864
Messel, L., *A Garden Flora: Trees and Flowers grown in the gardens of Nymans*, Sussex, 1916
Meynell, Esther, *Sussex*, 1947
Montague, C., *The Right Place*, 1928
Moore, George, *Esther Waters*, 1894
Morton, J.B., *Hilaire Belloc: A Memoir*, 1955
Muggeridge, Malcolm, 'Collective Insecurity' in *Decade*, 1931-41
    Chronicles of Wasted Time, Vol. 1: The Green Stick, 1972
Nairn, I. and Pevsner, N., *The Buildings of England: Sussex*, 1965
Nairn, I., 'Outrage', *Architectural Review*, vol. ii, 1955, pp.127-45
Noyes, Alfred, *Collected Poems*, 1950
Olson, Stanley (ed.), *Harold Nicolson: Diaries and Letters, 1930-1964*, 1980
Oliver, Reggie, *Out of the Woodshed: The Life of Stella Gibbons*, 1998
Parish, W.D., *A Dictionary of Sussex Dialect*, Chichester, 1957 edn,
Parry, J.D., *The Coast of Sussex*, 1833
Pater, Walter, *Miscellaneous Studies*, 1917, pp.197-247
Patmore, Coventry, *How I Managed my Estate*, 1886
Pichot, M.W., *Voyage historique…en Angleterre*, Paris, 1825
Piozzi, Mrs, *Anecdotes of the Late Samuel Johnson LL.D*, ed. Robina Napier, 1884
Plomer, William, *At Home: Memoirs*, New York, 1958
Porter, Valerie, *The Southdown Sheep*, Singleton, Sussex, 1991
Powys, J.C., *Autobiography*, 1967
Pragnell, V.P., *The Story of the Sanctuary*, Steyning, 1928
Price, Nancy, *Nettles and Docks*, 1933 edn
    The Heart of a Vagabond, 1955
Pruden, Winefride, 'The Guild of St Dominic and St Joseph', Ditchling unpublished, 1994
Radcliffe, A. (ed.), *Gaston de Blondeville*, 1892 edn, vol. 2, p.44

Raymond, Ernest, *All the Days of my Life*, 1924
  Don John's Mountain Home, 1936
Reclus, E., *The Universal Geography, Vol. 4, The British Isles*, 1881, p.141
Rees, Simon, *The Charlton Hunt*, Chichester, 1998
Roberts, Peter, *Shoreham Airport; A Brief History*, Airport Visitor Centre, 2008
Robinson, Maude, *A South Down Farm in the Sixties*, 1938
Robinson, William, *The Wild Garden*, 1870
  Gravetye, 1911
  Home Landscapes, 1914
Rutherford, M. (Hale White), *The Autobiography of Mark Rutherford*, 1881
Sassoon, Siegfried, *The Weald of Youth*, 1942
Saunders, Max, *Ford Madox Ford: A Dual Life*, two vols, 1996
Sawyer, Amy, *Sussex Village Plays*, Sussex, 1934
Schofield, Arthur, 'The West Sussex Coast and Downs Report of the Arundel, Littlehampton and East Preston Joint Town Planning
  Advisory Committee', 1929
Seldon, Anthony, *Brave New City: Brighton and Hove, Past, Present and Future,* Sussex, 2002
de Selincourt, Hugh, *The Cricket Match*, 1924
Shanks, Edward, *Kipling*, 1924
Sharp, Thomas, *Town and Countryside*, 1932
Shone, Richard, *The Art of Bloomsbury*, Tate Gallery, 1999
Short, Brian, 'The Ashdown Forest Dispute, 1870-1882', *Sussex Record Society*, vol. 80, 1987
Shrubshall, Dennis and Coustillas, Pierre, *Landscape and Literati: unpublished letters of W.H. Hudson and George Gissing*, 1985
Sidgwick, R., *Walking Essays*, 1912
Simpson, Jacqueline, *The Folk-lore of Sussex*, 1973
Smart, Gerald and Brandon, Peter (eds), *The Future of the South Downs*, Chichester, 2007
Smith, Charlotte, *The Emigrants*, 1792-3
Solnit, Rebecca, *Wanderlust*, 2001
Spotts, F., *The Letters of Leonard Woolf*, 1990
Stephen, Leslie, 'Stray Thoughts on Scenery', *Cornhill Magazine*, 1878
Stockwood, M., *Chanctonbury Ring*, 1984
Taylor, James, *The Sussex Garland*, Newick, Sussex, 1851
Thirkell, Angela, *Three Houses: Reminiscences*, 1957
Thomas, Edward, *The Happy Go-Lucky Morgans*, 1912
Thomas, Helen, *Under Storm's Wing*, 1990 edn
Thorne, C., *Country Within Thirty Miles of London*, 1844
Towner Art Galley, *Henry George Hine*, Eastbourne, 2003
Trevelyan, G.M., *Clio, a Muse and other Essays*, 1931
Verrall, William, *William Verral's Cookery Book*, Haly, Ann (ed.), Lewes, 1988
Walker, Ted, *The High Path*, 1982
Walpole, Horace, *Letters*, Cunningham, P. (ed.), Edinburgh, 1906
Ward, Mrs Humphry, *Robert Elsmere*, 1888
Watkin, D., *Thomas Hope and the Neo-Classical Idea*, 1968
Waugh, Evelyn, *Labels*, 1930.
Waugh, Mary, *Smuggling in Kent and Sussex, 1700-1840*, Sussex, 1985
Wellesley, Dorothy, *Far Have I travelled*, 1955
  Early Light, the Collected Poems, 1955
Wellesley, Jane, *A Journey through my Family*, 2008
Wells, H.G., *Tono-Bungay*, 1909
  The Research Magnificent, 1915
  Experiment in Autobiography, vol. 1, 1924
  The Wheels of Chance, B. Bergonzi (ed.), Everyman edn, 1984
White, Gilbert, *The Natural History and Antiquities of Selborne*, 1836 edn
Whitford, Frank, *Bauhaus*, 1984
Wiener, Martin J., *English Culture and the Decline of the Industrial Spirit, 1850-1980*, Cambridge, 1981
Wilkinson, Walter, *A Sussex Peep Show*, 1933
Wills, Barclay, *Downland Treasure*, 1929
  Shepherds of Sussex, 1938
Williams, Albert N., *Travels in England*, 1845
Williams, Raymond, *The Country and the City*, 1973
Wolseley, Lady, *Some of the Smaller Manor Houses of Sussex*, 1925
Wood, William, *A Sussex Farmer*, 1938
Wooldridge, S.W., 'The Weald and the Field Sciences', *British Association for the Advancement of Science*, new series, vol. 1, 1949
Wooldridge, S.W. and Linton, D.L., *Structure, Surface and Drainage in South-East England*, 1939
Wooldridge, S.W. and Goldring, F., *The Weald*, 1953
Woolf, Leonard (ed.), *The Death of the Moth*, New York, 1942
  Beginning Again, 1968
Woolf, Virginia, *The Essays of Virginia Woolf*, McNellie, Andrew (ed.), vols. i-iv, 1986-94
  ed. Clarke, S.N., vol. v, 2009
Worlters, Neb, *Bungalow Town: Theatre and Film Colony*, Shoreham-by-Sea, Sussex, 1985
Wyndham, Richard, *South-Eastern Survey: A Last Look around Sussex Kent and Surrey*, 1940
Young, Gerard, *The Cottage in the Fields*, Bognor Regis, 1939
  Down Hoe Lane, Bognor Regis, 1950
Young, the Rev. Arthur, *General View of the Agriculture of the County of Sussex*, 1813

INDEX

Page numbers in bold refer to illustrations; Roman numerals at end of entries refer to colour plates.